1

TO
BE
CONTINUED....

A scene from *Son of Kong?* No, it's from *Tom Tyler's Luck.*

Football great Jim Thorpe greets Tom Tyler in *Battling with Buffalo Bill.*

TO
BE
CONTINUED...

Ken Weiss and Ed Goodgold

CROWN PUBLISHERS INC., NEW YORK

Acknowledgments

There are many individuals and organizations without whose cooperation this book could not have been completed. We are especially
indebted to John Serrano for providing help with facts and source
material. His tremendous knowledge of movies in general, and
serials in particular, was invaluable.

We would like also to extend our sincere appreciation to
Charles Powell, Ernie Kirkpatrick, Alan Eisenson, *Movie Star News,*
Columbia Pictures Corporation, King Features Syndicate, Marvel
Comics Group, National Periodical Publications, Inc., National Tele-
film Associates, Republic Pictures International, Screen Gems, Inc.,
and Universal Pictures Corporation.

Contents

Introduction

A great thing used to happen on Saturdays if you were lucky enough to be growing up in the Bronx about twenty-five years ago.

You would get to the local movie house at 9:30 in the morning, and for about a dime you'd receive a candy bar, an old comic book with the name removed, and you'd enter a world structured entirely for kids. The theatre lights would dim, and the show would start: first, five cartoons, then the "funny races," then the morning's special feature (usually a Western), and at last, what you'd been waiting for all along, the serial. (Except you never called it a "serial." It was always a "chapter.")

The faces in these chapters were all ones you had grown to know and love. The adults had their Clark Gables, their Robert Taylors, Jimmy Stewarts, and George Brents. But you had stars like Robert Lowery, Buster Crabbe, Kane Richmond, and Tom Tyler. And better yet, you had villains by the carload: insidious fiends such as Charles Middleton, Bela Lugosi, Eduardo Cianelli, Henry Brandon, and Roy Barcroft. And their henchmen: George Lewis, Kenne Duncan, and Ken Terrell.

The serials were a world of their own. For approximately twenty minutes you were totally involved in a series of hair-raising escapes, spectacular battles, mile-a-minute chases, hidden treasures, secret plans, and diabolical scientific devices, all held together by a plot which was at once highly tenuous and at the same time complicated almost beyond comprehension.

The chapter's end usually signaled the day's halfway point. It was nearly noon, and during the ensuing coming attractions and newsreel, the theatre would begin to take on the aroma of salami and cream cheese and jelly as sandwiches were taken from brown paper bags and removed from wax paper wrappers.

If you were lucky, the main double feature would be some of the kid classics—*King Kong* and *Gunga Din,* or *Thief of Bagdad* and *Jungle Book.* After the main features were over, the theatre generally repeated the serial, and naturally you watched it again with great interest, looking for clues you might have missed the first time around. After seeing the chapter for the second time, you went home. It was usually about 3:30 P.M. You'd gotten your dime's worth.

Curiously, despite the fact that millions of kids lined up to see the "chapters" every Saturday, the major studios avoided serial production. MGM, Warner Brothers, 20th Century-Fox, and Paramount never produced a sound serial. Aside from those produced by independent companies, sound serials were produced by four studios—Universal, Columbia, Mascot, and Republic. Universal led the way with the first sound serial, *Ace of Scotland Yard* (1929), and dominated the field until 1931, when Mascot and Universal each released five serials. The two studios shared the market (challenged only by the independent producers) until 1936. By that time, through a series of corporate mergers, Mascot had become part of Republic Studios and it released three serials in 1936. Columbia jumped into serial production in 1937, and from that year on until the mid-40s, the big three were Republic, Universal, and Columbia. At the end of World War II, the popularity of the serial diminished somewhat. By 1947 Universal had decided to discontinue serial production, leaving the field to Republic and Columbia, who persisted, despite a waning market, well into the 50s. In 1955, Republic produced its last serial, the wholly unworthy *King of the Carnival,* and, in 1956, the era came to a whimpering end with the release of Columbia's *Blazing the Overland Trail.*

Universal has the distinction of producing the most expensive, and perhaps the most popular, serial ever made, *Flash Gordon.* The studio had been successful with two other serials based on a comic strip character—*Tailspin Tommy* (1934) and its sequel *Tailspin Tommy and the Great Air Mystery* (1935)—and, noting *Flash Gordon's* amazing comic-strip success, contracted with King Features for the serial rights.

Flash Gordon cost a reputed $350,000 to produce, well over three times the cost of average serial production at the time. Much of the cost was due to expensive special effects and elaborate sets not generally indulged in by serials: elaborate "Kingdoms," a wide variety of costumes, rocket ships, monsters, electrical devices and weaponry, all prepared with startling fidelity to the comic strip.

The casting itself was a coup. Selected to star as Flash was the 1932 Olympic free-style swimming champion Buster Crabbe, who had embarked upon a movie career. Handsome and athletic, Crabbe was every youngster's idea of a serial hero. Eventually, he was to star in a total of nine serials, from 1933 to 1951, and appear in innumerable feature films. Jean Rogers, who had already been featured in *Tailspin Tommy and the Great Air Mystery, Ace Drummond,* and *The Adventures of Frank Merriwell,* played Dale Arden. But as Dale Arden, Jean portrayed what may be the sexiest heroine ever to grace a serial. Even today some of Dale's scenes are delightfully erotic. It's no wonder that shortly after completing a sequel, *Flash Gordon's Trip to Mars,* Jean was lured away to a contract with Fox. Beyond question, the best piece of casting was Charles Middleton, as Ming, the Merciless. Decked out in regal splendor, Middleton was every inch the demonic Ruler of the Universe.

Movie serials were innocently devoid of anything that might even be considered "social consciousness." Questions of a higher morality were blithely contradicted in the incessant, ever-menacing battle against evil. Second only to warehouses (which were constantly being destroyed by flame or explosives), human life was the most expendable of resources. Friends and cohorts met their makers with barely a "tsk-tsk" from the hero or a frown of annoyance from the villain. Captain Marvel, in particular, seemed to take great sadistic glee in tossing his opponents off of roofs. (I sometimes wondered about the safety of passersby—a concern apparently not shared by Captain Marvel.)

The racial attitudes of the period were also none too enlightened. For the most part Orientals were portrayed as sinister cultists bent upon the destruction of the white race; blacks were merely ignorant natives who followed the leader who most successfully played upon their primitive superstitions. The most blatant examples of white chauvinism occur in one of the best serials of the 30s, *The Lost City.* (You'll find a detailed synopsis on page 64.) As the hero races toward shrieks coming from the distance, he mentions to his sidekick, "That sounds like a *white* woman screaming." Later on, our hero learns that Dr. Manyus, the story's benevolent scientific genius, has invented a serum that can make black men white. "Dr. Manyus," our hero says, awestruck, "this is the greatest invention in history." Dr. Manyus smiles modestly and answers, "Science can accomplish *anything*!" I wonder what good old Dr. Manyus would have to say to Huey Newton or Bobby Seale.

There was one thing that could be counted on with clocklike regularity: the consistent stupidity of both the hero and the villain. Deep down in his heart of hearts, each kid sitting in the theatre knew that he was smarter than the hero. Each kid could anticipate the villain's moves and knew when the hero was walking into a trap. How come the hero never seemed to *learn*? Why did he keep walking into the same traps and keep making the same mistakes? For crying out loud, couldn't he tell just by *looking* at him that Anthony Warde was not to be trusted? And the villain was no smarter. There he was, supposedly the cream of the villainous crop, and it was obvious that he couldn't organize a game of hide-and-seek, no less dominate the world. Often we'd find the villain at a late stage in his plan to achieve his diabolical aim. All he needs is the atom-radar-cyclotizer developed by Dr. Genius. And so, for fifteen chapters he tries to get the atom-radar-cyclotizer, and Bruce Hero, assigned to protect it, attempts to thwart him. Somewhere in the middle chapters the villain gains possession of the device and stands at the brink of success. But he inevitably discovers that the essential dyno-tube is missing. His attempts to steal the tube are good for another few chapters. Naturally, he eventually obtains the dyno-tube and stands once again at the brink of success, only to discover that he needs compound X, the special fuel required to start the damn thing. And this went on chapter after chapter, serial after serial, until our hero finally caught up with him. By the time chapter fifteen finally rolled around, both the hero and villain had very often forgotten what it was they were originally after and were enmeshed in schemes that had nothing at all to do with atom-radar-cyclotizers.

Time after time the hero relived his blunders. For example, picture this situation, my nominee for the most oft-repeated sequence of events in serial history: The hero, revolver in hand, enters the villain's hideout warehouse (or cave, or cellar) and discovers two of the villain's cohorts working among barrels and crates ominously marked TNT or Dynamite. The room is lit by a lantern sitting on a frail table. Our hero gets the drop on the outlaws and demands that they tell him where their boss is. Suddenly, one of the villains reaches for a nearby object and throws it at the hero, knocking the gun from his hand. A fight ensues. Each outlaw is stunned and knocked down, and (conveniently for our hero) unable to resume the fight until his partner is knocked down. During the battle the lantern falls from the table, and burns unnoticed, at the foot of a TNT crate. Meanwhile the fight continues until both heavies manage to attack at the same time, at which time the hero is knocked unconscious—usually by a blow from behind. At this point one of the outlaws notices that the crates of TNT are a raging inferno, and both villains run like hell. Our poor hero lies unconscious as the flames lick hungrily at the explosives. A tremendous explosion occurs as the warehouse and, supposedly, our hero are blown to smithereens. That is, until next week.

The old "villain-will-knock-gun-from-hero's-hand" maneuver is most hilariously executed in *Spy Smasher,* otherwise a quite credible serial. In one scene, Spy Smasher and a comrade are aboard a Nazi submarine. They plan to escape through a torpedo hatch while Spy Smasher holds some Nazi crewmen at bay with a pistol. But each time Spy Smasher turns away from the Germans to assist his friend into the hatch, one of the Germans starts to feint toward Spy Smasher's gun. Spy Smasher knows that the German is going to go for his gun; the German knows that Spy Smasher knows. But rather than order the Nazis to move back a few feet, the charade continues until Spy Smasher looks away a bit too long, the gun is knocked from his hand, and the inevitable fight ensues.

Motivation was at best tenuous for hero and villain alike. The villain was invariably determined to get something (land, treasure, the world) for his own. The hero was equally determined to stop him. But what of the lesser characters? What compelled the master criminal's cohorts, chapter after chapter, to face deadly situations? What possible rewards could have tempted the likes of Frank Lackteen, Tom London, Charles King, Anthony Warde, and Kenne Duncan? God only knows. But fortunately for us, they obeyed, with complete loyalty, ridiculous orders which most often sent them to their doom.

In view of the obvious incompetence of the heroes, and the utter predictability of the plots, what was it that kept us going back week after week? Well, the answer could possibly be the subject of a long psychological study of a child's mind. But allow us to venture a few simple theories, based strictly on our own experience.

First of all there was very little dialogue, lots of action, and no "love stuff." Practically all of the action movies of the period followed a fairly rigid formula: battles at the beginning and the middle, with a big, climactic battle at the end. Everything in between was either "love stuff" or plot development (talk, talk, talk). (There are exceptions, however, to every rule. The first third of *King Kong* was all "plot development," and the last two-thirds all action.) In the serials practically everything was action. And with such a profusion of fights, chases, and explosions, what red-blooded ten-year-old needed a *plot*? When a sensible one existed it was, of course, appreciated but only if it didn't get in the way of the action.

Secondly, and perhaps most important, was the relationship of the serials to comic books. The importance of comic strips in our lives (to a youngster of the 30s or 40s) can't be overestimated, and in the serials we actually saw in action the people we read about in the comics. And not just the comic characters themselves, but the trapdoors, secret passageways, death rays, and the complicated scientific devices.

It didn't even matter that the serials took liberties with the comic book characters. We all knew that boy radio reporter Billy Batson didn't acquire his Captain Marvel powers while on an archaeological expedition. We noticed that Captain America lost his sidekick Bucky; that Spy Smasher suddenly inherited a twin brother; and that every superhero's costume had *wrinkles,* an upsetting discovery that never occurred in the comic strips. And very often the casting left a lot to be desired. Kirk Alyn was fine as Clark Kent, but was certainly no Superman. Dick Purcell, as Captain America, had none of the lean tautness of the Simon-Kirby strip, Douglas Croft's Robin looked as though he couldn't fight his way out of a Girl Scout meeting, and William Tracy was a disaster in *Terry and the Pirates.* But that was all trivial, and not nearly as important as the thrill of seeing a living, breathing superhero going through his paces on screen.

The majority of serial authorities seem to enjoy referring to the Republic productions of the early 40s as the "Golden Age" of sound serials. We're not so sure. Certainly the Republic products of those years were consistently superior to the Columbia or Universal serials made during the same period. Production values were excellent and Republic's attention to detail in miniatures and stuntwork was superior. But selecting a "Golden Age" in sound serial history is much like selecting a "Golden Age" for beautiful women. Were "flappers" more attractive than "flower children"? It's pretty much a matter of taste.

Our own preferences run to the serials of the 30s, and if we *had* to choose among studios, we'd lean toward Universal for their relatively strong, complicated story lines. In general, though, the serials of the 30s had an exotic graininess that lingers long in the memory. For some reason perhaps understood only by Marshall Mac-Luhan, what remains most in the mind are grainy mood qualities, best exemplified in serials such as *The New Adventures of Tarzan, Red Barry,* and *Buck Rogers.*

Selecting a favorite serial hero is equally difficult. A front-runner would certainly be Buster Crabbe, who appeared in nine serials: *Tarzan the Fearless, Flash Gordon, Red Barry, Buck Rogers, Flash Gordon's Trip to Mars, Flash Gordon Conquers the Universe, The Sea Hound, Pirates of the High Seas,* and *King of the Congo.* In terms of quantity a strong case could be made for the marvelous Tom Tyler who fought his way through seven serials: *Phantom of the West, Battling with Buffalo Bill, Jungle Mystery, Clancy of the Mounted, Phantom of the Air, Captain Marvel,* and *The Phantom* (in which Tyler's physical resemblance to the comic-strip character was almost uncanny). The Western serial champ would have to be Buck Jones, who appeared in six serials: *Gordon of Ghost City, The Red Rider, Roaring West, Phantom Rider, White Eagle,* and *Riders of Death Valley.*

Our own favorite, though, is Kane Richmond, whose ten-year serial career included seven serials: *Adventures of Rex and Rinty, The Lost City, Spy Smasher, Haunted Harbor, Brick Bradford, Jungle Raiders,* and *Brenda Starr, Reporter.* Kane combined good looks with a quality of performance unusual in serials, and his career, like Buster Crabbe's, included dozens of feature films. (Unlike Buster, however, Kane almost always played the leading man, albeit in low-budget, small-studio films. Buster Crabbe, on the other hand, played the mustached, sinister, second-string "heavy" in a whole procession of Paramount features in the late 30s.)

One final word about the synopses in this book. The serials which receive detailed treatment were selected more or less arbitrarily, and constitute for the most part some of our personal favorites. In each case we've made every attempt to be accurate, but, as we've indicated, serial plots don't always lend themselves to logical narrative explanation. Of necessity, even in our most detailed synopses, many "adventures" and sequences have been omitted. What we've tried to do wherever possible is retain the essence, or "flavor," of each serial.

Now get a salami or cream-cheese-and-jelly sandwich and a box of jujubes, sit back, relax, and prepare to enter a world that will never again exist, but will never completely disappear either.

Ken Weiss
Ed Goodgold
1971

1929

The Ace of Scotland Yard

10 Episodes
Universal, 1929

Directed by
Ray Taylor

(Publicized by Universal as the "First Talking Serial.")

CAST

Inspector Blake	Crawford Kent
Lady Diana	Florence Allen
Lord Blanton	Herbert Pior
Prince Darius	Albert Priscoe
Jarvis	Monte Montague
Queen of Diamonds	Grace Cunard

The formidable Queen of Diamonds, mastermind of a thoroughly professional band of thieves, plots to steal a ring belonging to Lord Blanton and his daughter, Lady Diana. In the guise of Prince Darius, the Queen convinces Lady Diana that she was a Babylonian Princess during a previous incarnation and, at that time, owned the ring. Darius also maintains that during a previous lifetime he was the Emperor Darius. Images of the past, conjured up by Darius in order to get Lady Diana to relinquish the ring, constantly haunt the confused maiden.

Fortunately, Lady Diana's friend and suitor is Inspector Blake, the Ace of Scotland Yard. His keen, analytical mind senses danger and sees the valuable ring as the natural cause. It isn't long before Blake figures out that Diana's visions are part of the scheme to get the ring and that Darius is a front for the Queen of Diamonds. In short order the Queen and her whole gang are rounded up and Blake wins the hand of his beloved Lady Diana.

Crawford Kent and Florence Allen, alone together.

Crawford Kent and Monte Montague are frisked by agents of the Queen of Diamonds.

Frank Merrill seems perplexed by the attentions of Natalie Kingston and the competing Lillian Worth.

Tarzan the Tiger

10 Episodes	Directed by
Universal, 1929	Henry McRae

CAST

Tarzan	Frank Merrill
Jane	Natalie Kingston
Queen La	Lillian Worth
Bobby Nelson	Al Ferguson

Native slave traders interested in capturing Jane and selling her at a high markup are diverted from their primary calling by a cache of stolen jewels from the jungle city of Opar. Meanwhile, an international band of jewel thieves is distracted from its day-to-day routine by Jane. Tarzan has to combat both of these evil forces. He is forced to deal with a spell-casting priestess, Queen La of Opar; a scheming tribal chief, a mammoth ape, and the cunning of sophisticated European thieves.

In the end, he saves both Jane and what he refers to as "pretty pebbles" from the evil clutches of both villainous forces.

TO BE CONTINUED

Frank Merrill hugs Natalie Kingston as Lillian Worth and the natives rejoice over the return of the fabulous treasure of Opar.

1930

The Indians Are Coming

12 Episodes
Universal, 1930

Directed by
Henry McRae

CAST

Jack Manning	Tim McCoy
Mary Woods	Allene Ray
Amos	Charles Royal
George Woods	Edmund Cobb
Rance Carter	Francis Ford
Bill Williams	Don Francis
Dynamite	Ring

Jack Manning arrives in a Midwest town from Gold Creek. He brings with him a message from George Woods to his brother Tom and niece Mary, informing them he has struck gold and asking them to join him via wagon train. Jack and Mary fall in love to the displeasure of Rance Carter who has a hankerin' after Mary himself.

But Jack and Mary not only have to be wary of Carter's machinations but also of Indian uprisings occurring in the West. They escape burning buildings, put out prairie fires, and outlast hundreds of Indians who are on the warpath. Unfortunately, Mary's father is killed by Rance, and Jack's friend Bill Williams is killed by Indians. Although Jack and Mary are happily united in the end, their joy is tinged with sorrow for those who have sacrificed their lives to make their own happiness possible.

Tim McCoy

The Jade Box

10 Episodes
Universal, 1930

Directed by
Ray Taylor

CAST

Jack Lamar	Jack Perrin
Helen Morgan	Louise Lorraine
Martin Morgan	Francis Ford
Edward Haines	Wilbur S. Mack
Percy Winslow	Leo White
John Lamar	Monroe Salisbury

When Martin Morgan steals the Jade Box which his friend John Lamar had purchased in the Orient, Lamar is spirited away by the members of an Eastern cult. When they discover that the box has been stolen, Morgan encounters the enmity of the leaders of an Oriental sect who vow to get him. Meanwhile, Jack Lamar, son of the vanished John, becomes engaged to Morgan's daughter Helen.

One day, a mysterious shadow flits across the living room as Morgan is talking to Helen and Jack. It leaves a message that Jack's father is in the land of the shadow and won't return until the Jade Box is returned to the sect.

The box contains a vial that holds the secret of invisibility. Jack sets out on a search that ranges from the United States to the Middle East. But Morgan stands in the younger Lamar's way—he is determined to find out the secret of invisibility himself and use it for his own selfish ends. He is killed by the shadow and the box is returned to its resting place. John Lamar is reunited with his son who, in turn, is reunited with his sweetheart Helen.

A wild melee, in which Jack Perrin and Louise Lorraine are seized by Eastern Cultists.

Louise Lorraine watches in astonishment as a thug makes an amazing escape.

Louise Lorraine in the clutches of the enemy.

The mysterious shadow claims the Jade Box from Francis Ford (*right*).

Jay Novello and Monroe Salisbury watch as Louise Lorraine and Jack Perrin receive the blessings of the Cult Chieftain.

The Lightning Express

10 Episodes	Directed by
Universal, 1930	Henry McRae

CAST

Jack Venable	Lane Chandler
Bobbie Van Tyme	Louise Lorraine
Whispering Smith	Al Ferguson
Kate	Greta Granstedt
Frank Sanger	J. Gordon Russel
Bill Lewellyn	John Oscar
Hank Pardelow	Martin Clichy
Henchmen	Floyd Criswell,
	Jim Pierce, and
	Robert Kelly

The Lightning Express, built by John Venable, is the crack train of the B & M railroad. Frank Sanger, guardian of Bobbie Van Tyme, refuses to let the road cross beautiful Bobbie's land. Jack Venable, son of the builder, is persuaded by his friend Whispering Smith to desert his round of wild parties and help carry out his father's ambition. He masquerades as Victor Jones, a new construction foreman.

Bobbie learns that Sanger is plotting against Smith and Jack, but is persuaded by Sanger that Jack is a worthless rake. Love at first sight, however, makes her an ally of Jack and the railroad extension. Sanger's attempts to block their efforts involve the friends in train wrecks, explosions, and near-drownings.

Sanger, hearing that the three friends are bound for the city, plans a wild party in Jack's apartment and manages to persuade Bobbie that "Victor Jones" is really Jack Venable and a complete rounder. But Jack is determined to win back Bobbie's affection, and, with Smith's help, discovers the real will of Bobbie's father, in which Smith, not Sanger, was appointed Bobbie's guardian. The men dash back to tell Bobbie. A fight ensues and Sanger and his men are taken to jail. Bobbie and Jack are married on the Lightning Express as it rides through Bobbie's land.

A wild party at the Venable estate, typical of the wastrel's life led by Jack Venable.

Louise Lorraine rescues Lane Chandler from drowning.

Louise Lorraine gets the drop on the three villains trying to subdue Lane Chandler.

Lane Chandler pleads for someone to help the injured Louise Lorraine.

It looks like a bullet in the back for Lane Chandler as a pair of menacing hands grab Louise Lorraine.

An innocent Louise Lorraine tries to lead Lane Chandler from an apparent life of debauchery.

The Lone Defender

12 Episodes	Directed by
Mascot, 1930	Richard Thorpe

CAST

Rinty	Rin-Tin-Tin
Ramon	Walter Miller
Dolores	June Marlowe
Buzz	Buzz Barton
Juan Valdez	Josef Swickard
Halkey	Lee Shumway
Burke	Frank Lanning
Jenkins	Bob Kortman
Limpy	Arthur Morrison
Sheriff	Lafe McKee
Deputy Sheriff	Bob Irwin
Dutch	Arthur Metzeth
Henchman	Bill McGowan

As they return from their secret mine in the desert, prospectors Valdez and Burke are ambushed. Burke escapes but Valdez is shot and killed. The Cactus Kid, a notorious bandit, is suspected of the crime. Ramon, a mysterious figure, overhears a conversation between two townsmen, Halkey and Jenkins, in which they discuss their failure to get a map of the mine from the dead man.

Rinty, recognizing Jenkins as his master's killer, attacks him but Jenkins is saved. Halkey decides to capture Rinty because he believes the dog can lead him to the mine. Meanwhile, Rinty becomes a suspect in the killing of a young colt, a colt he had tried to protect from the onslaught of a wolf. He is about to be shot when Ramon saves him.

Ramon turns out to be a special officer of the Department of Justice. He uncovers the Cactus Kid's real identity (Halkey), and turns over Valdez's rich mine to its rightful owner—his daughter Dolores.

Terry of the *Times*

10 Episodes	Directed by
Universal, 1930	Henry McRae

CAST

Terry	Reed Howes
Eileen	Lotus Thompson
Macy	Sheldon Lewis
Rastus	John Oscar
Patch Dugan	Will Hays
Moll	Mary Grant
Blindman	Norman Thomson
Hunchback	Kingsley Benedict

Terry of the *Times,* the son of the newspaper's founder, is assigned to investigate and report on a mysterious warning signed "30" that has been received by a local politician. (In newspaper parlance "30" means "the end.") In the course of his investigation, Terry is captured at a clandestine meeting of the "Mystic Mendicants," an outlaw band, where he overhears the plans of a plot to kill his uncle Robert Macy, publisher of the *Times.* Terry barely manages to escape in time to foil the plot.

Terry learns that, according to provisions of his father's will, he must get married within a short period of time if he is to inherit the newspaper. As he is in love with a girl named Eileen, this doesn't seem to pose a very serious problem. But Robert Macy's treacherous brother (he later turns out to be a *fake* brother) disguises himself as the paper's publisher and does everything in his power to prevent Terry from stopping the Mendicant band's forays and his attempts to get married.

In the end, a few reformed Mendicants help Terry subdue the false Macy. Terry finally gets married and accepts rightful possession of the *Times*.

Reed Howes and Lotus Thompson seem upset at Sheldon Lewis's displeasure at the morning headlines.

Lotus Thompson, Sheldon Lewis, and Reed Howes are startled by John Oscar's (*in blackface*) announcement.

Sheldon Lewis is less than cautious in passing on a secret message.

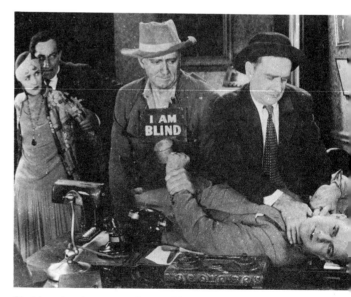

Sheldon Lewis grasps Lotus Thompson as not-so-blind Norman Thomson makes it easy for a cohort to get a good grip on Reed Howes's neck.

1931

Battling with Buffalo Bill

12 Episodes	Directed by
Universal, 1931	Ray Taylor

CAST

Buffalo Bill	Tom Tyler
Dave Archer	Rex Bell
Miss Archer	Lucile Browne
Jim Rodney	Francis Ford
John Mills	William Desmond
Swift Arrow	Jim Thorpe
Jack Brady	Yakima Canutt
Chief Thunderbird	Chief Thunderbird
Joe Tempas	Bud Osborne

When gold is discovered in a small Western town, Jim Rodney, the local gambler, decides to seize possession of the claim by having the townspeople either murdered or frightened away by Indians. In order to get the Indians into the right frame of mind, Rodney has his gang murder one of their squaws and steal their horses. When the town comes under attack by the enraged Indians, Buffalo Bill arrives with a U.S. cavalry troop and drives the Indians off.

Rodney is not totally discouraged, however. He pursues his goal by having himself elected town marshal, defeating Buffalo Bill's friend Dave Archer in a rigged election. Buffalo Bill then takes on the double-barreled task of bringing Rodney to justice while fighting off attacks by the still hostile Indians. He not only manages to accomplish both, but also convinces the Indians to smoke the peace pipe, bringing total tranquillity to the grateful town.

Rugged Westerner, Tom Tyler.

Tom Tyler has both hands full in this deadly predicament.

14

Rex Bell and William Desmond try to revive Lucile Browne.

Tom Tyler takes refuge behind his dead horse.

Danger Island

12 Episodes	Directed by
Universal, 1931	Ray Taylor

CAST

Harry Drake	Kenneth Harlan
Bonnie Adams	Lucile Browne
Professor Adams	Tom Rickells
Ben Arnold	Walter Miller
Bull Black	W. L. Thorne
Aileen Chandos	Beulah Hutton
Briney	Andy Devine
Lascara	George Regan
Cebu	Everett Brown

Before Professor Gerald Adams dies in the arms of his daughter Bonnie, he tells her of his discovery of a rich radium deposit located on an African island. Ben Arnold, a rich clubman, and Aileen Chandos, an adventuress, feigning friendship for Bonnie, decide to secure the rich mine for themselves.

Captain Harry Drake, who is noted for his honesty, falls in love with Bonnie and tries to help her see through the conspirators' facade. But he himself is discredited in the eyes of his beloved by their carefully calculated schemes.

On the island, the two villains try to induce a savage tribe to sacrifice Harry in a religious ritual. They encourage the natives to harass Harry and Bonnie at every turn. When Ben threatens Aileen's life, she deserts him and joins Harry and Bonnie. Ben and his henchman Bull are finally killed by the native Cebu, and Bonnie and Harry set sail for the States.

Lucile Browne is mildly distraught by the attention Kenneth Harlan is paying to the tempting Beulah Hutton, as Andy Devine looks on appreciatively.

Kenneth Harlan and Andy Devine are too busy examining the bucket to notice the natives surrounding them.

Kenneth Harlan and Andy Devine (*replaced by two stunt men*) about to be burned alive.

Lucile Browne, in the clutches of a jungle ape.

Finger Prints

10 Episodes	Directed by
Universal, 1931	Ray Taylor

CAST

Gary Gordon	Kenneth Harlan
Lola Mackey	Edna Murphy
Kent Martin	Gayne Whitman
Jane Madden	Gertrude Astor
John Mackey	William Worthington
Joe Burke	William Thorne
Officer Rooney	Monte Montague

Gary Gordon, Secret Service Agent, is commissioned to apprehend a band of smugglers known as the River Gang which numbers John Mackey, the father of Lola, the girl Gary loves, as one of its members.

When Joe Burke, Mackey's partner, is killed, Kent Martin claims to have evidence that would convict Mackey of the crime. He tries to blackmail Mackey and gain his consent to a marriage with Lola over the protests and threats of his sweetheart Jane, who is deeply in love with him.

When this ploy fails, Martin kidnaps Lola and takes her to his cave hideout. She is soon rescued by Gordon, however, who relentlessly pursues the investigation of Burke's murder. Methodically compiling evidence, he builds the investigation to a nerve-racking climax and Martin, unable to stand the suspense, breaks down and confesses to the crime. Others in the gang are arrested in a police raid. Mackey is cleared and Gordon and Lola plan to get married.

The Galloping Ghost

12 Episodes	Directed by
Mascot, 1931	Reeves Eason

CAST

Red Grange	Harold (Red) Grange
Barbara	Dorothy Gulliver
Elton	Walter Miller
Irene	Gwen Lee
Buddy	Francis X. Bushman
Jerry	Tom Dugan
Mystery Man	Theodore Lorch
Mullins	Tom London
Harlow	Eddie Hearn
Brady	Ernie Adams
Tom	Frank Brownlee
Snowball	Stepin Fetchit

The Clay-Hampton annual football game looks like a walkaway for Hampton. Red Grange and Buddy Courtland, Clay's big stars, are on the bench. With five minutes to play, Coach Harlow puts his two stars into the game. Spectacularly, Grange engineers a one-point victory for Clay. At the game are Brady and Mullins, two crooked gamblers who have lost heavily by Clay's victory. Red's girl friend and Buddy's sister, Barbara, meets Red and Buddy after the game to congratulate them.

Late that evening, in violation of training regulations, Buddy leaves his room. Red follows him to a roadhouse. A mysterious man follows Red. Buddy meets Irene, to whom he is secretly married. She demands money, threatening to announce the marriage if he refuses. Since announcement of the marriage would mean dismissal from the school and a break with his family, Buddy accepts a bribe to throw a game. Red, who has seen the transaction, takes the money from Buddy after a bitter fight. The man who bribed Buddy indirectly informs Coach Harlow that Red prevented Buddy from playing so that Clay would lose the game. Thus, Red is dismissed from the team in disgrace.

Red begins his own campaign to clear his name, eventually tracks down the brains behind the gang, and returns to school a hero.

While he is being choked, "Red" Grange gets set to deliver a hard right, as Dorothy Gulliver is abducted by Tom London.

King of the Wild

12 Episodes	Directed by
Mascot, 1931	Richard Thorpe

CAST

Robert Grant	Walter Miller
Muriel Armitage	Nora Lane
Mrs. LaSalle	Dorothy Christy
Harris	Tom Santschi
Mustapha	Boris Karloff
Bimi	Arthur McLaglen
Tom Armitage	Carroll Nye
Peterson	Victor Potel
Mrs. Colby	Martha Lalande

Robert Grant, an American adventurer who has recently escaped from an Indian prison, discovers that two men, Harris and Mustapha, have learned that a third man, Tom Armitage, knows the whereabouts of a diamond mine. The two conspirators hire a Mrs. LaSalle to help them get at Armitage's secret. When Mrs. LaSalle is mysteriously shot and killed, Peterson, a secret agent, accuses Harris of the crime. Harris, in turn, accuses Peterson. Meanwhile, Mrs. Colby, another secret service agent, appears. In addition, an inscrutable man wearing black glasses arrives on the scene giving almost everyone a helping hand at one time or another.

Grant unravels the mysterious tangle, he exposes the man in black glasses, overcomes Harris and Mustapha and wins exoneration, and Muriel (Armitage's sister) for himself.

The Lightning Warrior

12 Episodes
Mascot, 1931

Directed by
Armand Schaefer and
Ben Kline

The pioneers of the Kern River valley live in constant terror. They are menaced both by Indians and by a mysterious creature whom they know only as the Wolf Man. While a group of settlers are discussing their plight in the general store, an arrow whizzes through the front door. It bears a message telling the settlers to abandon their homes before the new moon.

While this drama is unfolding in town, Jimmy Carter and his father are paddling downstream toward the safety of the settlement. An arrow shot from the riverbank strikes Mr. Carter and the canoe overturns. Young Jimmy reaches the cabin of his father's friend Scott only to find Scott dead. But he also finds Rinty, Scott's dog, who not only tracks down his master's killer but unravels a plot to stir up the Indians against the whites.

The clever Rinty eventually points his tail at the Wolf Man, thereby revealing him as the mastermind behind the entire campaign of terror.

CAST

Rinty	Rin-Tin-Tin
Jimmy Carter	Frankie Darro
Dianne	Georgia Hale
Alan Scott	George Brent
Sheriff	Pat O'Malley
La Farge	Theodore Lorch
Hayden	Lafe McKee
Wells	Bob Kortman
Adams	George McGrill
Indian George	Frank Lanning
McDonald	Frank Brownlee
Carter	Hayden Stevenson

Georgia Hale is about to be abducted by the Wolf Man.

The Phantom of the West

10 Episodes　　　　Directed by
Mascot, 1931　　　 Ross Lederman

CAST

Jim Lester	Tom Tyler
Mona Cortez	Dorothy Gulliver
Martin Blain	William Desmond
Bud Landers	Tom Santschi
Oscar	Tom Dugan
Royce Macklin	Philo McCullough
Keno	Joe Bonomo
Peter Drake	Kermit Maynard
Cortez	Frank Lanning
Sheriff Ryan	Frank Hagney
Stewart	Dick Dickinson
Ruby Blain	Hallee Sullivan

Francisco Cortez, a lifer, escapes from prison. He is given shelter by rancher Jim Lester but escapes after he overhears two deputies who are searching for him tell Lester that the fugitive murdered his father. Before he departs, however, he leaves a note proclaiming his innocence and claiming that seven men in the town of Rawton know the name of the real murderer.

The mysterious Phantom soon starts terrorizing the town. Wherever he goes, he leaves strange warnings such as: "Will you talk or must seven pay for one man's crime?" Several people are killed when they are on the verge of disclosing something about the murder.

Throughout the intrigue, Jim Lester follows every clue that might lead to the solution of this double-barreled mystery. He is aided in his efforts by Cortez's daughter Mona, and by his ever-dependable horse. Eventually, the trail leads to the murderer, who is indeed one of the townsmen.

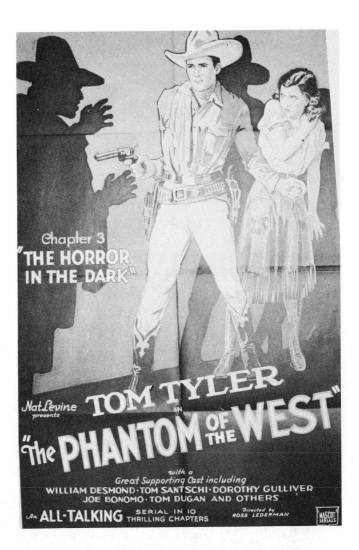

Spell of the Circus

10 Episodes   Directed by
Universal, 1931   Robert F. Hill

CAST

Jack Grant	Francis X. Bushman, Jr.
Marie Wallace	Alberta Vaughn
Butte Morgan	Tom London
George Wallace	Walter Shumway
Hank Harris	Charles Murphy
Totto	Monte Montague
Bobby	Bobby Nelson

Morgan, manager of The Big Circus, wants to marry Marie Wallace, the circus owner's daughter, so that he can gain control of the circus. Marie, in turn, is in love with Jack Grant, a Wild West Show cowboy.

Morgan hires someone to impersonate a minister, kidnaps Marie, and has a wedding ceremony performed. Jack finds out about the scheme and saves Marie from Morgan.

One night during a storm, Morgan returns while a performance is underway. With an off-beat desire to impress the Wallaces, he cuts the ropes holding the pole of the big tent and then attempts to kidnap Marie once again.

Grant prevents a disaster and injury to the hundreds attending the show and then fights a battle with Morgan in which the villain is vanquished and turned over to the police.

Bobby Nelson is prepared to clobber the villain with a pole, as Alberta Vaughn clings close to Francis X. Bushman, Jr.

Little Bobby Nelson pleads for help, as Francis X. Bushman, Jr., lies pinned under a car.

The Vanishing Legion

12 Episodes   Directed by
Mascot, 1931   Reeves Eason

CAST

Cardigan	Harry Carey
Caroline Hall	Edwina Booth
Rex	Rex
Jimmie Williams	Frankie Darro
Stevens	Philo McCullough
Sheriff of Milesburg	William Desmond
Stuffy	Joe Bonomo
Jed Williams	Edward Hearn
Sheriff of Slocum	Al Taylor
Hornback	Lafe McKee
Dodger	Dick Hatton
Dopey	Peter Morrison
Rawlins	Dick Dickinson
Larno	Bob Kortman
Laribee	Paul Weigel
Bishop	Frank Brownlee
Cowboy	Yakima Canutt
Warren	Tom Dugan
Allen	Bob Walker

Harry Carey (*left*) in jaw-to-jaw combat.

1932

The Airmail Mystery

12 Episodes
Universal, 1932

Directed by
Ray Taylor

CAST

Bob Lee	James Flavin
Mary Ross	Lucile Browne
Judson Ward	
(The Black Hawk)	Wheeler Oakman
Mason	Frank S. Hagney
Driscoll	Sidney Bracey
"Silent" Sims	Nelson McDowell
Holly	Walter Brennan
Jimmy Ross	Al Wilson
Captain Grant	Bruce Mitchell
Andy	Jack Holley

Bob Lee, airmail pilot, owns a gold mine whose operator is constantly harassed by the evil Black Hawk who has also kidnapped Jimmy Ross, Bob's best friend and the brother of his sweetheart Mary Ross.

Bob persistently tries to find Jimmy (who is saved and recaptured on several occasions) and get gold shipments from his mine to town despite the Hawk's determined effort to prevent him from doing so.

The Hawk is able to conduct a successful campaign of terror because of his aerial catapult—an amazing mechanism that throws an airplane into the sky without the use of a conventional runway.

In the end, Jimmy's cool thinking, Bob's strong nerves, and a bullet from Sims's rifle spell doom for the Hawk.

Lucile Browne and James Flavin.

Lucile Browne, Wheeler Oakman, and Frank S. Hagney.

Detective Lloyd

12 Episodes
Universal, 1932

Directed by
Henry McRae

CAST

Chief Inspector Lloyd	Jack Lloyd
Giles Wade, the Panther	Wallace Geoffrey
Sybil Craig	Muriel Angelus
Randall Hale	Lewis Dayton
Dion Brooks	Janice Adair
Chester Dunn	Tracy Holmes
The Manor Ghost	Emily Fitzroy
The Lodgekeeper	Humberstone Wright
Superintendent Barclay	John Turnbull
Inspector Walters	Shayle Gardner
Sergeant Sherwood	Clifford Buckton
Charwoman	Vic Kaley
Curator	Fewlass Llewillyn
Housekeeper	Ethel Ramsey
Egyptians	Gibb McLaughlin
	Earle Stanley
	Cecil Musk

Zealous and ruthless priests of the Temple of Amenhotep II vie against a band of international desperadoes for a valuable amulet that is in the possession of Lord Hale of Depedene Manor. The desperadoes are headed by the Panther, a master of disguise, who uses his talent to throw Detective Lloyd off of his track.

When the amulet disappears, each group believes the other has it; fiendish plans are made on both sides to get hold of it. Both the Egyptians and the crooks use every trick of the intrigue trade from kidnapping to gassing people to get their way.

Detective Lloyd, however, combines tenacity and endurance to withstand the efforts of both villainous factions. He not only recovers the amulet, but also becomes engaged to Lord Hale's niece.

The Devil Horse

12 Episodes   Directed by
Mascot, 1932   Otto Brower

CAST

Norton Roberts	Harry Carey
Canfield	Noah Beery
The Wild Boy	Frankie Darro
The Devil Horse	Apache
The Wild Boy at Five Years	Carli Russell

A fiery wild steed is spotted by Canfield and his group of unscrupulous villains who decide that such a magnificent animal would be of great value. Canfield will stop at nothing—including murder—to gain possession of the beast, called the Devil Horse. The Devil Horse is the leader of a herd of wild horses and is protected by a young Wild Boy, who has been reared by the herd since he wandered among them at the age of five.

Canfield kills a forest ranger who stands in the way of his efforts. But the ranger's brother, Norton Roberts, vows revenge, and, in the course of tracking down the murderer, crosses paths with the Devil Horse and Wild Boy, enlisting their aid in the hunt. At last justice catches up with Canfield! The Devil Horse tramples him to death and finds its way back to the wilderness to run with the herd again.

Harry Carey and Frankie Darro try to help the wounded Devil Horse.

Frank Lackteen creeps up on a blissful Diane Duval and Onslow Stevens.

Heroes of the West

12 Episodes   Directed by
Universal, 1932   Ray Taylor

CAST

Noah Blaine	Noah Beery, Jr.
Ann Blaine	Diane Duval
Tom Crosby	Onslow Stevens
John Blaine	William Desmond
Martha Blaine	Martha Mattex
Rance Judd	Philo McCullough
Butch Gole	Harry Tenbrook
Buckskin Joe	Frank Lackteen
Bart Eaton	Edmund Cobb
Missouri	Jules Cowles
Captain Donovan	Francis Ford
Thunderbird	Thunderbird

The building of the transcontinental rail- road is fraught with great danger and calls for supreme courage on the part of John Blaine who is awarded a contract to build a section of the road. With his eighteen-year-old son Noah and his daughter, Ann, Blaine treks across the treacherous country and establishes his construction camp in the heart of Wyoming, on the border of hostile Indian territory.

Many forces unite to stop Blaine from completing the road on time—crookedness within the camp and the consequent delay, the conspiracy of Blaine's political enemies to take his building contract away from him, and the repeated attacks of hordes of Indians. But with the leadership of plucky young Noah and engineer Tom Crosby, the hardships of railroad pioneering are overcome and the railroad is successfully built.

Indians encircle the wagon train in the classic tradition.

Kneeling behind his horse, Noah Beery, Jr., prepares to defend his sister Diane Duval.

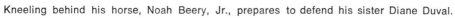

The Hurricane Express

12 Episodes
Mascot, 1932

Directed by
Armand Schaefer
and J. P. McGowan

CAST

Larry Baker	John Wayne
Gloria Martin Stratton	Shirley Grey
Mr. Edwards	Tully Marshall
Stevens	Conway Tearle
Jim Baker	J. Farrell MacDonald
Jordan	Matthew Betz
Hemingway	James Burtis
Walter Gray	Lloyd Whitlock
Matthews	Joseph Girard
Stratton	Edmund Breese
Carlson	Al Bridge
Barney	Ernie Adams
Mike	Charles King
Jim	Glenn Strange

The father of young air transport pilot Larry Baker is killed in one of a series of mysterious train wrecks. Baker determines to track down and demolish "The Wrecker," a shadowy figure who has been causing the crashes. But the search for the Wrecker is complicated by his diabolical ability to assume the appearance of anyone he may choose.

Rivalry between the L. & R. Railroad and the air transport line is keen. Gray, the head of the airline, is under suspicion, as is Stratton, an escaped convict who had been falsely prosecuted by an official of the L. & R. for embezzlement. And then there's Jordan, a discharged employee of the railroad, who has vowed to get even. Stratton's daughter Gloria, whom Larry loves, helps the young pilot in his quest.

Railroad wrecks . . . the armed air transport's night attack on the "Hurricane" as it roars over the rails carrying a huge shipment of gold . . . Larry and Gloria trapped in a blazing passenger plane as it careens madly through space—these are just some of the hazards faced by the intrepid couple as they attempt to bring the master criminal to justice. But finally the young pilot captures the Wrecker, avenges his father's death, and looks forward to a happy life with Gloria.

The Jungle Mystery

12 Episodes
Universal, 1932

Directed by
Ray Taylor

CAST

Kirk Montgomery	Tom Tyler
Barbara Morgan	Cecelia Parker
Mr. Morgan	William Desmond
Shillow	Philo McCullough
Fred Oakes	Noah Beery, Jr.
Belle Waldron	Carmelita Geraghty
Zungu	Sam Baker

While hunting in Africa, Kirk Montgomery and his friend Fred Oakes encounter Shillow, a rival hunter, who is searching for a vast store of ivory. Kirk and Fred later meet Barbara Morgan and her father who are seeking the girl's missing brother. The two friends decide to team up with the Morgans and aid them in their quest. Shillow and his gang, which includes the treacherous adventuress Belle Waldron, do their best to obstruct and discourage the Morgan party, fearing that the latter group is also after the ivory.

Shillow's schemes are aided when the friends encounter wild beasts and unfriendly natives, and get entangled in a series of captures and escapes. The friends are helped by a mysterious jungle ape-man named Zungu who has a sympathetic disposition toward virtue as well as a split-second sense of timing. With his help, the friends soon rout the Shillow party, and find Barbara's brother. Tom and Cecelia can look forward to a more relaxed relationship.

It looks like a hopeless situation for Tom Tyler.

Sam Baker appears to menace Cecelia Parker as Tom Tyler gets set to swing his rifle butt, Frank Lackteen stands alert and Noah Beery, Jr. takes aim.

Frank Lackteen prepares to make an incision on Tom Tyler's arm as Noah Beery, Jr., holds his friend steady.

Noah Beery, Jr., and William Desmond grip Tom Tyler's wrists and pull him to safety, as Cecelia Parker (*right*) looks on.

The Lost Special

12 Episodes
Universal, 1932

Directed by
Henry McRae

CAST

Tom Hood	Frank Albertson
Betty Moore	Cecilia Parker
Bob Collins	Ernie Nevers
Kate Bland	Caryl Lincoln
Botter Hood	Francis Ford
Sam Slater	Frank Glendon
Dink	Tom London
Gavin	Al Ferguson
Spike	Edmund Cobb
Lefty	George Magrill
Joe	Joe Bonomo
Professor Wilson	Harold Nelson
Doran	Jack Clifford

The "Gold Special," a train from the rich Golconda Mines, is stolen without a sign of where it might have been taken. The combined efforts of secret service agents, special detection officers, and local police meet with no success. Then two college athletes, Tom Hood and Bob Collins, and Betty Moore, a young lady newspaper reporter, and her girl friend enter the scene.

After diligently pursuing clues and avoiding numerous attempts on their lives, the friends discover that the train has been hidden in a secret mine shaft and that the mastermind behind the theft is Sam Slater, half-owner of the Golconda. The youngsters resolve the mystery before it's time to return to school.

Frank Albertson and Ernie Nevers help Cecelia Parker to her feet.

The powerful Joe Bonomo about to help Frank Albertson down a flight of stairs the hard way.

Frank Albertson and Cecelia Parker look for a way through a raging forest fire.

Frank Albertson, Cecelia Parker, and an ally are trapped in a dungeon rapidly filling with water.

The Last Frontier

12 Episodes
RKO-Radio, 1932

Directed by
Spencer Bennet

CAST

Tom Kirby	Creighton Chaney (Lon Chaney, Jr.)
Betty Halliday	Dorothy Gulliver
Aggie Kirby	Mary Jo Desmond
Jeff Maillad	Francis X. Bushman, Jr.
Blackie	Joe Bonomo
Happy	Slim Cole
Rose Matland	Judith Barrie
Tiger Morris	Richard Neil
Custer	William Desmond
Buch	Leroy Mason
Wild Bill Hickok	Yakima Canutt
Hank	Pete Morrison
Colonel Halliday	Claude Peyton
Mama Morris	Fritzi Fem
Tex	Bill Nesteld

Frontier newspaper editor Tom Kirby fights a band of outlaws, led by Tiger Morris. Morris has discovered a rich deposit of gold and is fomenting Indian uprisings in order to drive settlers off this valuable property. After Tom uncovers a cache of arms meant for the Indians, he is accused of being a renegade himself.

Despite this setback, Tom continues to fight the outlaws with the aid of Colonel Halliday, his daughter Betty, and General Custer. The most help, however, comes from the Black Ghost, a tireless range-riding fighter for law and order.

In a final gun encounter, Kirby vanquishes Morris and sets a wedding date with Betty.

The Shadow of the Eagle

12 Episodes
Mascot, 1932

Directed by
Ford Beebe

CAST

Craig McCoy	John Wayne
Jean Gregory	Dorothy Gulliver
Danby	Walter Miller
Ward	Kenneth Harlan
Evans	Richard Tucker
Ames	Pat O'Malley
Boyle	Yakima Canutt
Clark	Edmund Burns
Gardner	Roy D'Arcy
Clown	Billy West
Nathan Gregory	Edward Hearn
Green	Lloyd Whitlock

A sensational wartime flyer, Nathan Gregory, now owner of a traveling carnival, is accused of being "The Eagle," a criminal who has been sending mysterious threats to the officers of a large corporation, by means of skywriting. Gregory denies the charge, although he admits a motive for revenge, since the success of the corporation is due to an invention stolen from him. One of Gregory's troupe, Craig McCoy, is also a clever skywriter.

When Craig discovers that Gregory's plans for the invention have been stolen, he pursues Green, a director of the corporation, who is running from the scene. Green escapes from Craig and catches up with two ruffians, Boyle and Moore. When Boyle displays the stolen plans, Craig dashes past on his motorcycle, seizes the plans, and returns to the circus grounds. There he and Jean, Gregory's daughter, discover that Gregory has disappeared.

Gregory has been kidnapped by the Eagle, but by clever detective work is located by Jean, who quickly calls Craig for help. Craig comes to the rescue and, following an ever-widening trail of clues, succeeds in eventually unmasking the Eagle.

1933

Clancy of the Mounted

12 Episodes   Directed by
Universal, 1933   Ray Taylor

CAST

Sergeant Tom Clancy   Tom Tyler
Ann Louise   Jaqueline Wells
Steve Clancy   Earl McCarthy
Dave Moran   William Desmond
Maureen Clancy   Rosalie Roy
"Black" MacDougal   W. L. Thomas
Pierre LaRue   Leon Duval
Inspector Cabot   Francis Ford
Constable MacGregor   Tom London
Constable McIntosh   Edmund Cobb

Steve Clancy, the brother of Mountie Tom Clancy, is framed for the murder of John Laurie by LaRue and MacDougal who are after the dead man's gold mine. Tom is assigned to bring his brother in.

Fortunately, snowstorms, renegade Indians, a wolf pack, and fast-running rapids interfere with Tom's duties. These difficulties enable him to meet up with the real culprits. They also give him the opportunity to meet Ann, the dead man's daughter, who is also in danger of losing her life to the outlaws.

Tom walks a tightrope of peril, but eventually clears his brother, secures the Laurie mine, and kills the villain.

Tom Tyler is menaced from behind.

Tom Tyler (*right*) demands that outlaws release Jaqueline Wells and William Desmond.

Jaqueline Wells at the mercy of renegade half-breeds.

36

Fighting with Kit Carson

12 Episodes	Directed by
Mascot, 1933	Armand Schaefer
	and Colbert Clark

CAST

Kit Carson	Johnny Mack Brown
Joan Fargo	Betsy King Ross
Kraft	—Noah Beery
Nakomas	—Noah Beery, Jr.

A shipment of government gold is lost when the pack train headed up by famous scout Kit Carson is wiped out. Only Carson miraculously escapes. Aided by a detachment of cavalry, Carson rounds up the outlaw band known as the Mystery Riders.

Carson then leaves the soldiers and his Indian friend Nakomas to bring in the prisoners, and rides furiously back to the trading post, where his little friend Joan Fargo, disguised as a boy, has been keeping watch on Kraft—the man who Carson suspects is the secret leader of the Mystery Riders.

When he is accused of being the leader of the Mystery Riders, Kraft swears his innocence and makes a quick getaway. In order to trap him, Carson and the troopers don the garb of the Mystery Riders, with hopes that Kraft, upon seeing his men, will be fooled into giving away the location of his secret hiding place for the gold. However, Kraft spots a government badge on one of the riders, discovers the ruse, and leads the men to a false hideout, where gunpower is prepared to explode when the door is touched. In the nick of time, little Joan arrives with news that she has located Kraft's true hideout—underneath his barn. The gold is saved and scout Carson is on his way again.

Robert Warwick grips the neck of a menacing outlaw.

Gordon of Ghost City

12 Episodes
Universal, 1933

Directed by
Ray Taylor

CAST

Buck Gordon	℗ Buck Jones
Mary Gray	Madge Bellamy
Rance Radigan	Walter Miller
Ed	Hugh Enfield
John	William Desmond
Amos Gray	Tom Rickett
Jim Carmody	Francis Ford
Sheriff	Dick Rush
Scotty	Ed Cobb
Bob	William Steele
Tom	Bob Kerrick
Pete	Ethan Laidlaw
Jeff	Jim Corey
Hank	Bud Osborne
Silver	Silver

Buck Gordon is hired by John Mulford, a ranch owner, to hunt down a gang of cattle rustlers whose leader is Mulford's foreman Rance Radigan. Buck makes the acquaintance of Mary Gray whose grandfather, Amos, has discovered a rich vein of gold under his old store in Ghost City. He wants Mary to have it. A mystery man (who turns out to be Gray's old partner Jim Carmody), however, tries to stop the mining of the vein.

Faced with two diabolical foes, Buck calls on all his resources of mind and heart—plus those of his horse Silver—to protect Mary and reveal the outlaw's identity. Escaping prairie fires, stampedes, and outlaw bullets, Buck eventually succeeds in rounding up both opponents and wins Mary's heart as well.

Watched by Madge Bellamy, Buck Jones rounds up a trio of outlaws.

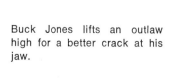

Buck Jones lifts an outlaw high for a better crack at his jaw.

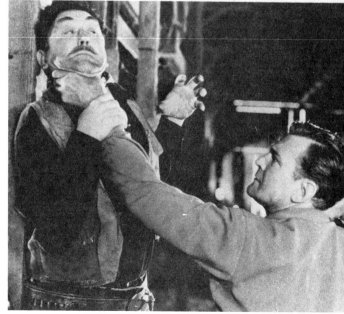

Buck Jones gets an interesting hold on a shocked Madge Bellamy.

A bound outlaw is brought in by Walter Miller, Buck Jones, and Madge Bellamy.

The clever Silver unties Buck Jones's bonds.

Madge Bellamy and Buck Jones, knocked unconscious after a wagon wreck.

Mystery Squadron

12 Episodes
Mascot, 1933

Directed by
Colbert Clark
and David Howard

CAST

Fred Cromwell	Bob Steele
Bill Cook	"Big Boy" Williams
Dorothy Gray	Lucile Browne
Davis	Jack Mulhall
Johnson	Purnell Pratt
Gray	Lafe McKee
The Black Ace	? ? ? ? ? ?

Stephen Gray, owner of a construction firm, is facing ruin as a result of mysterious airplane raids on the power dam which he is building. His foreman Hank Davis has enlisted the aid of two longtime friends and expert flyers—Fred Cromwell and Bill "Jelly Bean" Cook—in guarding the area. Davis, however, disappears shortly after.

The Black Ace, leader of the Mystery Squadron, has threatened to strike again unless Gray halts work on the dam. It seems that the proposed dam is to be built on the site of one of the richest gold mines in the country; if the dam is completed the gold will be submerged under fifty feet of water!

Lafe Johnson, a rival contractor, is suspected of being the Black Ace, but is soon able to prove his innocence. After a scuffle with the mysterious raiders, Cromwell finds Davis tied up in a car. Davis claims that he has been held prisoner all this time by the Mystery Squadron.

Bit by bit, all the evidence is pieced together and points to Davis as the guilty one. Realizing he has been successfully identified, Davis manages to make a getaway in his plane. Cromwell and Cook follow him into the air, fire at his plane, and Davis—the Black Ace—plunges to a flaming death!

The Phantom of the Air

12 Episodes
Universal, 1933

Directed by
Ray Taylor

CAST

Bob Raymond	Tom Tyler
Mary Edmunds	Gloria Shea
Mort Crome	LeRoy Mason
Blade	Hugh Enfield
Mr. Edmunds	William Desmond
Munsa	Sidney Bracey
"Skid"	Walter Brennan
Marie	Jennie Cramer
Joe	Cecil Kellog

Bob Raymond is hired by Thomas Edmunds to test his new invention the Contragrav, a device designed to overcome the effects of gravity and thereby revolutionize aviation.

Crome, disguised as a mild-mannered aviator and actually the head of a notorious gang of smugglers, would like to get his hands on the new invention to advance his own evil plans.

To ward off Crome's gang of thugs, Edmunds employs "The Phantom," a marvelous airplane that he can control from his underground headquarters. With the aid of the mechanical marvel, Crome's effort to steal Edmunds's invention is rendered futile.

Crome makes a last attempt to force Edmunds's secret from him in the inventor's workshop. However, Edmunds presses a button and the entire workshop is blown to atoms and Crome is killed. Fortunately Edmunds survives and is reunited with his daughter Mary and pilot Raymond.

Tarzan the Fearless

15 Episodes	Directed by
Principal, 1933	Robert F. Hill

CAST

Tarzan	Buster Crabbe
Mary Brooks	Jaqueline Wells
Dr. Brooks	E. Alyn Warren
Bob Hall	Edward Woods
Jeff	Philo McCullough
Nick	Matthew Betz
Abdul	Frank Lackteen
High Priest	Mischa Auer

Dr. Brooks is captured by followers of Zar, God of the Jeweled Fingers, but he is soon rescued from their lost city by Tarzan. Tarzan speaks no English but undertakes to locate Dr. Brooks's daughter Mary after seeing a photograph of her.

Meanwhile, Mary and Bob Hall are searching for Dr. Brooks. Their guides, Jeff and Nick, are more interested in unearthing a lost jungle treasure and in winning Mary than in finding Dr. Brooks. Jeff is in the possession of a message offering a large reward for Tarzan—dead or mortally wounded. A group of Arabs, who are also captivated by Mary, accompany the searchers.

During a series of robberies, kidnappings, plots and counterplots, everyone is captured by the followers of Zar, escapes, and is recaptured. The guides Jeff and Nick are killed and everyone promises never to return to the city.

Mary decides to remain with Tarzan in the jungle, and her father returns home.

Edward Woods and Jaqueline Wells discuss the fate of their expedition.

The Three Musketeers

12 Episodes   Directed by
Mascot, 1933   Armand Schaefer
            and Colbert Clark

CAST

Tom Wayne	John Wayne
Elaine Corday	Ruth Hall
Clancy	Jack Mulhall
Renard	Raymond Hatton
Schmidt	Francis X. Bushman, Jr.
Stubbs	Noah Beery, Jr.
Armand Corday	Creighton Chaney
Ali	Al Ferguson
El Kador	Hooper Atchely
Ratkin	Edward Piel
El Maghreb	George Magill
Colonel Duval	Gordon De Main
Captain Boncover	William Desmond
Major Booth	Robert Frazier
General Pelletier	Emile Chautard
Colonel Brent	Robert Warwick
Demoyne	Rodney Hildebrandt

Three Legionnaires get drawn into a circle of death by El Shasta, the Devil of the Desert, a man who never shows his face; a human vulture who plots death for anyone disagreeing with his destructive schemes. The three buddies are rescued from sure death at the hands of desert rebels by an American D'Artagnan who takes them out of the frying pan and into the fire of constant peril.

The Legionnaires and their new friend embark on a series of adventures to uncover the identity of El Shasta. But their task is formidable for El Shasta casts a shadow of evil wherever he and his men move and the desert is an extremely harsh environment. Eventually, however, they triumph.

Whispering Shadows

12 Episodes   Directed by
Mascot, 1933   Albert Herman
            and Colbert Clark

CAST

Professor Strang	Bela Lugosi
Bradley	Henry B. Walthall
Sparks	Karl Dane
Vera Strang	Viva Tattersall
Jack Foster	Malcolm MacGregor
Raymond	Robert Warwick
Steinbeck	Roy D'Arcy
Bud Foster	George Lewis
The Countess	Ethel Clayton
Dr. Young	Lloyd Whitlock
Slade	Bob Kortman
Dupont	Tom London
Martin Jerome	Lafe McKee

In the House of Mystery, a waxworks, the sinister Professor Strang makes wax figures that move and speak with lifelike precision.

Each time one of the radio-equipped trucks of a huge moving and storage company transports one of Strang's figures, its driver is attacked and killed by the henchman of the Whispering Shadow. Each holdup is preceded by the mysterious jamming of the broadcasting apparatus in the radio laboratory atop the warehouse.

No man has ever seen the Shadow in the flesh; but his fiendish genius for manipulating radio and television enables him to project his voice and shadow where he will. He can see through doors, hear through walls, and electrocute people by radio death ray!

Which of the several men bent on possessing the priceless jewels secretly stored in the transport warehouse is the Whispering Shadow?

Professor Strang? Steinbeck, the mysterious Russian who has charge of the warehouse radio room? Jerome, a suspicious official of the company, whose mysterious interests bring him to the radio room in dead of night? Slade, escaped convict and internationally famous jewel thief? These men and many others are under suspicion, but, when the Whispering Shadow is finally apprehended, he turns out to be the innocuous and trusted Sparks.

Bela Lugosi whispers instructions to Vera Strang in the House of Mystery.

The Wolf Dog

12 Episodes	Directed by
Mascot, 1933	Harry Frazer
	and Colbert Clark

CAST

Pal	Rin-Tin-Tin, Jr.
Frank	Frankie Darro
Bob	George Lewis
Irene	Boots Mallory
Jim Courtney	Henry B. Walthall
Stevens	Fred Kohler

Frank finds a wounded dog, nurses him back to health, and becomes his inseparable pal. The two comrades meet Bob, an inventor of an electric ray that can destroy ships at a distance of several miles. Bob intends to turn the device over to the government, but Bryan, the evil general manager of the Courtney Steamship Lines plans to steal it.

Bryan tries to kidnap Frank and kill Bob on numerous occasions. A speedboat chase, a desperate struggle on the running board of a fast-moving car, and a spectacular explosion caused by the electric ray are just a few of the dangers encountered.

But thanks to the heroism of the boy and the inventor and the intelligence of the dog, the crooks are brought to bay. Bob's invention is perfected and Frank and Pal are reunited.

1934

Burn 'Em Up Barnes

12 Episodes
Mascot, 1934

Directed by
Colbert Clark
and Armand Schaefer

CAST

Bobbie	Frankie Darro
Barnes	Jack Mulhall
Marjorie Temple	Lola Lane
Tony	Julian Rivero
Warren	Edwin Maxwell
Drummond	Jason Robards
Ray Ridpath	Francis McDonald
George—cameraman	James Bush
Joe Stevens	Stanley Blystone
Tucker—detective	Al Bridge
Frazer	Bob Kortman
Parsons	Tom London
Parker	Eddie Hearn
Chase	John Davidson
District Attorney	Lloyd Whitlock
Director—Lambert	Bruce Mitchell
Assistant Director	Jimmy Burtis

A speed demon and a "champ" at any style of racing, "Burn 'Em Up Barnes" adopts Bobbie, the kid brother of his buddy who was killed in a race. Barnes enters into partnership in an auto transportation business with Marjorie Temple, whose life he has saved in a battle with transportation racketeers.

Drummond, a scheming promoter, knows that land Marjorie has inherited contains very valuable oil deposits and tries every means to wreck her business and force her to sell her land at a low price.

"Burn 'Em Up Barnes" and his pal Bobbie take desperate chances to raise money and prevent Marjorie from losing her property. In every race Barnes enters, attempts are made on his life. Finally, aided by Bobbie, who has become an "ace" newsreel cameraman, Barnes overcomes the gigantic odds of men and money against him and wins out.

Could it be that hero Jack Mulhall has actually been shot in the heart by Wheeler Oakman?

The Law of the Wild

12 Episodes
Mascot, 1934

Directed by
Armand Schaefer
and Reeves Eason

CAST

Rex	Himself
Rin-Tin-Tin, Jr.	Himself
Sheldon	Bob Custer
Henry	Ben Turpin
Alice	Lucile Browne
Nolan	Richard Cramer
Raymond	Ernie Adams
Jim Luger	Edmund Cobb
Mack	Charles Whitaker
Salter	Dick Alexander
Sheriff	Jack Rockwell
Parks	George Chesebro

Sheldon, a young rancher, has roped and tamed Rex, King of the Wild Horses, and gained the animal's confidence and affection. Rinty, a magnificent police dog, is another of Sheldon's pals. The dog and horse soon become firm friends. Salter, one of Sheldon's men, conceives the idea of stealing Rex and training him for the track, and carries it off successfully.

After winning a race with Rex, Salter is killed by Luger, who has aided him and with whom Sheldon has refused to divide the purse. Sheldon, coming to reclaim Rex, is accused of the murder. Nolan, a crooked racetrack tout, claims the dead Salter had sold the horse to him. Realizing it is a frame-up, Sheldon with the aid of Rinty, flees until he can prove his innocence. He receives valuable aid from Alice Ingram, Alice's father, a well-to-do rancher and horse owner, and Henry, their cross-eyed stable boy.

Sheldon compiles evidence against Nolan and his henchmen and Alice wins a fortune on betting on Rex in a big sweepstakes race. Sheldon gets the necessary evidence to clear himself, and he and Rinty clean out Nolan's gang.

Rex and Rin-Tin-Tin, Jr., enjoy a rare moment of tranquility.

The Lost Jungle

12 Episodes
Mascot, 1934

Directed by
Armand Schaefer
and David Howard

CAST

Clyde Beatty	Clyde Beatty
Ruth Robinson	Cecelia Parker
Larry Henderson	Syd Saylor
Sharkey	Warner Richmond
Kirby	Wheeler Oakman
Thompson	Maston Williams
Explorer	J. Crawford Kent
Howard	Lloyd Whitlock
Bannister	Lloyd Ingraham
Captain Robinson	Edward Le Saint
Flynn	Lou Meehan
Slade	Max Wagner
Jackman	Wes Warner
The Cook	Jack Carlyle
Steve	Jim Corey
Sandy	Lionel Backus
Pete	Ernie Adams
Maitland	Harry Holman
Mickey	Mickey Rooney

A young Mickey Rooney.

Clyde Beatty, the world's greatest animal trainer and menagerie expert, is a shy young fellow except when he is putting his "cats" through their paces in a big cage. He is so shy, in fact, that he cannot summon up courage to propose to Ruth Robinson.

When Ruth's father, Captain Robinson, charters his ship to Professor Livingston to search for an uncharted island in the tropic seas, Ruth calls at the winter quarters of Maitland's Circus where Clyde is rehearsing his lions and tigers. She tells him she is going on the cruise with her father. Despite the opportunity this announcement presents, and the doleful prospect of losing her for a whole year, Clyde still lacks the courage to propose to her.

Later, word reaches him that Professor Livingston's party is lost in the jungle. Clyde, intent on saving Ruth, joins the rescue party which sets out in a giant dirigible. Although the airship is wrecked in a terrific hurricane, Clyde and a few other survivors manage to land in the lost jungle on the uncharted island.

Clyde finds Ruth and her father but learns that Professor Livingston has mysteriously disappeared. Clyde, Ruth, and Captain Robinson, accompanied by Larry, the circus press agent, and Sharkey, a jealous assistant, feverishly organize search parties to find Professor Livingston. Progress is further impeded by a group of white men searching for gold. Clyde overcomes these human obstacles, as well as the additional danger of man-eating animals, to find the professor and return to the mainland with Ruth, his bride-to-be.

Clyde Beatty offers a few helpful hints on animal training to Mickey Rooney and his pals.

Syd Saylor and Clyde Beatty take care at the edge of an animal pit.

Mystery Mountain

12 Episodes
Mascot, 1934

Directed by
Otto Brower
and Reeves Eason

CAST

Ken Williams	Ken Maynard
Jane Corwin	Verna Hillie
Blayden	Edward Earle
The Rattler	Eddie Cobb
Matthews	Lynton Brent
Breezy	Syd Saylor
Little Jane	Carmencita Johnson
Mr. Corwin	Lafe McKee
Henderson	Al Bridge
Lake	Eddie Hearn
Hank	Bob Kortman

When the B. & L. Railroad builds a tunnel that will put the Corwin Transportation Company out of business, Jane Corwin's father is the first person in a long line of people who are mysteriously murdered.

Behind these murders is the sinister figure of "the Rattler"—the Menace of the Mountain. But another stranger—Ken Williams—appears on the scene, determined to solve the multiple crimes.

Williams picks up the Rattler's trail and learns that the Rattler, operating from his headquarters deep within the mountain, has a grand design to control the entire area. After numerous gunfights with the Rattler's henchmen, as well as split-second escapes from crashing stage-coaches and exploding mines, Williams corners the Rattler in his lair, destroys the criminal's sophisticated electrical equipment, and escapes just before the damaged machinery explodes, blowing up half of the mountain and burying the Rattler in the rubble of his phantom empire.

The Rattler, complete with cape, mask, and false mustache, about to deliver a hard right to the struggling Ken Maynard.

Perils of Pauline

12 Episodes
Universal, 1934

CAST

Pauline Hargrave	Evalyn Knapp
Robert Ward	Robert Allen
Professor Hargrave	James Durkin
Dr. Bashan	John Davidson
Willie Dodge	Sonny Ray
Fang	Frank Lackteen
Aviator	Pat O'Malley
Professor Thompson	William Desmond
Captain	Adolph Muller
Foreign Consul	Josef Swickard
American Consul	William Worthington

Dr. Hargrave, a noted scientist, is in Indo-China seeking an ivory disc that is engraved with the formula for a deadly gas. Dr. Bashan and his henchmen are also after the secret formula and will stop at nothing to get it.

Dr. Hargrave's daughter Pauline and air engineer Robert Ward discover Bashan's fiendish designs and protect Dr. Hargrave from him. Bashan and his assistant Fang try to blow them up on several occasions. In addition, the two friends have to contend with bands of murderous natives.

In the end, Bashan and Fang are in possession of the disc and seem to be on the verge of discovering the deadly gas when Robert attacks their lab. Both villains are killed.

Hargrave can now perfect the poison gas without fear of further trouble from Bashan, and Robert and Pauline take a slow train to China.

Robert Allen (*left*) greets William Desmond as Evalyn Knapp, Sonny Ray, and James Durkin watch.

50

Two durable villains, John Davidson and Frank Lackteen.

ever-sinister John Davidson.

Evalyn Knapp tries to discourage whatever it is that John Davidson has in mind.

Pirate Treasure

12 Episodes
Universal, 1934

Directed by
Ray Taylor

CAST

Dick Moreland — Richard Talmadge
Dorothy Craig — Lucille Lund
Stanley Brasset — Walter Miller
John Craig — Pat O'Malley
Captain Carson — William Desmond
Drake — William E. Thorne
Robert Moreland — Del Lawrence
Curt — Ethan Laidlaw
Jed — George de Normand
Tony — Al Ferguson
Marge — Beulah Hutton

During a reception at the Aeroclub, Dick Moreland announces that he is going to search for a treasure buried on a tropical island by one of his piratical ancestors. He has recently found a map to guide him. Stanley Brasset, a criminal lawyer, decides to steal the map and go after the treasure himself.

Despite the help of his henchmen—Curt, Tony, Mike, and Marge—Brasset's efforts at robbery fail. He then tries to sabotage Dick's boat but fails in that attempt also. Once on the island, however, he does manage to steal the treasure from Dick. But as soon as his gang opens the chest, they are attacked and captured by the island's natives. Dick befriends the tribe by giving them some jewels and ransoms the villains. The gang is then taken to the ship and put in irons.

The Red Rider

15 Episodes
Universal, 1934

Directed by
Louis Friedlander

CAST

Red Davidson	Buck Jones
Silent Slade	Grant Withers
Marie Maxwell	Marion Shilling
Jim Breen	Walter Miller
Joe Portos	Richard Cramer
Joan McKee	Margaret LaMarr
Robert Maxwell	Charles French
Johnny Snow	Edmund Cobb
Scotty McKee	J. P. McGowan
Sheriff	William Desmond

Red sacrifices his job as sheriff and his good name to save his best pal Silent Slade from the noose, following a court decision in which Slade has been sentenced to hang for the murder of Scotty McKee. Believing Slade innocent, Red allows him to escape from jail and pledges to aid him in proving his innocence.

Red is forced to turn in his badge and leaves Marlin City that night. Several months later, Red arrives in a small town near the Mexican border. There he meets the sheriff who tells him that he might find a job at the ranch of Robert Maxwell. Red arrives at the ranch in time to save Marie, Maxwell's daughter, from the unwelcome attentions of Jim Breen. Red discovers the man with Breen is his pal Slade but is warned to say nothing.

While working on the ranch, Red makes friends with Johnny Snow and tells him he suspects Breen is the man who killed McKee. Johnny promises to aid Red in proving Breen's guilt. They learn that Maxwell has been tricked into a smuggling deal with Breen. As Maxwell and Breen leave the house, Red and Johnny follow them to a cantina. Soon, four men bring Maxwell out of the place and tie him to a horse. Red knocks out one of the men and saves Maxwell.

Eventually, Red proves that Breen is guilty of the crime, and Slade is once again a free man.

Buck Jones and a half-breed ally.

52

The Return of Chandu
(The Magician)

12 Episodes	Directed by
Principal, 1934	Ray Taylor

CAST

Frank Chandler (Chandu)	Bela Lugosi
Princess Nadji	Maria Alba
Dorothy Regent	Clara Kimball Young
Vindhyan	Lucien Prival
Betty Regent	Phyllis Ludwig
Bob Regent	Dean Benton
Prince Andre	Bryant Washburn
Judy	Peggy Montgomery
Sertia	April Armbuster
Bara	Elias Lazaroff
Morta	Dick Botellier
Nito	Frazer Acosta
Voice of Ubasti	Murdock McQuaine
Vitras	Jack Clark
Tyba	Josef Swickard
Tagora	Harry Walker
Mr. James	Charles Meecham
Mrs. James	Isobel LeMall

On the magic island of Lemuria, the followers of the Black Magic Cult of Ubasti prepare for their reemergence as a great power in the world. Before this can happen, however, their grand priest tells them that a proper sacrifice must be made, in this case the lovely Nadji, Princess of Egypt. Peering into the sacred flame, the grand priest locates the whereabouts of the princess and dispatches several underlings to kidnap her.

Frank Chandler, known as Chandu the magician, has been entertaining Nadji. When he prepares to embark by boat on a voyage, he leaves Nadji with his sister Frances and his neice and nephew Betty and Bob. As Chandu departs, the sinister henchman of Ubasti uses his magical power to cast a spell over Nadji, convincing her to come immediately to a nearby cottage. Suspicious of Nadji's behavior, Frances, Betty, and Bob go along with her.

Meanwhile, at sea, Chandu receives strange vibrations that warn him of Nadji's danger. Looking into his crystal ball, Chandu contacts "the great yogi," his "teacher across the sea," who advises him to return to port immediately. Chandu quickly has the boat turned around and heads back with all possible speed.

In the cottage, Nadji is tricked into entering a room with the Ubasti agent, who has set up a small flaming urn and black magic implements. He explains the purpose of his mission to Nadji, and, as the princess struggles in his arms, he ignites a flaming circle around them, causing them both to vanish. At this point, Chandu bursts into the room, to find that only the still smoking circle and the religious artifacts remain. Chandu recognizes them instantly and surmises that Nadji has been taken to the Magic Island of Lemuria. He sets sail for Lemuria immediately. Frances, Betty, and Bob decide to accompany him.

But Chandu's progress is being watched by the evil grand priest, who has planted an agent on Chandu's ship. As the craft approaches the Magic Island, the agent executes various acts of sabotage and sinks the ship. Only Chandu, Frances, Betty, Bob, and the ship's captain survive, washed up on the shore of Lemuria. When Chandu leaves his friends to explore the island, Frances, Betty, Bob, and the captain are captured by Ubasti followers and taken to the imperial palace where they are imprisoned. As Chandu approaches the entrance to the palace, a trapdoor opens and Chandu finds himself in a vast underground labyrinth from which there is no escape.

As he wanders through the endless tunnels, Chandu comes across a grating built into the ground. Peering into the grating, Chandu spies a bearded, white-robed old man looking up at him. The old man explains that he is the benevolent leader of the followers of White Magic who has been deposed and imprisoned by the high priest of Black Magic. Chandu lifts the heavy grating from its place, lowers himself into the cell, and explains his situation to the old man. Together they plan to thwart the high priest's

Sol Lesser presents
BELA LUGOSI in
'THE RETURN OF CHANDU
(THE MAGICIAN)

EPISODE No. 6
CHANDU'S FALSE STEP
Distributed by PRINCIPAL DISTRIBUTING CORP.

scheme. To help Chandu rescue the others the old man summons his own magic powers and makes Chandu invisible. But Chandu's invisibility will last only as long as sand remains in the upper half of a magic hourglass.

Meanwhile, Bob has been brought to a torture room and strapped to a table; an enormous razor-sharp sword swings above him and is slowly lowered toward his body. Bob strains at his bonds as the sword swings closer and closer. Suddenly, to everyone's amazement, the sword stops in its arc and Bob's straps are mysteriously loosened. As the frightened guards flee, Chandu's voice tells Bob to join a friend in the next room. In the hallway Bob finds the old man, who introduces himself as an ally and leads Bob to a safe chamber.

As Chandu disrupts the grand priest's men, he suddenly loses his invisibility and is seized. The evil grand priest orders Chandu tied to the floor, where a huge stone is to be slowly lowered upon him, crushing him to death. As a burly guard releases the stone, Bob and the old magician appear. Bob grapples with the guard

and subdues him as the old man frees Chandu. The three fugitives then flee through the endless tunnels.

Meanwhile, Princess Nadji is being prepared for her role as a sacrifice to the Gods of Black Magic. She is brought to the great sacrificial chamber, but refuses to declare allegiance to the powers of Black Magic. As Chandu, Bob, and the Old Man make their way through the tunnels, they pass the sacrificial chamber and observe Nadji's situation. The noble Chandu refuses to run any farther, and, followed by his two friends, marches directly to Nadji's side, much to the astonishment of the grand priest and his followers. Nadji quickly realizes that Chandu is doomed because of his devotion to her.

She tells the grand priest that if he frees Chandu and his companions, she will willingly pledge her devotion to Black Magic and accept the sacrifice. The grand priest agrees, and Chandu, Bob, Betty, Aunt Frances, and the captain are escorted out of his kingdom. Chandu, however, decides to return and rescue Nadji.

He suddenly receives vibrations from the great Yogi, who tells him that, in order to save Nadji he will be permitted to employ "the great incantation," a chant of such awesome power that even Chandu is overwhelmed at being allowed to use it.

Chandu makes his way back into the imperial palace, where Nadji is about to be sacrificed. As Chandu recites "the great incantation," the place begins to tremble. The walls shake, the foundations of the sacrificial chamber begin to shift, and the building starts to collapse. As Chandu rushes to Nadji and leads her outside to safety, the palace comes crashing down, killing the grand priest and his followers.

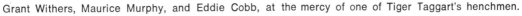

Tailspin Tommy

12 Episodes
Universal, 1934

Directed by
Louis Friedlander

CAST

Tailspin Tommy	Maurice Murphy
Betty Lou Barnes	Patricia Farr
Skeeter	Noah Beery, Jr.
Mrs. Tompkins	Belle Daube
Deacon Grimes	Lee Beggs
Milt Howe	Grant Withers
Bruce Hoyt	Walter Miller
Paul Smith	Charles A. Browne
Speed Walton	Edmund Cobb
Tiger Taggart	John Davidson
Cliff	Monte Montague
Al	Jack Leonard
Grease Rowley	Bud Osborne
Sloane	William Desmond

Tommy Tompkins, a youthful auto mechanic, is chosen by pilot Milt Howe of Three Points Airline to fly with him in a race against time for a mail-delivery contract. Thanks to Tommy, Milt wins the contract. But, in the process, he earns the emnity of Tiger Taggart who would like nothing more than to see Three Points fail.

Tommy soon becomes a Three Points pilot himself and battles Taggart's aerial pirates. He also prevents a runaway plane from crashing into a crowd of children, dangles from a refueling hose, survives an earthquake, crashes into the ocean, prevents a railroad catastrophe, and sees to it that Taggart and his henchmen are brought to justice.

In addition, Tommy wins a movie contract for himself and his sweetheart and fills his mother's heart with pride.

Grant Withers, Maurice Murphy, and Eddie Cobb, at the mercy of one of Tiger Taggart's henchmen.

The Vanishing Shadow

12 Episodes
Universal, 1934

Directed by
Louis Friedlander

CAST

Stanley Stanfield	Onslow Stevens
Gloria	Ada Ince
Ward Barnett	Walter Miller
Carl Van Dorn	James Durkin
MacDonald	William Desmond
Dorgan	Richard Cramer
Denny	Sidney Bracey
Kent	Eddie Cobb

Stanley Stanfield seeks revenge against a political group that was responsible for hounding his father to death through a relentless smear campaign. With the aid of Professor Van Dorn, he develops a wide array of technological devices that enable him to confront the evil-doers, and especially their leader, Barnett.

When Barnett tries to frame Stanley with a murder rap for the killing of an underworld figure, the zealous avenger begins to employ his complex arsenal of weapons: a vanishing belt, a destroying ray, and a robot are among the technological tools Stanley uses in his crusade.

The only wrinkle in his plan is the fact that Barnett is the father of the girl he loves. But when Barnett eventually dies trying to escape the law, true love conquers and the couple look forward to an uncomplicated life together.

James Durkin and Onslow Stevens check their latest invention.

Eddie Cobb watches a robot clutch Ada Ince and Onslow Stevens lies unconscious.

Once again Eddie Cobb watches as Richard Cramer, Monte Montague, and Al Ferguson grab Onslow Stevens. Ada Ince, held back by Walter Miller, is a horrified witness.

Ada Ince, James Durkin, and Onslow Stevens face the enemy, protected by the most advanced scientific weaponry.

Young Eagles

12 Episodes
First Division, 1934

CAST

Bobby Ford   Bobbie Cox
Jim Adams   Jim Vance

This film dedicated by the Boy Scouts to President Franklin Delano Roosevelt.

Two Eagle Scouts, Bobby Ford and Jim Adams, are awarded trips to South America for meritorious service. A storm disables their plane somewhere over Central America and their pilot's leg is broken in the resulting crash. The boys administer first aid to him and then begin a journey through the jungle to bring help. On several occasions they are captured by Mayan natives but escape.

Bobby and Jim stumble across a treasure which brings them in conflict with Candylos, a crooked trader, and Jose Pinardo and his bandits. U.S. planes and marines dispatched to the area save the scouts from Pinardo and Candylos and the two young scouts return to the states as heroes.

1935

The Adventures of Rex and Rinty

12 Episodes
Mascot, 1935

Directed by
Ford Beebe
and Reeves Eason

CAST

Rex	Himself
Rinty	Rin-Tin-Tin, Jr.
Frank Bradley	Kane Richmond
Dorothy Bruce	Norma Taylor
Tanaga	Mischa Auer
Jensen	Smiley Burnette
Crawford	Harry Woods

Deep in the interior of a small island, guarded by jungles and roving beasts, nestles a sacred shrine. For ages a devout group has worshiped the God-Horse of Sujan, treasuring him as sincerely as did the Assyrians the Bull and the Egyptians the Cat.

A trio of unscrupulous Americans visits Sujan to buy horses. There, the High Priest Tanaga innocently lets them view the God-Horse Rex, a beautiful black stallion. The unscrupulous trio steal the horse and bring it to the United States, where they sell it to Crawford, a wealthy and greedy ranch owner.

The new owner futilely attempts to train Rex as a polo horse, but Rex escapes and takes to the open road. On the range he meets another wanderer, Rinty. The animals team up to avoid capture by Crawford. Crawford's attempts draw the attention of Frank Bradley, polo player, who befriends Rex and Rinty and takes them both back to the Island of Sujan.

Crawford follows Frank and his party to Sujan and convinces the natives to turn against their God-Horse. But Bradley and the loyal priest join forces and rescue Rex just as he is about to be burned as a sacrifice.

Rin-Tin-Tin, Jr., overpowers an enemy.

The Call of the Savage

13 Episodes
Universal, 1935

Directed by
Louis Friedlander

CAST

Jan	→ Noah Beery, Jr.
Mona Andrews	Dorothy Short
Borno	H. L. Woods
Dr. Harry Trevor	Bryant Washburn
Dr. Frank Bracken	Walter Miller
Dr. Charles Phillips	Fredric McKaye
Andrews	Russ Power
Emperor	John Davidson

Dr. Harry Trevor, Dr. Frank Bracken, and Dr. Charles Phillips are sent into the jungles of Africa to search for a formula that will cure infantile paralysis. Dr. Trevor is accompanied by his wife, Georgia, and their small son Jan. Although Dr. Trevor's intention is purely altruistic, the motives of his associates are purely selfish; they want the formula only for the money it will bring them.

When Dr. Trevor discovers the formula, Bracken and Phillips conspire to steal it. But Trevor has grown wary of his two "friends." He writes half the formula on a piece of parchment and the other half on a flexible metal band which he places on the wrist of young Jan. One day, the boy and his chimpanzee playmate Chicma wander into the post menagerie among some lions. Georgia rushes in in an attempt to protect her son, but a lion leaps upon her and kills her. Trevor tries to rescue his wife, but is knocked unconscious. In the confusion, Jan is led into the jungle by Chicma, as a fire breaks out and the entire post is destroyed. Bracken and Phillips, believing that everyone else is dead, leave Africa and head back to the U.S.A.

Fifteen years later, Bracken and Phillips return to Africa and discover Trevor there, his memory partially gone. They find the parchment half of the formula in Trevor's possession and are able to determine that Jan has the other half. Meanwhile, Mona Andrews, the daughter

Noah Beery, Jr., and his faithful friend H. L. Woods.

Noah Beery, Dorothy Short, Bryant Washburn (*background*) confer with John Davidson.

Russ Power, Dorothy Short, Noah Beery, and Bryant Washburn face a slowly descending spiked ceiling.

of a prominent trader, is also en route to Africa to visit her father's trading post. When her boat stops at a port, two prisoners who have been captured in the jungle are brought on board—a white wild boy and his pet chimpanzee. They are, of course, Jan and Chicma.

As the boat proceeds on its voyage, a violent storm comes up, and the boat springs a serious leak. Mona, Jan, Chicma, and Borno, another passenger, are thrown overboard. All four cling desperately to a raft as the ship sinks. The survivors reach shore and Borno introduces himself as a banished member of the lost Kingdom of Mu. By an incredible coincidence, Borno recognizes a small tattoo on Mona's palm and declares that she is a Princess of Mu.

As the friends wend their way toward the Andrews trading post, they meet with Trevor and are set upon by unfriendly natives and vicious animals. Finally, they encounter Bracken and Phillips. At one point Borno meets Andrews and learns that Mona is not the trader's real daughter, but was found as an infant in front of the post. This confirms the fact that Mona is actually a Princess of Mu.

Borno convinces the entire group, including Trevor and Andrews, to return to Mu with him. But as they proceed they are followed and constantly harassed by a safari led by Bracken and Phillips, who are determined to seize the formula. When they arrive at Mu, they are briefly interrupted by a dissident faction within the kingdom led by Prince Samu, who is trying to wrest control from the benevolent emperor. Bracken and Phillips arrive on the scene and are quickly captured.

Prince Samu's schemes are dashed when Borno gains an audience with the emperor and convinces him that Mona is his long-lost daughter. The formula is restored to Trevor, and Andrews is richly rewarded for caring for Mona. Bracken and Phillips are set free, but as they return to the jungle they are killed by lightning. Mona asks that Jan stay with her, and the emperor gladly agrees.

Fighting Marines

12 Episodes
Mascot, 1935

Directed by
Reeves Eason
and Joseph Kane

CAST

Corporal Lawrence   Grant Withers
Sergeant McGowan   Adrian Morris
Frances Schiller   Ann Rutherford
Colonel Bennett   Robert Warwick

Colonel Bennett is trying to establish a landing field on Halfway Island, but each of his attempts has been sabotaged. The Marines, however, are hot on the trail of the suspect—the mysterious Tiger Shark. Corporal Lawrence and Sergeant McGowan have trailed the Tiger Shark to a deserted warehouse where they prepare to capture the criminal.

But the warehouse turns out to be a base for the Tiger Shark and he quickly outwits the Marines. With the Marines close behind, he heads for his secret hideout on Halfway Island. Immediately upon landing, he destroys the Marine plane with his radio gravity gun. Lawrence and McGowan, however, parachute out.

Realizing that he will be caught, and loath to surrender the king's ransom of treasures that his men have pirated, the Tiger Shark decides to flee the island with as many valuables as he can carry. Lawrence and McGowan arrive in time to stop him. During the ensuing gun battle in the cave hideout an ill-placed bottle of nitroglycerin is hit by a bullet and the cave and the Tiger Shark blow up.

Corporal Grant Withers in mortal combat with one of Tiger Shark's men.

The Lost City

12 Episodes
Krellberg, 1935

Directed by
Harry Revier

CAST

Bruce Gordon	Kane Richmond
Zolok	William "Stage" Boyd
Natcha	Claudia Dell
Manyus	Josef Swickard
Butterfield	George F. "Gabby" Hayes
Jerry	Eddie Fetherstone
Gorzo	William Bletcher
Andrews	Milburn Moranti
Queen Rama	Margot D'use
Appolyn	Jerry Frank
Reynolds	Ralph Lewis
Colton	William Millman
Ben Ali	Gino Corrado
Hugo	Sam Baker

After a series of electrical storms disrupt the world, electrical engineer Bruce Gordon develops a machine to trace the cause of the disasters. He discovers that the source is in central Africa and, backed by the nations of the world, sets out on an expedition. His loyal companion Jerry and two professional colleagues, Colton and Reynolds, accompany him.

Bruce's African journey leads to a trading post run by Butterfield, a shrewd slave trader. There Bruce sets up his machine and finds that the disturbances emanate from an area called the Magnetic Mountain. Unknown to Bruce, the Magnetic Mountain contains a city ruled by a scientific wizard named Zolok who has unleashed the electrical fury threatening civilization as part of his plan to conquer the world. Utilizing his own advanced television system, Zolok is closely observing Bruce's progress.

Viewing the arrival of the Gordon party with Zolok is Dr. Manyus, the captive scientific genius behind Zolok's power. The good doctor is forced to do Zolok's bidding because his lovely daughter Natcha is also held prisoner, and Manyus fears for her life if Zolok is displeased. Zolok is also aided by Gorzo, a hunchback, who hopes that his evil master will someday make him strong and straight, and by Appolyn, Zolok's muscular right-hand man.

Zolok also commands a cadre of brainwashed native giants who are the product of one of Manyus's inventions, a brain-destroying and enlarging machine which can create a brainless behemoth from a normal-sized native.

It is with an army of such giants that Zolok intends to conquer the world.

Zolok decides to lure the Gordon party to his headquarters. While Bruce and his friends are heading for the Magnetic Mountain, Zolok forces Natcha to scream into a microphone wired to a distant thatched hut. Jerry responds, "That sounds like a white woman's scream." Bruce and Jerry dash into the hut, fall through a trapdoor, slide down a chute, and find themselves within Zolok's Lost City.

Bruce asks Zolok who he is and Zolok answers, "As you may know, the Ligurians were a race of master scientists. I am the last of that race, carrying on the electromagnetic tradition of my people." Zolok then vows he will exploit Bruce's engineering knowledge to further his scheme of world conquest or, failing that, change him into a mindless giant.

Meanwhile, Colton and Reynolds have also been captured by Zolok's men and brought to the Lost City. When they see what Manyus's scientific skills have brought Zolok, they start to think about the power they could command if they controlled him. Gaining the old doctor's confidence, they convince him to show them the way to a cave leading to the outside world. Then, despite his protests, they force him to escape with them.

When Natcha learns that her father has left with Colton and Reynolds, she draws Bruce and Jerry aside and leads them out of the Lost City by the same cave route. Enraged, Zolok sends Appolyn, Gorzo, and a few giants out to capture the escapees and keeps track of all concerned through his vast jungle television network.

Meanwhile, back at the trading post, Butterfield hears, via the jungle grapevine, rumors of Dr. Manyus's ability to create giants. "With an army like that," he sighs, "I could control Africa." Summoning his trusted natives, Butterfield goes out hunting for Manyus.

In the jungle, Butterfield comes upon the camp of Ben Ali, a veteran Arab slave trader. Ben Ali, too, has heard about the giants and figures they'd be a hot item on the auction block. Butterfield, however, convinces Ben Ali that no such giants exist.

In the jungle, Bruce, Natcha, and Jerry come upon the Arab camp. Bruce quickly decides that Natcha and Jerry should enter the camp and rest, while he continues the search for Manyus. While Ben Ali is entertaining his guests, Hugo, a brainless native giant, and Gorgo capture Colton and Manyus. They barely start back to the Lost City when they are captured by Ben Ali's men and taken to the Arab's encampment.

Ben Ali is impressed when he spies Hugo; Colton, in order to save his own skin, tells the Arab of Manyus's scientific brilliance and suggests that the two of them become partners in exploiting the doctor. But Ben Ali doesn't see how Colton fits into the picture and has him shot. The Arab chieftain also has Butterfield imprisoned for lying about the giants.

In an adjacent tent, Gorzo and Hugo are shackled to a pole. As soon as they are alone, Gorzo commands Hugo to break their bonds, which the powerful giant proceeds to do. Obeying Gorzo's commands, Hugo then kills the Arab guarding their tent and the two flee into the jungle. Meanwhile, Natcha, left unguarded, slips out of her tent and also heads for the jungle, where she runs into Bruce.

Bruce quickly decides to infiltrate the Arab camp and help the others escape. He is met by Jerry, who had overpowered his Arab guard and donned his cloak as a disguise. Together, the two friends free Manyus and Butterfield and flee, with Ben Ali's men in close pursuit. Butterfield returns to his trading post, rounds up his

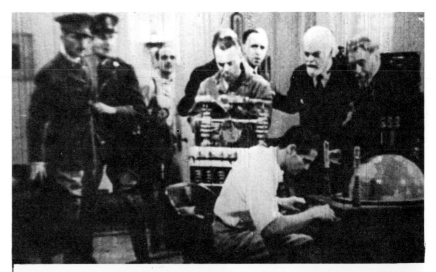

Kane Richmond (*seated*) works intently to discover the source of the earth's disturbances, while Eddie Fetherstone (*center*) and world dignitaries offer encouragement.

Claudia Dell and Josef Swickard discuss the possibility of rescue from the Lost City.

Claudia Dell is comforted by Josef Swickard as William Bletcher watches.

(*Left to right*) Eddie Fetherstone and Kane Richmond confront William "Stage" Boyd and Jerry Frank in Zolok's headquarters.

William "Stage" Boyd demands more electrical energy from the reluctant Josef Swickard.

George "Gabby" Hayes strikes a bargain with Margot D'use.

Kane Richmond dines with Margot D'use.

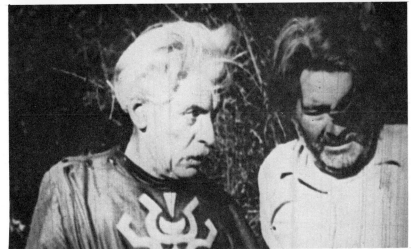

Josef Swickard saves the life of George ''Gabby'' Hayes.

George ''Gabby'' Hayes, Kala, and Claudia Dell watch as Kane Richmond regains his sight.

Kane Richmond flinches at the approach of the destroying Ray as William ''Stage'' Boyd smiles in maniacal glee. In the background, Claudia Dell and Josef Swickard recoil in horror.

friendly natives, and attacks Ben Ali's men, putting the Arabs to flight.

Butterfield then turns on his former rescuers and sends his natives to capture Dr. Manyus. Pursued through the jungle, Bruce, Natcha, Jerry, and Manyus cross a trail called the "Path of Skulls" and enter the dreaded Spidermen's village. Because of a local superstition, Butterfield's natives refuse to cross the Path of Skulls and retreat in panic when they come to it.

As the friends enter the village, Dr. Manyus explains that the white, Pygmy-sized inhabitants were once black Pygmies, but have been turned white by another of Dr. Manyus's remarkable formulas. After being greeted by the natives, our heroes watch as a black Spiderman pleads with Manyus to change him into a white man. The doctor quickly obliges and performs the necessary operation. Jerry, awestruck, says, "Doc, you're a genius." Manyus answers, "Science can accomplish anything." Bruce adds, "Doc, this is the greatest scientific discovery yet." Manyus points out that Gorzo is a Spiderman whom he had turned white. Little do they know that Gorzo is right outside the window of the hut, listening to their words.

Meanwhile, the discouraged Butterfield returns to his trading post to find that the lovely Queen Rama, queen of the slave trade, is looking for him. He explains what has been happening and makes a deal to share control of Africa with her once they get hold of Manyus. Butterfield sets out once again to capture the doctor, but this time with Rama's natives, the Wangas, who have no qualms about invading the Spidermen's village.

The Spidermen are quickly routed and Butterfield returns with his prisoners. Queen Rama is immediately taken by Bruce's good looks, and imagines that he would make a much more attractive partner than Butterfield. Butterfield, therefore, is tied to stakes in the middle of the jungle and left to die. Rama invites Bruce to dinner in her room, and makes an offer of marriage. Bruce is flattered, but suggests "a long friendship" instead. Rama is outraged and, to vent her spleen, orders that a clumsy servant girl Kala be whipped. When Bruce objects, Rama relents, but her fury has not subsided and she slips a potion into Bruce's wine that causes him to go blind. Rama also has plans for Natcha. She orders that the young girl be thrown into a lion pit.

While all of this is going on, Dr. Manyus escapes into the jungle and, after wandering about, comes upon Butterfield and releases him. The old slave trader is touched by this act of mercy and, admitting that he'd been an "awful rotter," promises to make amends.

At the trading post, the native girl Kala, whom Bruce had saved from the sting of the lash, leads the blind engineer to the lion pit and helps him save Natcha. The trio then escapes into the jungle where they run into Manyus and Butterfield. The ex-villain brews up a pot of antidote tea the natives had taught him to make. This restores Bruce's vision.

Butterfield and Bruce decide to go back to recapture the trading post from Rama. They leave Manyus and his daughter in a cave, which happens to contain one of Zolok's many television cameras. No sooner do Bruce and Butterfield leave, then Appolyn captures the doc and Natcha.

At the trading post, Bruce frees Jerry, and Butterfield discovers that Rama has been stabbed to death. He smiles and walks over to congratulate Kala. Bruce and Jerry quickly return to the cave and discover that Manyus and Natcha have disappeared. Bruce tells Jerry to get Butterfield and his natives to follow him.

As for Bruce himself, he runs into Appolyn and his giants and is quickly subdued. Along with Manyus and Natcha, he is returned to the Lost City.

Jerry and Butterfield are on their way to the Lost City when they come upon Gorzo, who says that he, too, is relenting and will help them find the cave entrance to the Lost City. Meanwhile, Zolok has greeted his captives in typical merciless style, deciding to kill Bruce with yet another of Manyus's inventions—a Destroying Ray. Bruce is tied to a chair and the death machine is turned on. But just as Bruce is about to be destroyed, Gorzo and his group come to the rescue.

Zolok is tossed into a dungeon, but quickly escapes and returns to his vacant laboratory. By now Zolok has gone completely insane, and proceeds to turn on all of his powerful electrical equipment full blast. Bruce and his friends escape through the cave just as a mighty explosion rips through the Lost City, destroying it completely.

The Miracle Rider

15 Episodes   Directed by
Mascot, 1935   Armand Schaefer
                     and Reeves Eason

CAST

Tom Morgan	Tom Mix
Ruth	Jean Gale
Zaroff	Charles Middleton
Carlton	Jason Robards
Janes	Edward Hearn
Sam Morgan	Pat O'Malley
Chief Black Wing	Robert Frazer
Stelter	Ernie Adams
Burnett	Wally Wales
Longboat	Bob Kortman
Chief Two Hawks	Black Hawk
Chief Last Elk	Chief Standing Bear

Tom Morgan, the "Miracle Rider" and captain of the Texas Rangers, is made a blood brother of the Ravenhead tribe because of his service to them. Unscrupulous oil interests, led by Zaroff, covet the Indian reservation, which contains valuable supplies of a deposit called X-94, a powerful explosive.

With the aid of Longboat, a treacherous half-breed who wants to become a chieftain, and by means of an invisible ray and a radio-controlled glider, Zaroff's men play on the superstitions of the Indians and attempt to get rid of Tom, their chief menace. Black Wing, the Ravenhead chief, is killed in an attack on Tom. Ruth, the bereaved daughter of the murdered chief, falls in love with Tom, and so, with Ruth's help, Tom manages to expose the plot and route the villains.

Tom Mix hushes an outlaw.

Herman Brix, a captive in the Mayan City.

The New Adventures of Tarzan

12 Episodes	Directed by
Dearholt-Stout	Edward Kull
and Cohen, 1935	and W. F. McGaugh

CAST

Tarzan	Herman Brix
Ula Vale	Ula Holt
Major Martling	Frank Baker
Alice Martling	Dale Walsh
Gordon Hamilton	Harry Ernest
Raglan	Don Castello
George	Lewis Sargent
Bouchart	Merrill McCormick
Nkima	"Jiggs"

An educated Tarzan leaves Africa to help a friend who has been captured by the Mayan inhabitants of a city in Guatemala. On his voyage to Guatemala he agrees to help the Martling party search for the lost Green Goddess, an idol containing a fortune in jewelry. The valuable statue also contains a formula for a deadly explosive which a group of revolutionaries is after.

Other people, however, are also searching for the Goddess: Operator 17 of the Secret Service; Raglan, a killer who sometimes acts on behalf of the revolutionaries; and the mysterious Ula Vale. All the parties looking for the Goddess alternately fight each other, the elements, hostile natives, and ferocious animals before they even reach the Mayan city and locate Tarzan's friend. After arriving at their destination, the ruler, Queen Maya, offers to let Tarzan remain as her consort but orders the others thrown into her crocodile pit. Tarzan refuses and helps everyone escape, but not before they seize possession of the Green Goddess.

The party finds its way to a freighter where each faction makes a final bid for the Goddess's treasure and Operator 17 places all of the criminals under arrest. He also reveals that Ula, too, is a secret service operator. The idol and its contents are returned to Major Martling, who expresses the wish to present the statue to the government of Guatemala. Tarzan, his mission accomplished, returns to Africa.

Phantom Empire

12 Episodes
Mascot, 1935

Directed by
Otto Brewer
and B. Reeves Eason

CAST

Gene	Gene Autry
Frankie	Frankie Darro
Betsy	Betsy King Ross
Queen Tika	Dorothy Christy
Argo	Wheeler Oakman
Mal	Charles R. French
Rab	Warner Richmond
Professor Beetson	Frank Glendon
Oscar	Lester "Smiley" Burnette
Pete	William Moore

Gene, a dude rancher, and his young pals Frankie and Betsy are battling a gang of crooks who covet his radium-laden land. Pursued by Gene, the crooks stumble upon the entrance to Murania—a futuristic metal city 20,000 feet underground—and enter its gates. They discover that Murania is filled with supermen possessing death-dealing inventions far ahead of any earthly weapons. There they meet up with Queen Tika and Argo, her rebellious prime minister.

Still on the trail of the interlopers, Gene finds his way into the kingdom and soon becomes a prisoner of the Muranians. When Frankie and Betsy follow Gene into Murania, they too are captured. Then yet another "rescuer" enters the city. Oscar, Gene's friend, tries to disguise himself as one of Murania's mechanical robots, but this ploy is discovered and he too becomes a captive.

Fortunately for the friends, a revolt breaks out in Murania. While rival factions battle each other, Gene and his group make good an escape via an elevator that carries them 20,000 feet to the surface of the earth. Just as Gene and his friends reach safety, the Muranian dissidents turn loose an awesome death ray which totally destroys the Muranian empire.

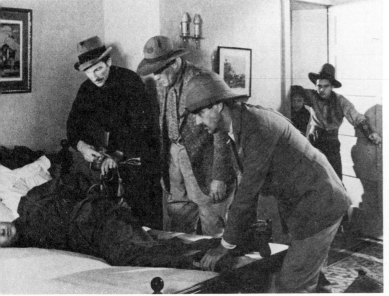

Gene Autry is bound by the outlaws seeking his property, as Betsy King Ross and Frankie Darro watch.

Gene Autry, standing over some vanquished foes, is saved from a blow on the head by Smiley Burnette.

The Roaring West

15 Episodes
Universal, 1935

Directed by
Ray Taylor

CAST

Montana Larkin	Buck Jones
Mary Parker	Muriel Evans
Gil Gillespie	Walter Miller
Jinglebob Morgan	Frank McGlynn, Sr.
Clem Morgan	Harlan Knight
Jim Parker	William Desmond
Marco Brett	William Thorne
Ann Hardy	Eole Galli
Steve	Pat O'Brien

Montana Larkin and Jinglebob Morgan, cowpunchers and partners, ride into a new territory to participate in an impending land rush. They have with them a map giving the location of valuable mineral deposits which the two friends hope to secure in the land rush. They stop overnight at the ranch of Jim Parker and meet Jim's daughter Mary. That night, the overtalkative Jinglebob plays cards with ranch foreman Gillespie, who is jealous and suspicious of Montana. Jinglebob inadvertently reveals to Gillespie the secret of the map and, during the night, Gillespie has his aide, Hank, steal the map and copy it, without arousing Montana's suspicions.

After the land rush, Montana is astonished to discover that Gillespie has already filed claim to the property, and Parker is doubly astonished when Gillespie offers to share the property if Parker's daughter Mary will marry him at once. Mary indignantly refuses and Gillespie is discharged as ranch foreman. Montana and Jinglebob meet Jinglebob's brother Clem, who reveals that the original map did not give the accurate location of the mineral deposits, and the three quickly ride off to file the proper claim. Learning of this, Gillespie has his men begin a reign of terror, aimed at securing the mine for himself. When these attempts fail, Gillespie gathers his outlaw band and mounts a raid on the town bank, where the mined gold is stored. But by this time, Montana has anticipated this move, has had himself sworn in as deputy sheriff, and the entire Gillespie gang is captured and lodged in jail.

William Desmond, Frank McGlynn, Sr., Buck Jones, and Muriel Evans, prepared for the worst.

Rustlers of Red Dog

12 Episodes
Universal, 1935

Directed by
Louis Friedlander

CAST

Jack Woods	John Mack Brown
Mary Lee	Joyce Compton
Deacon	Walter Miller
Laramie	Raymond Hatton
Rocky	H. L. Woods
Snakey	Fredric McKaye
Tom Lee	Charles K. French
Bob Lee	Lafe McKee
Ira Dale	William Desmond
Captain Trent	J. P. McGowan
Buck	Edmond Cobb
Jake	Bud Osborne
Kruger	Monty Montague

Jack Woods, Deacon, and Laramie are the Three Musketeers of the Old West. They fight their way across the plains and mountains to protect the settlers who are constantly threatened by Indians, rustlers, and badmen.

Jack had been marshal in another western town. Now, he and his friends come riding into the Red Dog country. The former marshal hopes to find peace and quiet—and perhaps a gold strike. Laramie, however, is never averse to stirring up a fight, while Deacon is happiest when he is teaching some cowhand the intricacies of poker.

Tom Lee, a leading citizen of the town of Nugget, prevails on the trio to remain in town as protectors. But Jack, Laramie, and Deacon ride out of town to team up with a wagon train bringing Tom's daughter Mary and his brother Bob into Red Dog. The wagon train has also been infiltrated by a gang of rustlers, led by Rocky, who plan to rob the train of fifty-thousand dollars in gold being carried in one of the wagons.

Attacked by renegade Indians, all hands join in defending the wagon train, and the Indians are beaten off. A convoy of soldiers arrives and escorts the train to a nearby fort. No sooner have the travelers settled down than the Indians attack the fort in great number. Rocky and his gang seize this moment as the opportunity they've been waiting for; they occupy the gold-laden wagon and crash through the fort's gate in their escape. The hordes of hostile redskins, seeing the opening, rush through the gate and capture the defenders.

Jack is recognized by a young Indian chief as one who had once saved his life and is told that, in return, his own life will be spared. But Mary is to become a squaw, while Laramie and Deacon must die. They are all taken to the Indian village and Jack's two friends are to be burned at the stake that night.

Walter Miller and Raymond Hatton face a fiery death as Johnny Mack Brown watches helplessly.

As army reinforcements arrive at the fort to rescue the settlers, Jack manages to stampede the Indians' horses and, in the ensuing excitement, the four comrades escape from the Indian village.

Rocky and his men discover that the gold is contained in a thick safe which they are unable to open, so they carry it to a cave and attempt to blast it open. But Jack, Mary, Laramie, and Deacon, who happen to be passing by, see what is happening and, unnoticed by the rustlers, enter the cave, retrieve the safe, and elude the outlaws.

The four comrades overtake the wagon train and return the gold in time for a triumphant arrival in Nugget, where the gold is hidden in Lee's home for safekeeping. Jack now accepts Lee's invitation to serve as the town's marshal, in order personally to bring Rocky to justice.

While Jack and his two pals are out following Rocky's trail, an old prospector arrives in Nugget with a tale of a gold strike. He has been sent by Rocky to depopulate the town so that the rustlers can raid it. The townspeople fall for the story and evacuate the town in a mad rush for gold. On the trail, Jack and his friends rescue a stage from Indians. The old prospector, whom they also rescue, confesses that his story was a hoax.

In town, Rocky and his gang are looting the bank and stores when the stage arrives. Rocky lets it through, so that he can use it to carry off his swag. But when he approaches the stage, he finds himself looking down the barrels of Jack's guns and is forced to make his men lay down their arms. Determined to avoid prison, Rocky attempts to escape, and, in a final gun duel with Jack, is fatally shot.

With this, Mary and Jack proceed to make plans for their future.

Tailspin Tommy in the Great Air Mystery

12 Episodes
Universal, 1935

Directed by
Ray Taylor

CAST

Tommy	Clark Williams
Skeeter	Noah Beery, Jr.
Betty Lou	Jean Rogers
Inez Casmetto	Delphine Drew
Ned Curtis	Bryant Washburn
Mrs. Tompkins	Helen Brown

Tailspin Tommy and Skeeter try to foil an unscrupulous plan concocted by Manuel Casmetto and Horace Raymore to steal Nazil Island's valuable oil reserves. They are aided in their efforts by Bill McGuire, a newspaperman who poses as Raymore's right-hand man, and pilot Milt Howe.

The young aviators have to escape belching volcanoes, time bombs, and antiaircraft shells. They not only manage to come out of their adventure in one piece, but they also get a movie contract.

Noah Beery, Jr., and Clark Williams emerge from a plane crash.

74

1936

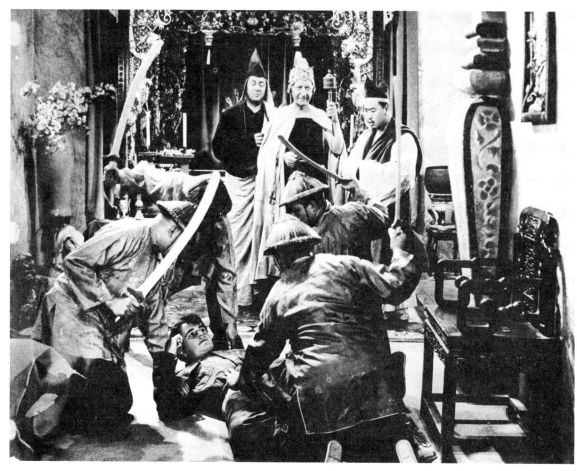

Guy Bates Post (*wearing the white cape*) arrives with Arthur Loft and Chester Gan to save the life of Noah Beery, Jr.

Ace Drummond

13 Episodes	Directed by
Universal, 1936	Ford Beebe
	and Cliff Smith

CAST

Ace Drummond	John King	Henry Kee	James B. Leong
Peggy Trainor	Jean Rogers	Johnny Wong	James Eagle
Jerry	Noah Beery, Jr.	Meredith, Sr.	Selmer Jackson
Grand Lama	Guy Bates Post	Winston	Robert Warwick
Chang-Ho	Arthur Loft	Trainor	Montague Shaw
Kai-Chek	Chester Gan	Bauer	Fredrick Vogeding
Billy Meredith	Jackie Morrow	Wyckoff	Al Bridge
		Ivan	Lon Chaney, Jr.
		Sergei	Stanley Blystone
		Nicolai	Ed Cobb
		Boris	Richard Wessel
		Lotan	Louis Vinzinot
		Le Page	Sam Ash
		Caldoni	Hooper Atchley

An international effort to establish a globe-circling airplane service is frustrated by a mysterious, evil power known as "The Dragon." This archvillain is resolved to stop the construction of the vital Mongolian link necessary for the completion of the project.

Ace Drummond, one of the aviation world's leading pioneers, volunteers to foil the Dragon's scheme. In addition, he takes it upon himself to help Peggy Trainor search for her lost father. Moreover, he volunteers his services to help find a hidden mountain containing enormous quantities of jade.

Whenever Ace has a free moment, he sings his favorite song: "Give Me a Ship and a Song." His singing, however, does not interfere with his tenacious hunt for the Dragon and resourceful wrap-up of his investigations.

John King keeps a watchful eye on villains Al Bridge and Fred Vogeding.

Sam Ash and Robert Warwick (*seated*) exchange glances as Jackie Morrow points an accusing finger at James Leong. Jean Rogers, John King, Hooper Atchley, and Selmer Jackson look on.

The Adventures of Frank Merriwell

12 Episodes
Universal, 1936

Directed by
Cliff Smith

CAST

Frank Merriwell	Don Briggs
Elsie Belwood	Jean Rogers
Bruce Browning	John King
Carla Rogers	Carla Laemmle
Harry Rattletown	Sumner Getchell
Wallace Reid	Wallace Reid, Jr.
House Peters	House Peters, Jr.
Allan Hersholt	Allan Hersholt
Daggett	Bentley Hewett
Black	Allen Bridge
Monte	Monte Montague
Gorman	Bud Osborne

Frank Merriwell, Fardale's star pitcher, receives a wire from his mother to come home at once. She has found a mysterious stranger rifling the desk of Frank's dad who has vanished. On his arrival Merriwell's mother gives him a ring which his father entrusted to her care and for which she thinks the mysterious visitor was looking.

Frank returns to Fardale with the ring.

Under a laboratory microscope, the boys find that the ring carries a Spanish inscription but neither they nor Elsie can translate it.

The boys and girls go to the Kirkland theatre where Mr. Belwood, Elsie's father, translates the inscription on the ring. The deciphered ring inscription directs them to Timbergold, a deserted mining camp. Hoping to find buried treasure they try to elude a stranger and his gang who are pursuing them. Frank discovers a chest filled with $30,000 in gold nuggets, which the stranger nearly steals from them.

While escaping from the stranger Frank discovers his father imprisoned in a cave. They are attacked by Indians, but Frank manages to escape and bring help.

The stranger reveals himself as Daggett, a distant relative, who is anxious to obtain Mr. Merriwell's fortune. In desperation he kidnaps Frank and demands information from Dr. Merriwell on the whereabouts of the treasure. Frank's father is about to reveal the treasure's location when the radio announces that Frank has escaped. Dr. Merriwell and Jeff promptly seize Daggett and turn him over to the police.

Frank arrives back at Fardale in the middle of the school's big game with rival Calford. The score as Frank enters is 19 to 6, Calford leading. With a remarkable display of hitting and pitching skill, Frank enables Fardale to win 20 to 19.

Jean Rogers and Don Briggs get good news from coach Jack Donovan.

The chest is opened to reveal its treasure in golden nuggets to Walter Law, Wallace Reid, Jr., Herchell Mayall, a lumberjack, Sumner Getchell, Carla Laemmle, and (*kneeling*) Jean Rogers, Don Briggs, John King.

Eddie Cobb and Bud Osborne discuss the captured Don Briggs.

The Black Coin

15 Episodes
Weiss-Mintz, 1936

Directed by
Albert Herman

Ozzie	Joe Garcia
Juan	Juan Duval
Ortega	Lou Meahan
Anderson	Carter Wayne
Slim	Milburn Morante

CAST

Prescott	Ralph Graves
Dorothy Dale	Ruth Mix
Terry Navarro	Dave O'Brien
Virginia Caswell	Constance Bergen
Jensen	Mathew Betz
Hackett	Robert Frazer
Vic Moran	"Snub" Pollard
Shark Malone	Robert Walker
Caswell	Bryant Washburn
Donna Luise	Clara K. Young
Don Pedro	Josef Swickard
McGuire	Blackie Whiteford
Ed McMahan	Yakima Canutt
Bobbie	Jackie Miller
Sir Philip	Lane Chandler
Hank	Richard Cramer
Bartender	Bill Desmond
Gleason	Roger Williams
Herb	Walter Taylor
Ali Ben Aba	Pete de Grasse

Terry Navarro, an employee of the Caswell Shipping Company, is entrusted to deliver some valuable papers to Mr. Caswell at a deserted port. But other forces attempt to obtain the papers, which are believed to hold the key to a smuggling ring using the Caswell ships. Dorothy Dale and Walter Prescott, American secret agents, attempt to intercept the papers, as do Hackett (a cohort of Caswell's) and an Arab tribesman, Ali Ben Aba.

As one faction after another gains temporary possession of the papers, two black coins of indeterminate, but apparently great significance, are occasionally offered as barter for the papers. After a quest that ranges from Africa to the United States, the papers are recovered, the smuggling ring is smashed, and Terry looks forward to a pleasant future with Caswell's daughter Virginia.

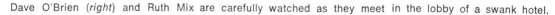

Dave O'Brien (*right*) and Ruth Mix are carefully watched as they meet in the lobby of a swank hotel.

The Clutching Hand

15 Episodes
Stage and Screen,
1936

Directed by
Albert Herman

Warden — Henry Hall
"Snub" — Snub Pollard

CAST

Craig Kennedy	Jack Mulhall
Verna Gironda	Marion Shilling
Number Eight	Yakima Canutt
Sullivan	Reed Howes
Shirley McMillan	Ruth Mix
George Gaunt	William Farnum
Walter Jameson	Rex Larse
Mrs. Gironda	Mae Busch
Denton	Bryant Washburn
Dr. Gironda	Robert Frazier
Louis Bouchard	Gaston Glass
Montgomery	Mahlon Hamilton
Mitchell	Robert Walker
Cromwell	Joseph W. Girard
Wickham	Frank Leigh
Hobart	Charles Locher
Nicky	Franklyn Farnum
Captain Hanson	Knute Erickson
Olaf	Dick Alexander
Marty	Milburne Morante
Mrs. White	John Elliot

After he claims that he has found a formula for making synthetic gold, Dr. Paul Gironda is kidnapped. The eminent detective Craig Kennedy is brought into the case by Walter Jameson, a newspaper reporter and the fiance of Dr. Gironda's daughter Verna. But the two men are consistently thwarted in their investigation by the mysterious Clutching Hand.

After escaping many traps and pitfalls arranged by the Clutching Hand, Kennedy calls a meeting of the International Research Foundation. At the meeting he produces Gironda's missing formula book. Dr. Gironda appears out of nowhere demanding his formula book back. Kennedy grabs him and introduces him to the assembled group as the Clutching Hand. The doctor runs to his laboratory and commits suicide.

Afterward, Kennedy explains that the doctor—who was really Verna's guardian and not her father—misappropriated vast sums belonging to his ward. In order to cover up this deception, he faked a gold formula which he thought would bring him a great deal of money and enable him to leave the country a wealthy man.

Ruth Mix, at a slight disadvantage, faces the Clutching Hand.

Custer's Last Stand

15 Episodes	Directed by
Stage and Screen,	Elmer Clifton
1936	

CAST

Kit Cardigan	Rex Lease
Fitzpatrick	William Farnum
Tom "Keen" Blade	Reed Howes
Lieutenant Cook	Jack Mulhall
Major Trent	Josef Swickard
Hank	Creighton Hale
Buckskin	Milburn Moranti
Belle Meade	Lona Andre
Red Fawn	Dorothy Gulliver

Young Wolf, who leads the Dakotas in a series of attacks on settlers, loses a sacred medicine arrow that is the key to an Indian cave of gold. Major Trent, former Confederate Army doctor, and his daughter Barbara recover it without knowing its value.

Renegade Tom Blade—Keen Blade to the Indians—aids Young Wolf in his attempts to recover the valuable arrow while secretly seeking the gold for himself. In the midst of this Indian upheaval and settler unrest, General Custer and army scout Kit Cardigan try to restore peace.

In the final battle, Kit rides with a troop that barely survives a hopeless attempt to reach the ill-fated Custer. He returns to kill Blade and see the hope of a brighter day.

Darkest Africa

15 Episodes	Directed by
Republic, 1936	B. Reeves Eason
	and Joseph Kane

CAST

Clyde Beatty	Clyde Beatty
Baru	Manuel King
Valerie	Elaine Shepard
Dagna	Lucien Prival
Bonga	Naba
Samabi	Ray Benard
Durkin	Wheeler Oakman
Gorn	Edward McWade
Craddock	Edmund Cobb
Hambone	Ray Turner
Negus	Donald Reed
Driscoll	Harrison Greene
Tomlin	Henry Sylvester
Nagga	Joseph Boyd

Clyde Beatty, famous lion trapper, meets Baru, a jungle boy who has come to the outland for assistance in rescuing his sister Valerie, the Goddess of Joba, a lost city in an unexplored part of Africa. Beatty agrees to help Baru and organizes a safari. With the aid of Bonga, an ape who is Baru's protector, they all manage to get to Joba, but only after wending their way through Africa, and encountering hostile natives, lions, tigers, and a tribe of winged men called Bat Men.

Once in Joba, they meet Dagna, the high priest, who relies on Valerie's influence with the natives to help him retain power; he tries to prevent them from leaving. Aiding Dagna are Durkin and Craddock, rival animal traders who have followed the Beatty safari because they believe a fortune in jewelry exists in the lost city. When the villains gain the upper hand and the entire troupe is held captive, Valerie volunteers to perform the great sacrifice of leaping from Pinnacle Rock so that her brother and Clyde may be released from the clutches of Dagna. At the last moment, however, Gorn, her devoted teacher, changes places with Valerie. Wearing her cloak, he makes the leap! Dagna, meanwhile, has released the two. All three man-age to escape Joba just in time—for the city is wrecked in an earthquake. Craddock and Durkin are stuffing their pockets with diamonds in the lost city when the earthquake hits. Both men are killed instantly and the city is totally de-stroyed.

Although onlookers appear worried, Clyde Beatty knows that if the chair and whip don't work, the pistol will.

On Safari with Clyde Beatty.

TO BE CONTINUED

Eddie Cobb takes a hard right from Clyde Beatty.

Clyde Beatty begins to get the point that he's surrounded.

Elaine Shepard and Clyde Beatty face the future together.

Flash Gordon

13 Episodes   Directed by
Universal, 1936   Frederick Stephani

CAST

Flash Gordon	Larry "Buster" Crabbe
Dale Arden	Jean Rogers
Emperor Ming	Charles Middleton
Aura	Priscilla Lawson
Vultan	John Lipson
Prince Barin	Richard Alexander
Dr. Zarkov	Frank Shannon
King Kala	Duke York, Jr.
Officer Torch	Earl Askam
High Priest	Theodore Lorch
King Thun	James Pierce
Zona	Muriel Goodspeed
Gordon, Sr.	Richard Tucker

The planet Mongo is heading toward earth, and severe atmospheric disturbances are causing worldwide panic. Flash Gordon and Dale Arden are in an airplane that, due to the disturbances, is thrown into a dive. They parachute to safety and land near the laboratory of Dr. Alexis Zarkov, a brilliant scientist. Zarkov has built a rocket ship in which he hopes to reach Mongo and in some way avert that planet's headlong rush toward earth. Flash decides to join Zarkov, and Dale asks to be taken along.

The ship blasts off and hurtles through space, finally landing on Mongo. They are captured by soldiers of a ruthless dictator called Ming the Merciless.

Flash and his companions are taken before Ming, and Zarkov convinces the ruler that if earth is destroyed, Mongo will be, too. Ming, impressed with Zarkov's brilliance, decides to use his services. Ming has also become drawn to the beautiful Dale, and, in order to get Flash out of the way, throws the young earthman into an arena to battle three monkey-men.

But Aura, Ming's daughter, is attracted to the handsome Flash, and, armed with a ray gun, comes to his aid. As they are battling Ming's soldiers, a lever is pulled, and Flash and Aura drop through a trapdoor into a pit filled with horrible reptiles. Aura discovers a secret passageway through which they escape.

Suddenly, another resident of Mongo, a sworn enemy of Ming, King Thun and his Lion Men attack in their gyro ships. During the battle, Flash encounters Thun and overpowers him, but does not kill him. When Thun learns that Flash is Ming's enemy, he joins forces with the Earth people.

Meanwhile, Ming has put Dale into a trance-like state, with the intention of marrying her. Flash observes this on a "spaceograph" viewer and determines to rescue Dale. Flash, Aura, and King Thun are making their way through a secret tunnel leading to Ming's headquarters, when they are confronted by a gocko, an enormous dragon-dinosaur beast with lobsterlike claws. The gocko seizes Flash and begins to crush him in its huge claws, but a blast from Thun's ray gun kills the monster and saves Flash's life. Then, with Thun's help, Flash invades Ming's castle and prevents the ceremony, making off with Dale.

The group escapes through another tunnel leading to the underwater palace of the sharkmen, denizens of Mongo's oceans, led by Kala. In the underwater kingdom, Flash is separated from Thun and Dale who go to the palace's throne room to wait for him. But Aura, jealous of Flash's devotion to Dale, tells him that Thun and Dale have left the underwater kingdom via submarine and that they are to follow in another sub. As she and Flash depart, Aura confesses the truth to Flash. He immediately tries to turn the submarine around, but Aura knocks him unconscious.

Ming, learning that the escapees had headed for the underwater kingdom, uses his powerful magnetic equipment to raise the sharkmen's palace to the surface of the sea. Flash regains consciousness in time to see the winged

Jean Rogers is held by Ming's slaves as Charles Middleton (*center*) and Priscilla Lawson watch Flash in combat.

Frank Shannon is introduced to his new laboratory by Charles Middleton.

hawk-men from the Sky City, led by Vultan, swoop down to the palace and carry off Dale and Thun.

Meanwhile, in Ming's fortress, Zarkov is visited by Prince Barin, who enters through a secret passageway and reveals that he is the true ruler of Mongo, dethroned by Ming, who killed his father. Barin offers to aid the Earth people if they will help him overthrow Ming. They head for Barin's rocket ship and, meeting Flash and Aura, take off to rescue Dale and Thun. But upon arrival at Vultan's domain, a wondrous city that floats on antigravity ray beams, they are captured, and Flash and Barin are sent as slaves to the atom furnace rooms which supply the power that keeps the city suspended in space. In the furnace room Flash and Barin find Thun, also enslaved.

While he has held her captive, Vultan has fallen in love with the beautiful Dale, and, recognizing Flash as his rival, has the Earth man taken to the "static room," where electric current is sent through his body. Dale promises Vultan that she will marry him if he stops torturing Flash. But Vultan's reaction is to lead Dale away after ordering that Flash be killed.

Aura, however, has uncovered a ray gun and forces the static machine operator to turn off the device. She then takes Flash to the laboratory, where Zarkov has been made to work, and has the doctor treat him to counteract the electric shocks. Flash recovers and enters Vultan's room, where he battles the king. But Vultan overcomes the still weakened Flash and has him wired to the atom furnaces, so that he will be electrocuted if he tries to escape.

Zarkov frees Flash and rewires the circuit so that a terrific explosion occurs and the furnaces are destroyed, thus threatening the Sky City. Zarkov then confronts Vultan and announces that in return for Flash's freedom, he will turn over to Vultan a new type of ray that will save the city. Vultan agrees, but before the Earth people can be set free, Ming visits the Sky City and forbids their liberation.

Instead, Ming suggests that the entire group return to his kingdom and that a tournament be held there. If Flash wins, he gains his liberty and can choose his bride. Recognizing Ming's power, Vultan agrees. The "Tournament of Death" begins and Flash faces a number of assorted monsters, vanquishing them one by one. When Flash finally emerges victorious, a livid Ming promises to give Flash his freedom and to allow him to choose his bride in three days.

As the third day approaches, Aura slips Flash a drug of forgetfulness, so that Flash does not recognize his Earth friends. When Ming asks him to choose his bride, Aura answers, stating that Flash has chosen her. Much to the astonishment of Zarkov, Barin, and Dale, the drugged Flash offers no protest. Barin and Zarkov, suspecting foul play, bring Flash to the laboratory and submit him to a ray treatment which restores his memory.

Meanwhile, the treacherous Ming orders a firing squad to the lab to execute Flash. As they enter, Zarkov thrusts Flash into a machine that makes him invisible, allowing him to escape. Still jealous, Aura sends a vicious tigron, a tiger-like beast, to track down and kill Dale. Flash, regaining visibility, appears just as the tigron is attacking Dale, and leaps upon the beast. The enraged tigron turns and attacks Aura, but Prince Barin arrives and leaps to Aura's defense, killing the tigron. Aura is drawn to Barin for his bravery, and the prince confesses that he is in love with her.

The repentant Aura goes to Ming to plead for the lives of her friends, but Ming orders their seizure. Just as Ming's forces are about to execute Flash, Thun and his lion-men attack the palace and break into Ming's headquarters. Trying to escape, Ming heads through one of the secret tunnels. But he is seized by a gocko and killed. Barin assumes his rightful place as ruler of Mongo, Aura at his side. And Flash, together with Dale and Zarkov, blast off for the return trip to Earth.

In the Sky City, John Lipson offers Jean Rogers a bite to eat, as Priscilla Lawson watches.

Larry "Buster" Crabbe battles an ape-creature during the Tournament of Death.

In the furnace room of the Hawk Men, James Pierce tries to hold back an enraged Larry "Buster" Crabbe.

Theodore Lorch (*left*) smiles craftily as Charles Middleton tells Priscilla Lawson of his plans for Flash.

Jean Rogers (*left*) recoils in horror and Charles Middleton and Priscilla Lawson watch with interest as Flash fights for his life.

It's obvious to James Pierce (*left*) that Charles Middleton has foul plans in mind for tender Jean Rogers.

James Pierce, Frank Shannon, and Jean Rogers help a nearly electrocuted Larry "Buster" Crabbe.

Larry "Buster" Crabbe and Priscilla Lawson face a new onslaught from Ming's men.

Larry "Buster" Crabbe and Jean Rogers head for home.

The Phantom Rider

15 Episodes
Universal, 1936

Directed by
Ray Taylor

CAST

Buck Grant	Buck Jones
Mary Grayson	Maria Shelton
Helen Moore	Diana Gibson
Steve	Joey Ray
Harvey Delaney	Harry Woods
Judge Holmes	Frank LaRue
Spooky	George Cooper
Sheriff Mark	Eddie Gribbon
Lizzie	Helen Shipman
Dirk	James Mason
Roscoe	Charles Lemoyne

Under orders from the state governor, Buck Grant and his partner Spooky arrive in Maverick on a secret mission to investigate reports of outlaw activity. Buck soon discovers that this activity is directed against the Hidden Valley Ranch, and immediately allies himself with ranch owner Mary Grayson, whose father has just been killed by the outlaws.

Donning the mask and cloak of the Phantom Rider to disguise his identity, Buck moves against the criminals. He finds out that they intend to seize control of Hidden Valley Ranch as potential railroad land and also to gain possession of a rich gold mine discovered by Mary's father.

The outlaws, led by town rancher Harvey Delaney, attempt in a number of ways to drive Mary from her property, but each effort is thwarted by the Phantom Rider. At one point Delaney suspects that Buck is the Phantom Rider, but changes his mind when the Phantom Rider appears while Buck is talking to Delaney. (Buck has had Spooky put on the Phantom Rider costume to avoid suspicion.)

Eventually, Buck is captured by Delaney and his gang of thieves. Mary is told that unless she signs her ranch over to the outlaw, Buck will be killed. To protect the life of the man she has come to love, Mary prepares to sign. But before she can sign, Buck breaks loose and, using Delaney as a shield, rounds up the outlaws and turns them over to the authorities.

The ghostlike Phantom Rider.

Robinson Crusoe of Clipper Island

14 Episodes
Republic, 1936

Directed by
Mack V. Wright
and Ray Taylor

CAST

Mala	Mala
Rex	Rex
Buck	Buck
Princess Melani	Mamo Clark
Jackson	Herbert Rawlinson
Hank	William Newell
Tupper	John Ward
Canfield	Selmer Jackson
Ellsworth	John Dilson
Porotu	John Piccori
Draker	George Chesebro
Wilson	Bob Kortman
Goebel	George Cleveland
Lamar	Lloyd Whitlock
Eppa	Tiny Roebuck
Larkin	Tracy Layne
Stevens	Herbert Weber
Radio Operator	Anthony Pawley
Taylor	Allen Connor

Mala, a Polynesian in the employ of the U.S. Intelligence Service, is sent to Clipper Island to investigate sabotage which resulted in the wrecking of the giant dirigible *San Fran-*

Mala is greeted by his dog Buck and his man Friday, William Newell.

cisco. Accompanied by Hank, his "man Friday," and his dog Buck, he proceeds to the island, and discovers that sinister members of an international spy group have been ordered to kill him.

Mala finds a wrecked radio station on the island, repairs it, and sends out messages, only to have them intercepted by the spy gang, who, infuriated because he has not been killed as they had planned, manipulate electrical contraptions causing the eruption of Pele, sacred volcano.

The eruption of this volcano brings Princess Melani and her warriors to the ceremonial island. Mala is sentenced to death in a pit of fire for "provoking the gods," but is rescued by Hank and Buck.

Encountering the beautiful Princess Melani later, he convinces her that he is a friend, not an enemy, and unites with her in an effort to quell the uprising headed by Porotu, high priest of Pele, who is plotting to overthrow her.

Porotu, believing that Mala and Melani perished in a second eruption of the volcano, seizes her sacred feather headdress and proclaims himself king of the Clipper Islands. Mala recovers the headdress, and proceeds to San Francisco for aid.

With evidence he has accumulated, he learns who is backing the spy ring and engages the aid of the police to round up the gang before returning to Clipper Island for the final battle to rescue Melani from Porotu's power.

Mala interrupts George Chesebro (*right*) and four other spies.

Mamo Clark clings close to Mala for protection.

Shadow of Chinatown

15 Episodes   Directed by
Victory, 1936   Bob Hill

CAST

Victor Poten	Bela Lugosi
Joan Whiting	Joan Barclay
Martin Andrews	Herman Brix
Sonya Rokoff	Luana Walters
Willy Fu	Maurice Liu
Healy	William Buchanan
Captain Walters	Forrest Taylor
Wong	James B. Leong
Dr. Wu	Henry F. Tung
Tom Chu	Paul Fung

A European importing firm, finding Chinese competition too great for it, instructs its West Coast representative, the beautiful Eurasian woman Sonya Rokoff, to close the West Coast Chinatown to tourists. Sonya engages Victor Poten, a mad Eurasian chemist and inventor, who hates both the Chinese *and* the white races, to help her. Well-planned raids follow and the Chinese merchants, headed by Dr. Wu, are at a loss to account for them. Not realizing that she is the author of these disturbances, they engage Sonya to help solve the mystery.

Joan Whiting, a young newspaperwoman who has lately been elevated from Society Editor to the rank of reporter, interests Martin Andrews, a young novelist and author of a book concerning Chinatown, in the matter. When Martin's theories strike close to home, Poten disguises himself as an employee of the telephone company and, poisoning a needle which he hopes to insert in Martin's telephone, leaves for Martin's house. However, Poten is interrupted before he has a chance to insert the needle. Never one to waste a poisoned needle, Poten inserts the needle in Dr. Wu's telephone. Dr. Wu, returning from a restaurant, is saved in the nick of time by Joan who suspected the presence of the needle because she had been studying Martin's book, and thus far all of the trouble in Chinatown had run according to the plot outlined in the book.

Captain Walters, calling on Martin, tells him he is under suspicion for having started the Chinatown troubles because of the similarity between these troubles and his. While all this is

EPISODE 11
THUNDERING DOOM

Bela LUGOSI
SHADOW OF CHINATOWN

happening, Sonya has a change of heart and decides to join Martin's cause, and reveals to him all that she knows about Poten's schemes. Martin sends his servant Willy, Sonya, and Joan to his house to wait for him there while he tries to find Poten. There, at Martin's house, Sonya sinks into an exhausted sleep on the living room couch while Willy and Joan go up-stairs and are captured and bound by Poten and Healy, one of the scientist's henchmen. Poten fixes the heavy chandelier over the front door so that it will fall on the head of anyone opening the door.

Sonya, awakening, sees this, as Poten and Healy hurriedly exit when they hear Martin coming up the walk. Martin opens the door just as Sonya rushes forward to warn him and the chandelier comes crashing down on both of them. Sonya is killed by the chandelier but Martin escapes. Martin captures Healy as the latter tries to make his getaway and forces the fact out of him that Poten has a boat tied up at dock No. 13 on which he hopes to escape. Poten's license number is broadcast and a chase is started in which he goes over the dock into the ocean and is apparently drowned. Shortly afterward, the Chinese merchants give a cere-monial dinner in celebration, but at the dinner, one of the waiters is Poten in disguise. As he is about to poison the wine, Martin discovers him and turns him over to Walters. Martin and Joan are about to be married at the final fade-out.

Undersea Kingdom

12 Episodes Republic, 1936	Directed by B. Reeves Eason and Joseph Kane

CAST

Crash Corrigan	Ray "Crash" Corrigan
Diana	Lois Wilde
Khan	Monte Blue
Sharad	William Farnum
Ditmar	Boothe Howard
Professor Norton	C. Montague Shaw
Billy Norton	Lee Van Atta
Briny	Smiley Burnette
Salty	Frankie Marvin
Hakur	Lon Chaney, Jr.
Darius	Lane Chandler
Lieutenant Andrews	Jack Mulhall
Joe	John Bradford
Martos	Ralph Holmes
Gourck	Ernie Smith
Captain Clinton	Lloyd Whitlock
Naval Sentry	David Horsley
Naval Doctor	Kenneth Lawton
Gasspon	Raymond Hatton
Magna	"Rube" Schaeffer

At the bottom of the ocean lies the fabled Lost Continent of Atlantis, beset by two factions in deadly combat. The White Robes, the followers of Sharad, high priest of the true Atlantians, are engaged in a power struggle with Unga Khan, the tyrant ruler of the Black Robe Guards.

Having harnessed the atom, Unga Khan has built a disintegrating machine and is directing it at North America as part of his scheme to gain control of the upper world.

In America, a brilliant scientist, Professor Norton, theorizes that the unprecedented earthquakes disturbing the continent emanate from a human source, probably the legendary Lost Continent of Atlantis at the bottom of the ocean. He announces to a waiting world that he has built an earthquake-countering ray and plans to descend with it to the ocean's floor in another of his inventions, a rocket-powered submarine. Accompanying the professor as he departs are Crash Corrigan, naval officer and superathlete; Diana Compton, a newspaperwoman; Billy, the professor's young son; and two sailors, Briny and Salty.

Their descent is traced by Unga Khan, who has the submarine electrically drawn to Atlantis through an inland sea in the center of the dome-covered continent. As Crash and the others step out of the sub, they are met by a tanklike device called a Juggernaut, from which four mechanical men called "Volkites" emerge. Crash, Diane, Norton, and Billy flee from the monsters by running through a nearby tunnel. But Briny and Salty are captured and taken to Unga Khan's metal tower.

As Crash and his party head back to the submarine they are captured by a detachment of White Robes, led by Martos and Darius, and are led off to Sharad's palace. But en route they are attacked by Black Robes. In the battle that ensues, Diana and Norton are captured and taken to Khan's tower. Crash follows close behind, overpowers two guards, and disguises himself as a Black Robe. In the tower's throne room, Khan urges Norton to aid him in his plan for world conquest. When the professor refuses, the tyrant has Norton placed in a "transforming cabinet" which can alter his mind to do Khan's bidding. Just as this transformation is about to take place, Crash enters the room, rescues the professor, and attempts to escape with Norton and Diana. Their way, however, is blocked by Volkites and Black Robe guards, and Crash is forced to abandon his friends. In a display of his great athletic skill, he slides down an elevator-shaft cable, overcomes several guards, then mounts a horse and gallops toward Sharad's palace.

Crash is brought before Sharad, accused of being a Black Robe, and sentenced to mortal combat with other Black Robes in the arena. Back in Khan's throne room, Norton is placed in the transformation cabinet and becomes the evil tyrant's tool. Through a televisionlike device

TO BE CONTINUED

called a "reflectoplate," Khan shows Diana Crash—imprisoned and waiting to do battle.

Crash is led into the arena and pits his brawn against three Black Robes. He overpowers all three, but refuses to kill them. As punishment, Sharad has Crash tied by a rope to a chariot and plans to drag him to his death. At that moment, Magna and Gourck, two of the defeated Black Robes, attempt to escape. They tackle Sharad, throw him into the chariot, and ride away, dragging Crash behind them. Magna drives the chariot through the city gates and across the countryside toward Khan's tower.

Drawing himself hand over hand into the chariot, Crash hurls the Black Robes to the ground and returns with Sharad to the high priest's palace. There, Sharad displays his gratitude by reuniting Crash with Billy and placing the naval athlete in complete charge of his army. And not a moment too soon. For Crash is soon informed that Khan's entire army, led by Hakur, is advancing upon the city. During the fierce battle that follows, Juggernauts, flame-throwers, and catapults are brought into deadly use. Finally, Black Robe laddermen attempt to swarm over the walls. In the heat of battle Crash overpowers Hakur and, disguising himself in the enemy officer's uniform, gives the order to retreat, thus saving the city. Billy is forced to hide in the chariot of one of the retreating Black Robes and finds himself heading for Khan's fortress. Wandering around the enemy city, he bumps into Diana.

Meanwhile Crash, still disguised as Hakur, decides to go back with the Black Robes to rescue Diana and Norton. Once there, he climbs the wall of Khan's tower, peers through a window, and sees Diana about to be placed in the transformation cabinet. He bursts into the room and is promptly overpowered and knocked unconscious. However, at that moment Billy, armed with an atom gun, enters and rescues Diana, holding Khan, the transformed Norton, and a contingent of Black Robe guards at bay while Diana escapes. As soon as Crash recovers consciousness, he and Billy make good their escape; they join Diana in Sharad's kingdom.

Crash learns that Norton is working on a rocket motor which requires a priming powder,

a supply of which is in their submarine. Immediately, he and Billy head for the inland sea in a chariot. After loading the powder onto the chariot, Crash sends Billy back to Sharad's palace, while he sets out to the tower on foot to destroy the rocket motor. But no sooner has Crash sneaked into Khan's fortress than he is captured, and a diabolical scheme enters Khan's mind.

Diana and Billy are conferring with the high priest of Sharad's kingdom when they are interrupted by the arrival of one of Khan's Juggernauts outside of the city gates. To their horror they discover Crash strapped to the nose of the Juggernaut. Hakur, who is driving the vehicle, demands the vital powder, threatening to ram Crash against the gates unless it is delivered. Stalling for time, resourceful Billy sneaks down from the balcony and slips unseen into the Juggernaut. He frees Crash and enables him to capture Hakur.

Crash and Billy drive the Juggernaut back to Khan's fortress, where unsuspecting guards allow them to enter the city. They make their way to Professor Norton, but he resists their rescue attempts so vigorously that Crash has to knock him unconscious. Finding their way back to the Juggernaut blocked, Crash and Billy carry Norton to one of Khan's Volplanes and succeed in taking off from the tower. When he tries to avoid enemy torpedoes, however, Crash sends the Volplane into a steep dive and makes a forced landing. The threesome return to Sharad's kingdom on foot. But as soon as they arrive, Norton steals away and heads back to Khan's tower.

When Norton returns, Khan determines to destroy the high priest's city once and for all by using the dreaded "projector machine," which hurls a barrage of deadly projectiles. During this devastating attack, Sharad's temple is destroyed and the high priest is killed. Khan then prepares for his final blow: his metal tower is to serve as a huge rocket in which he will be launched into the upper world. Norton informs Khan that, before he blasts off, he must have some maps and charts which were left in the submarine. Khan sends a Black Robe and two Volkites to the submarine but they are spotted by Crash, Billy, Diana, Briny, and Salty. Crash overpowers the Black Robe and puts the Volkites out of commission. The intrepid Crash then decides to return to Khan's fortress once more to rescue Norton, this time disguised as a Volkite.

Once again, Crash makes his way to the tower, confronts Khan, and forces him to change Norton back to his former self. As Crash and the professor flee, Khan notices that they are at the base of the rock tower and commands that the rocket motors be turned on. Crash and Norton escape destruction from the rocket's exhaust by slipping through a manhole before the flames consume them. Realizing that the rocket

is about to take off, both men climb into the tower to avoid being left behind.

Diana, Billy, Salty, and Briny, at the submarine, watch the tower take off and move up toward the roof of Atlantis. They quickly submerge and head for the ocean through the inland sea. Aboard the tower, Crash comes upon a reflectoplate and, using it as a wireless, contacts the navy, which promptly dispatches a battle fleet to deal with the approaching menace. As the tower surfaces, Crash and Norton take off in a Volplane, just as navy shells hit the tower, destroying it completely.

Diana and Crash are reunited and announce their marriage plans.

Ray "Crash" Corrigan demonstrates his superathletic prowess.

C. Montague Shaw and Lois Wilde are captured by Volkites and Black Robes, in front of the Juggernaut.

"Crash" Corrigan (*center, left*) directs the White Robe army in defense of Sharad's fortress.

Boothe Howard, Monte Blue, a Black Robe, and C. Montague Shaw are held at bay by Lee Van Atta, as a wounded Crash Corrigan recovers.

Lon Chaney, Jr., Monte Blue, and Boothe Howard are held at sword point as Crash Corrigan tries to rescue C. Montague Shaw.

Crash is about to be dragged to his death, as a kneeling Lee Van Atta looks on.

As Crash Corrigan attends to a Volkite, a "transformed" C. Montague Shaw prepares to clobber him.

After a forced landing in a Volplane, Crash Corrigan helps C. Montague Shaw while Lee Van Atta lies unconscious.

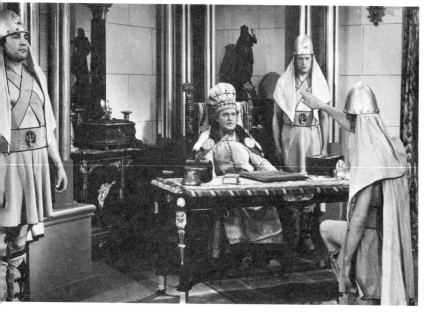

A White Robe messenger brings news to High Priest Sharad.

Boothe Howard and Monte Blue listen as C. Montague Shaw explains how the Tower can be transformed into a huge rocket.

The Vigilantes Are Coming

12 Episodes
Republic, 1936

Directed by
Mack V. Wright
and Ray Taylor

CAST

Don Loring	Bob Livingston
Doris	Kay Hughes
Salvation	Guinn "Big Boy" Williams
Whipsaw	Raymond Hatton
Burr	Fred Kohler
Raspinoff	Robert Warwick
Father Jose	William Farnum
Petroff	Bob Kortman
Talbot	John Merton
Captain Frémont	Ray Corrigan
Colton	Lloyd Ingraham
Anderson	William Desmond
Barsom	Yakima Canutt
Peters	Tracy Layne
Ivan	Bud Pope
Pedro	Steve Clemente
Harris	Bud Osborne
Robert Loring	John O'Brien
Señor Loring	Henry Hall
Dick Feather	Philip Armenta
Kramer	Stanley Blystone

In 1840, General Jason Burr, wealthy California settler, conceives the idea of establishing himself as dictator of the country in order to exploit it for gold. To this end, he imports Cossacks and enlists the aid of the "Imperial Russian Empire," led by Count Raspinoff, the Russian emissary.

But Burr needs the rich mines and lands of Señor Loring to rise to power, so he arranges for Loring and his son Robert to be murdered while the eldest son, Don, is away in the Northwest with Captain Frémont and the U.S. soldiers. When Don returns, he finds his family's lands appropriated by Burr. Unable to fight Burr in the open, he dons a mask and black robe and, as the mysterious Eagle, sets off to reclaim his property. With the aid of Captain Frémont and his troops, he ends the plot to establish a foreign empire in America.

William Farnum and Kay Hughes listen appreciatively as Bob Livingston strikes a note for freedom.

Guinn "Big Boy" Williams enjoying the local color.

The mysterious "Eagle" leads his men against a would-be tyrant. The big man in the saddle, just left of center, is "Big Boy" Williams.

1937

Blake of Scotland Yard

15 Episodes
Victory, 1937

Directed by
Bob Hill

CAST

Blake	△Ralph Byrd
Hope Mason	Joan Barclay
Bobby	Dickie Jones

and

Herbert Rawlinson
Lloyd Hughes
Nick Stuart

Sir James Blake, former Scotland Yard inspector, has financed and perfected a death ray, invented by Jerry Sheehan and Blake's niece Hope Mason. After seeing a demonstration of the ray, munitions maker Count Basil Zegelloff offers a mysterious black-robed individual called "The Scorpion" a fabulous sum to steal the machine. After numerous attempts, the Scorpion, whose right hand closely resembles a lobster's claw, succeeds.

Discovering that a vital part of the machine is missing, the Scorpion embarks upon a campaign of terror which includes kidnapping, dynamiting, and attempts at murder in order to get the vital component. Blake conducts his own campaign, aimed at learning the identity of the Scorpion. When Blake determines that Count Basil is behind the Scorpion's attempts, he disguises himself as the Scorpion and plans a meeting with the count.

He is just about to gain some very useful information from the count when the real Scorpion drops on him from a ceiling trapdoor, and the enemies stand face to face. Blake attacks, but when the police rush in, the Scorpion and the count disappear.

Eventually, direct suspicion falls on the mild-mannered Dr. Marshall, a supposed friend of Blake's. Confronted while trying to remove the ray from a safe, the Scorpion is revealed as Dr. Marshall. Despite his exposure, he attempts a getaway, still bent on stealing the machine. Blake leaves the ray in the safe and makes no attempt to stop Marshall when he grabs it. The machine is heavily charged with electricity and Marshall is unable to break his hold. Blake turns Marshall over to the police, and once again Blake and his associates are left in peace.

Dick Tracy

15 Episodes
Republic) 1937

Directed by
Ray Taylor
and Alan James

CAST

Dick Tracy	Ralph Byrd
Gwen	Kay Hughes
Mike McGurk	Smiley Burnette
Junior	Lee Van Atta
Moloch	John Piccori
Gordon Tracy (after)	Carleton Young
Steve	Fred Hamilton
Anderson	Francis X. Bushman
Brewster	John Dilson
Gordon Tracy (before)	Richard Beach
Clayton	Wedgewood Nowell
Paterno	Theodore Lorch
Odette	Edwin Stanley
Cloggerstein	Harrison Greene
Martino	Herbert Weber
Burke	Buddy Roosevelt
Flynn	George de Normand
Korvitch	Bryon K. Foulger
Oscar and Elmer	Oscar and Elmer

Dick Tracy is assigned to bring a halt to the terrorist activities of the Spider Gang, so called because their sinister chief operates under the name of "The Spider." The gang captures Dick's brother Gordon, and Dr. Moloch, the Spider's right-hand man, performs an operation on him. As a result of the operation Gordon becomes a mindless slave, unable to determine right from wrong or remember anything of his past life. He is only too willing to obey the Spider's orders.

Gordon is used by the Spider to keep Tracy off balance, although the ace detective persists in closing the gap between himself and the master criminal. The Spider uses all kinds of weapons to achieve his aims, the most impressive of which is a powerful death ray carried in his futuristic aircraft, the *Flying Wing*. In the end, though, the Spider's devices are no match for the tenacity and determination of Tracy, who succeeds in destroying the criminal and bringing his gang to justice.

A trussed-up Ralph Byrd reaches for a handy knife.

Lee Van Atta and Kay Hughes are shown some clues by Ralph Byrd.

Ralph Byrd looks for a way out of what will soon be a raging inferno.

Jungle Jim

12 Episodes
Universal, 1937

Directed by
Ford Beebe
and Cliff Smith

CAST

Jungle Jim	Grant Withers
Joan	Betty Jane Rhodes
Malay Mike	Raymond Hatton
The Cobra	Henry Brandon
Shanghai Lil	Evelyn Brent
Bruce Redmond	Bryant Washburn
Tyler	Selmer Jackson
Slade	Al Bridge
La Bat	Paul Sutton
Kolu	Al Duvall
Hawks	William Royale

Two safaris head into the jungle in search of a jungle-raised white girl, Joan, who has fallen heir to a fortune in America. The expedition headed by Jungle Jim wants to help her claim her fortune, but the other expedition, led by Redmond, wants her out of the way so that the inheritance would go by default to them. Naturally, these men become Jungle Jim's enemies. But Jim has another deadly foe—the Cobra, a sinister escaped convict who has found a haven in the jungle posing as a friend of Joan. His safety depends on Joan's power over the natives, for they believe her to be a white goddess. The Cobra will do anything to keep the girl in the jungle.

Although the Cobra tries to convince Joan that Jungle Jim is her enemy, and despite the frequent interference of the Redmond party,

Jim succeeds in convincing Joan of his friendship. As a result, Joan decides to leave the jungle and return to New York with Jim. This sets off a flurry of desperate maneuvers by the Cobra and Redmond. As Joan, aided by Jungle Jim and her native tribe, gains the upper hand, Redmond, trying to escape, is attacked and killed by a lion. The Cobra, trying to make good his escape, is pursued and captured by Jungle Jim who turns him over to the authorities. Joan and Jim leave for America and happiness together.

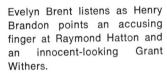
Evelyn Brent listens as Henry Brandon points an accusing finger at Raymond Hatton and an innocent-looking Grant Withers.

Bryant Washburn's escape is blocked by Betty Jane Rhodes and Grant Withers.

Grant Withers smiles sardonically and clutches Betty Jane Rhodes as Henry Brandon, Evelyn Brent, and Bryant Washburn face captivity.

Jungle Menace

15 Episodes
Columbia, 1937

Directed by
George Melford
and Harry Fraser

CAST

Frank Hardy	Frank Buck
Edward Elliott	John St. Polis
Dorothy Elliott	Charlotte Henry
Tom Banning	William Bokewell
Robert Banning	Richard Tucker
Murphy	Leroy Mason
The Tiger Man	Sasha Siemel
Chiang	Willie Fung
Rogers	Duncan Renaldo
MacLeod	Robert Warwick

In the province of Seemang in far-off Asia, where the Bay of Bengal meets the dangerous jungle, rubber planter Edward Elliott owns a large and prosperous rubber plantation. Elliott's attractive daughter Dorothy is engaged to neighboring planter Tom Banning. But problems are brewing for the planter.

When a load of rubber is put on a riverboat to be taken to port, the boat is attacked by river pirates. The crew is killed and the shipment stolen. Dorothy and Tom narrowly escape death by jumping into the river and swimming ashore.

There is an evil plot to force Elliott to sell his plantation. His plantation manager Murphy is helping the thieves, and when one of Elliott's men comes upon a clue he is murdered. Then Elliott himself, about to reveal his suspicions to the governor, is mysteriously shot through the heart from outside a window.

Adventurer Frank Hardy determines to find out who is behind the plot. But he faces danger after danger before he finally brings the murderers to justice.

The Mysterious Pilot

15 Episodes
Columbia, 1937

Directed by
Spencer Gordon
Bennet

CAST

Jim Dorn	Frank Hawks
Jean McNain	Dorothy Sebastian
Kansas	Rex Lease
Bergelot	Guy Bates Post
Snowden	Kenneth Harlan
Luke	Yakima Canutt
Yoroslaf	Frank Lackteen
Casper	Robert Terry
Fritz	George Rosener
Martha	Clara Kimball Young
Soft Shoe	Harry Harvey
Kilgour	Tom London
Carlson	Ted Adams
Jerry	Earl Douglas
Boyer	Robert Walker
McCarthy	Roger Williams
Vivian McNain	Esther Ralston

On a train traveling through the Canadian wilds, Jean McNain overhears a stranger accuse her host and potential fiancé, Carter Snowden, of murder. Alarmed, she slips off the train at Titan Pass and runs into the woods. When the stranger is found mysteriously shot through the head, Snowden directs his bodyguard to track Jean down.

Jim Dorn, a cartographer for the Royal Canadian Air Force, his pal Kansas, a Mountie, and Indian Luke hide Jean from Snowden. The industrious villain spares no efforts in tracking down the girl, who can not only point the finger of guilt at him, but whose beauty can also be of great value in his forthcoming political campaign. Discovering that she is being protected by Jim, Snowden lures Jean to his transport plane by sending her a message that Jim is hurt, and flies off with her. Jim and Kansas take to the air in pursuit and force Snowden's plane to crash. Jean drags herself from the wreckage and is rescued by Indian Luke, but Snowden is not as fortunate; he is killed in the crash. Jim bails out of his plane to help Jean, but his chute is carried by a high wind and gets entangled in the trees. Jean ends up rescuing Jim.

Stony-faced Frank Hawks gets a good grip on Frank Lackteen's neck.

The Painted Stallion

12 Episodes
Republic, 1937

Directed by
William Witney
and Ray Taylor

CAST

Clark Stewart	Ray Corrigan
Jamison	Hoot Gibson
Kit Carson	Sammy McKim
Escobedo Duprey	LeRoy Mason
Davey Crockett	Jack Perrin
Jim Bowie	Hal Taliaferro
Zamoro	Duncan Renaldo
The Rider	Julia Thayer
Oscar and Elmer	Oscar and Elmer
Tom	Yakima Canutt
Macklin	Maston Williams
Joe	Duke Taylor
Pedro	Loren Riebe
Juan	George de Normand
Governor	Gordon de Main
Bull Smith	Charles King
Oldham	Vinegar Roan

An American agent, Clark Stuart, is dispatched to Santa Fe to negotiate a trade agreement with the newly appointed Mexican governor. At the same time, the first American wagon train, led by Walter Jamison, leaves from Independence, Missouri, for Santa Fe, bearing goods for trade. The train is accompanied by

Jim Bowie, famed inventor of the Bowie knife, and by the youthful Kit Carson.

The former governor of Santa Fe, Alfredo Duprey, anxious to regain his lucrative control of the territory, plots to sabotage the treaty by substituting one of his own men for Stuart before the new governor arrives.

Duprey's confederate, Zamorro and Zamorro's henchmen attempt to destroy the wagon train, first by stirring up an Indian attack and later by luring it into a mountain pass where the Indians use dynamite to send a landslide down on it. They also make several attempts to kill Stuart, but each attempt is foiled by a mysterious girl rider on a painted stallion who warns of danger to the Americans by shooting a whistling arrow.

Duprey's men steal the papers from Stuart that authorize him to deal with the new Mexican governor. Stuart trails them into Santa Fe where he meets Davey Crockett. After more adventures and the arrival of the governor, the Americans trap the Duprey forces in their hideout in the caves. After a climactic battle, in which the rider on the painted stallion takes part, Zamorro and Duprey are killed and the rest of the gang routed.

The agreement establishing trade relations is signed by the governor, guaranteeing welcome and safety to American travelers.

Ray Corrigan appears trapped by LeRoy Mason, Duncan Renaldo (*far right*), and their comrades.

Mickey Rentschler finds a temporary haven in a radio patrol car.

Radio Patrol

12 Episodes
Universal, 1937

Directed by
Ford Beebe
and Cliff Smith

CAST

Pat O'Hara	Grant Withers
Molly	Catherine Hughes
Pinky Adams	Mickey Rentschler
Sam	Adrian Morris
Selkirk	Max Hoffman, Jr.
Thata	Frank Lackteen
Franklin	Leonard Lord
Pollard	Monte Montague
Zutta	Dick Botiller
Irish	Silver Wolf

A secret formula for flexible, bulletproof steel excites the interest of international crooks who will stop at nothing to get hold of it. They kill the inventor of the formula and try to adopt the inventor's young son Pinky in order to learn the secret of the steel.

Their nefarious scheme is stymied, however, by Pat O'Hara, a radio cop. With the aid of the lovely Molly Selkirk, Pat tries to keep the secret in Pinky's possession. He not only triumphs against the international band of crooks, but also reveals that Wellington, the owner of the steel factory, is the biggest crook of them all. This, of course, is social realism at its finest.

Silver Wolf gets a good grip on a gangster's gun arm.

Grant Withers seems to have this situation well in hand.

Secret Agent X-9

12 Episodes
Universal, 1937

Directed by
Ford Beebe
and Cliff Smith

CAST

Secret Agent X-9	Scott Kolk
Shara Graustark	Jean Rogers
Tommy Dawson	Henry Hunter
Pidge	David Oliver
Wheeler	Larry Blake
Baron Michael Karsten	Monte Blue
Blackstone (Brenda)	Henry Brandon
Maroni	Lon Chaney, Jr.
Marker	Max Hoffman, Jr.
Scarlett	Bentley Hewlett
Packard	George Shelley
Thurston	Robert Dalton
Ransom	Leonard Lord
Trader Delaney	Bob Kortman
The Fence	Edward Piel, Sr.
Rose	Lynn Gilbert

Secret Agent X-9 is assigned to track down the whereabouts of the stolen Belgravian crown jewels. He discovers that a notorious jewel thief, Brenda, is in the United States and tries to corner the crafty crook. With the aid of his diver Pidge and other G-men, he closes in on the pirate ship headquarters of Brenda's gang. Machine guns clatter, tear gas bombs are hurled into the ship, and the crooks are taken prisoner —except for Brenda who, disguised as a Belgravian baron, manages to slip ashore. X-9, however, doggedly follows the mysterious Brenda's trail and discovers that he is really Blackstone, a well-known local criminal. He proves Brenda-Blackstone to be the mastermind behind the jewel robbery and recovers the stolen gems.

While the wounded David Oliver stands beside him, Scott Kolk captures a group of Brenda's henchmen, the most prominent of which is Lon Chaney, Jr. (*third from left*).

Henry Hunter and Scott Kolk, disguised as a janitor, arrest Henry Brandon on suspicion of being implicated in the daring theft of the Belgravian crown jewels.

Max Hoffman, Jr., makes a break for liberty while being questioned at the Department of Justice. Using Monte Blue as a shield, Hoffman covers Scott Kolk.

SOS Coast Guard

12 Episodes
Republic, 1937

Directed by
William Witney
and Alan James

CAST

Terry	Ralph Byrd
Boroff	Bela Lugosi
Jean Norman	Maxine Doyle
Commander Boyle	Herbert Rawlinson
Thorg	Richard Alexander
Snapper McGee	Lee Ford
Rickerby	John Picorri
Rabinisi	Lawrence Grant
Jim Kent	Thomas Carr
Dodds	Carleton Young
Dick Norman	Allen Connor
Degado	George Chesebro
Wies	Ranny Weeks

Terry Kent, Coast Guard hero, discovers that Boroff, a half-mad inventor, has contracted to supply Morovania with his deadly disintegrating gas for purposes of warfare. Arnatite, the necessary raw material, is smuggled out aboard the freighter Carfax, which is driven aground by heavy storms. The Coast Guard effects a rescue while Jean Norman, newspaper girl, and Snapper McGee, her cameraman, recognize the fleeing Boroff. Anticipating an investigation, Boroff sends Thorg, a giant idiot under his power, to cut the cables of the grounded Carfax, sinking all evidence. Terry and Jean, trapped in the sinking boat, fortunately find themselves in an air pocket so they swim to a hatch and rise safely to the surface.

Terry enlists the aid of Jean's brother Dick, a chemist, to reproduce the ink notation found in Boroff's cabin, now undecipherable because of the water. It reads "Rickerby's Laboratories." Terry goes there and discovers Rickerby to be in league with the munition plotters. The outlaws overpower him, bind him, and take him aboard a launch, but Terry loosens his hands enough to send a code message which is picked up by the Coast Guard. In the ensuing battle, the boat is wrecked and starts to sink, Terry tied to the wheel.

Terry loosens his bonds and swims to safety. Boroff has an old kelp plant put into condition for the manufacturing of the disintegrating-gas bombs, and sends Thorg to dive for the tins of arnatite still in the hold of the sunken Carfax. These recovered, everything is ready for the manufacture of the deadly gas. Krohn, the scientist who is to make the gas, is spirited past the Coast Guard in the guise of a heavily bandaged scalded boiler stoker. Snapper blunders onto the scene, and the wicked scientists decide to use him in place of a dog as the "subject" to test the power of the gas. Terry comes to the rescue, and Boroff explodes one of the bombs at his feet.

Terry hastily joins Snapper in a glass cabinet which the gas cannot penetrate. Everything about them dissolves to atoms. They then pursue the mobsters to a lumberyard, but first, Terry gives Jean one of the gas pellets he has picked up to take to her brother for analysis. When Boroff learns where Jean has gone, he sends his men to Dick's laboratory; they appear just as Dick is about to learn the secret of the chemical. Terry trails the plotters to where they are holding Jean prisoner. There is a desperate fistfight, and Terry rescues Jean.

It is learned that a supply of zandoide, a product necessary for the manufacture of the gas, reached Honolulu but apparently disappeared. The America-bound freighter Adamic carries no record of zandoide being shipped, but Terry suspects that it is disguised as something else. To investigate, he hastens to Hawaii, via the China Clipper, and joins the crew of the Adamic on the eastbound voyage. Benton, the cargo master, is a Boroff man, and causes a boiler to explode in Terry's face.

But Terry escapes the steam through an iron door. Learning that the Boroff gang plans to ship the gas pellets to Morovania from a small railroad station, Pierport, Terry hastens there in a Coast Guard plane and finds Snapper already there. The only freight being shipped out is a consignment of electric light bulbs. But Terry's suspicions are aroused when one of the men registers great fright over Snapper's careless handling of one of the bulbs; it is plain that these bulbs conceal the deadly gas pellets. The police arrive and, in the ensuing gun battle, some of the bombs are exploded, but Terry taxis his plane so that the exhaust blows the gas away.

He then learns that the *Sea Wolf,* a notorious smuggling vessel, is anchored near the wreck of the *Carfax,* and suspects that the Boroff gang, thwarted because their gas bombs were destroyed at Pierport, have determined to raise the remaining tins of arnatite. Terry decides to do some diving himself, and comes into underwater conflict with Thorg. They grapple, and Thorg cuts the air hose of Terry's diving suit. Meanwhile, Boroff and his cutthroats are covering the operation from a launch and shooting at those who try to aid Terry.

Terry frees himself from the useless diving suit and swims to the surface. Suspecting some connection between the mysterious cargo of the sunken *Carfax* and the kelp plant, he arranges to visit the plant along with Jean and Snapper, supposedly to get a newspaper story. Boroff shows them around, and Snapper takes pictures. Later, when Boroff learns that the arnatite is radioactive and the rays will show on the developed film, he orders his followers to pursue Snapper and break the camera. In the chase, the villainous gang shoots through the rear tire of Jean's press car; it careens and plunges over a cliff but Terry, Jean, and Snapper jump from the doomed car just before it goes over.

The films are developed and disclose the radioactive arnatite. From this, Terry deduces that the disintegrating gas is manufactured at the kelp plant. He secures Coast Guard aid in raiding the plant. Boroff learns of Terry's plans and decides to evacuate the plant, first mining it with dynamite. The Coast Guard arrives and Terry spots the explosives; Jean and Snapper arrive, ignorant of the dynamite, and leisurely inspect the deserted plant. Terry rushes up to warn them, but the dynamite explodes.

Terry, Jean, and Snapper save themselves by taking refuge in Boroff's secret laboratory, which is shockproof. Finding one crate of the "light bulbs" left behind, they rush it to Dick's laboratory to complete the analysis and create a countergas formula. Terry goes to a chemical supply house for a compressor necessary for finding the countergas. Boroff's mob overpowers him and the supply-house drivers, dressed in Terry's clothes, gain access to Dick's laboratory. They slug Dick and drive him to an abandoned spot where they set fire to the supply-house truck. But Terry has followed a trail of leaking acid and arrives in time to rescue Dick.

Dick is taken to a hospital where he attempts to dictate to Jean the secret of the countergas. Meanwhile, Morovania is pressing Boroff for delivery and he promises that the consignment will sail immediately aboard the steamer *Agoura.* Learning that the *Agoura* is anchored out at sea awaiting a mysterious cargo, Terry goes there in a patrol boat and engages in a gunfight with Boroff's crew during which many of the gas pellets are exploded. The entire launch disintegrates. Boroff, seeing this from his cave hideout, orders Thorg to go out and kill Terry when he lands. There is a struggle with the giant Thorg in the sea cave, and Terry's body goes limp.

Terry, unconscious, is brought to Boroff who has the idea of using him as a pawn to call off all Coast Guard activities until the gas bombs are safe at sea. Terry burns his bonds by means of a smoldering cigarette, escapes, and summons the Coast Guard which closes in on Boroff's cave. Boroff rigs up an entire circle of the gas bombs, connecting them as a mine. This is exploded, with Terry and his men in the center. Jean flies her plane to the region just in time and releases a blast of the countergas, which clears away the fumes. The murderous plotters are all arrested—except Boroff, who escapes. Thorg, mortally wounded by Boroff's own bullet, appears, fiendishly set on revenge. He hurls a gas cartridge at Boroff, annihilating both of them.

Wild West Days

13 Episodes
Universal, 1937

Directed by
Ford Beebe
and Cliff Smith

CAST

Kentucky	Johnny Mack Brown
Dude	George Shelley
Trigger	Robert Kortman
Mike	Frank Yaconelli
Lucy	Lynn Gilbert
Larry	Frank McGlynn
Keeler	Russell Simpson
Purvis	Francis McDonald
Doc Hardy	Walter Miller
Red Hatchet	Chief Thunderbird
Steve	Al Bridge

Kentucky Wade and his two buddies Trigger and Mike ride to help Larry and Lucy Monroe, who are threatened by outlaws. Matt Keeler, the scheming owner of *The Brimstone News,* is anxious to discover the location of Larry's mine, which is rich in ore. Matt has Larry framed and jailed and instigates an attempt to lynch him but Kentucky rescues Larry and takes him away. They are pursued by Red Hatchet, chief of the marauding Indians, who captures Larry and hands him over to Keeler. Once again Larry escapes with the aid of Kentucky.

When Keeler hears of Larry's escape he uses a ruse to find the mine: in his newspaper he announces a fake gold rush hoping to grab the property when the rich lode is found. Thousands of gold-crazy men swarm in on horseback and in wagons. But Kentucky exposes the gold rush hoax and rounds up Keeler's men for trial.

However, Red Hatchet's Indians appear and wage a fierce battle against Kentucky's outfit. Reinforcements come to Kentucky's aid and drive away the redskins. Kentucky, suspicious of Keeler, confronts him in a saloon. Keeler pulls a gun but Kentucky knocks him cold and has him jailed. With the bandits out of the way, Kentucky, Trigger, and Mike start off to seek new adventures.

Two settlers seem suspicious of Johnny Mack Brown (*second from left*) and his friends. (That's Bob Kortman in the center.)

119

TO BE CONTINUED

Zorro Rides Again

12 Episodes
(Republic,) 1937

Directed by
William Witney
and John English

CAST

James Vega (Zorro)	John Carroll
Joyce Andrews	Helen Christian
Phillip Andrews	Reed Howes
Renaldo	Duncan Renaldo
Brad Dace (El Lobo)	Richard Alexander
Marsden	Noah Beery
Manuel Vega	Nigel de Brulier
Trelliger	Robert Kortman
Carter	Jack Ingram
Manning	Roger Williams
Captain of Rurales	Tony Martelli
Larkin	Edmund Cobb
Carmelita	Mona Rico
O'Shea	Tom London
O'Brien	Harry Strang
Duncan	Jerry Frank

Marsden, with his henchmen, is ruthlessly trying to gain control of the California-Yucatan Railroad, Inc., owned jointly by Phillip and Vega. A masked stranger, who gives his name as Zorro, comes to the aid of the railway and wins the admiration of all by his brave deeds. In one of the outlaw raids, Vega is mortally wounded, and as he lies dying, Zorro reveals himself as Vegas's nephew James, whom everybody believed to be a weak and spineless wastrel. Zorro vows to avenge his uncle's death, bides his time, rescuing Joyce and Phillip from efforts on the part of El Lobo, Marsden's chief henchman, to kill them and gain control of their road.

The outlaws succeed in destroying the warehouse which is the source of supply for the railroad, but James, without his Zorro disguise, tricks Marsden into buying new supplies on the pretext of selling Marsden a share in the railroad. Marsden, furious at the trick that has been played on him, plans to wreck the train carrying the supplies, but Zorro thwarts his efforts by throwing the switch in the nick of time with his Argentine whip.

Meanwhile, important land deeds have been stolen by El Lobo's men, and one of them plans to fly across the border to register them. Zorro disguises himself and stows away in the plane, but he is discovered, and the plane is shot down. Zorro miraculously escapes unharmed. Finally confronting the villains, Zorro sees El Lobo escaping, but Zorro's horse El Rey goes after El Lobo and kills him. And by this time, enough evidence has been presented to the authorities by Zorro to convict Marsden.

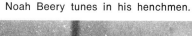
Zorro transfers from his horse El Rey to a hijacked truck.

Noah Beery tunes in his henchmen.

120

John Carroll faces a flaming death . . . his only hope, that open window. . . .

A well-armed Zorro opens fire upon Marsden's men.

Jerry Frank, atop the twin-prop airplane, talks to cohorts Richard Alexander (*right*) and Bob Kortman.

John Carroll disposes of an outlaw.

1938

Dick Tracy Returns

15 Episodes   Directed by
Republic, 1938   William Witney
and John English

CAST

Dick Tracy	Ralph Byrd
Gwen	Lynn Roberts
Pa Stark	Charles Middleton
Junior	Jerry Tucker
Ron Merton	David Sharpe
Mike McGurk	Lee Ford
Steve	Michael Kent
Champ	John Merton
Trigger	Raphael Bennett
Dude	Jack Roberts
The Kid	Ned Glass
Joe Hanner	Edward Foster
Snub	Alan Gregg
Rance	Reed Howes
Reynolds	Robert Terry
Hunt	Tom Seidel
Slasher	Jack Ingram

Dick Tracy, ace G-man, is assigned to a case on the West Coast. Ron Merton, a promising recruit, is sent with him. The case Tracy is to solve concerns a large criminal family, the Starks. Headed by Pa Stark, this notorious group includes the father and five sons: Champ, Slasher, Dude, Trigger, and the Kid.

While robbing an armored car, the Starks murder Ron Merton soon after he and Tracy arrive on the coast. Tracy catches the Kid, and orders a man brought from the east to testify against him. With the aid of his G-men, and Gwen, Junior, Mike McGurk, and others, Tracy keeps on the trail of the Starks. One by one the Starks are killed off. First the Kid, then Slasher, then Duke and Trigger. However, Pa Stark and Champ manage to escape each raid. Before the gang is wiped out, the Starks have stolen a government torpedo boat, have extorted thousands of dollars from various individuals, and have attempted to wreck a 200-inch telescope lens in an important observatory. They've caused a huge dam to be blown up, have stolen a powerful new welding device, and in general caused the G-men a considerable amount of trouble.

However, Pa Stark and Champ are finally cornered in their hideout, an abandoned rock-crusher plant. Champ is killed, but Pa Stark forces Tracy to enter a plane with him on the threat of blowing everyone up by means of two vials filled with nitroglycerin, which he has strapped to his wrists. Tracy gets in the plane with him and takes off. When they reach an altitude of 15,000 feet, Tracy quickly barrel-rolls the plane over, drops out, and floats to safety by parachute. The plane crashes and explodes, bringing to an end the last of the Stark gang.

Charles Middleton (*right*) and his cohorts subdue a struggling Ralph Byrd.

Fighting Devil Dogs

12 Episodes
(Republic, 1938)

Directed by
William Witney, John
English, Robert Beche

CAST

Lieutenant Tom Grayson	Lee Powell
Frank Corby	Herman Brix
Janet	Eleanor Stewart
General White	Montague Love
Warfield	Hugh Sothern
Colonel Grayson	Sam Flint
The Lightning	?
Crenshaw	Perry Ivins
Benson	Forrest Taylor
Gould	John Picorri
Johnson	Carleton Young
Lin Wing	John Davidson
Sam Hedges	Henry Otho
Parker	Reed Howes
Wilson	Tom London
Ellis	Edmund Cobb
Macro	Alan Gregg
Todd	Allan Mathews

Tom Grayson and his friend Frank Corby, lieutenants in the U.S. Marine Corps, are engaged in a campaign against organized bandits in a tropical protectorate. Tom leads his platoon away from the regular line of duty to investigate a fort, the occupants of which have all been mysteriously killed. While all his men are searching the building, it is struck by a curious projectile, which transforms it into a crackling mass of death-dealing electricity. The entire platoon except for Tom and Corby, who had been searching the grounds outside, are killed.

Tom is called back to the United States to face censure, and an inquiry is begun into the loss of his men. He is convinced that they were victims of a new weapon, an artificial thunder-bolt. His opinion is confirmed when a similar weapon is used against a steamship.

It develops that this thunderbolt has been created by a mysterious criminal, known only as "The Lightning." Tom and Corby are assigned to track him down, and a group of scientists is organized to develop some means of defense against the deadly thunderbolt. This group includes Colonel Grayson, Tom's father; Warfield, a prominent and wealthy manufacturer of electrical machinery; Janet, his attractive daughter who acts as his assistant; Crenshaw, a famous electrical inventor; and several other scientists. Before their work has even begun, the Lightning launches a torpedo from his superplane, known as the *Wing,* and electrifies the laboratory, killing Tom's father.

Tom redoubles his efforts to track down the identity of the Lightning. With the help of the Marines, he locates and attacks the Lightning's headquarters, but the villain escapes.

It becomes obvious that one of the scientists is the Lightning. But which one? All clues point to Crenshaw, who always manages to excuse himself just before the Lightning makes an appearance, enters with a bandaged arm after the Lightning has injured his own, and generally behaves suspiciously.

In the course of his search Tom avoids a flaming death aboard a burning ship by leaping overboard only to have his air hose cut while underwater in full diving gear. Fortunately there is enough air left in the diving suit to enable him to walk to shore. Despite these obstacles Tom eventually succeeds in exposing the Lightning, by gathering all the suspects together and claiming to know the Lightning's identity. Just before the name of the Lightning can be pronounced, a shot rings out, fired by Warfield, who is, in fact, the Lightning. In the confusion, Warfield flees. Trying to escape in his wing-shaped plane, Warfield and his crew are blown out of the sky by a ray machine invented by Crenshaw for just this purpose.

"Does Lieutenant Grayson expect us to believe this wild story of a military weapon unknown to science?" Herman Brix and Lee Powell (*left*) hear their story denounced at a military tribunal. Montague Love (*center*) listens grimly.

Lee Powell and his Marines are on the alert against the Lightning.

The Lightning and his men wreck the scientific equipment being used to develop a defense against his Thunderbolt.

Montague Love, Perry Ivins, Lee Powell, Forrest Taylor, Eleanor Stewart, and Herman Brix, about to blast the Lightning out of the sky with the Ray Machine.

Flaming Frontiers

15 Episodes	Directed by
Universal, 1938	Ray Taylor
	and Alan James

CAST

Tex Houston	John Mack Brown
Mary Grant	Eleanor Hansen
Tom Grant	Ralph Bowman
Ace Daggett	Charles Middleton
Bart Eaton	James Blaine
Breed	Charles Stevens
Tom Crosby	William Royle
Sheriff	Horace Murphy
Postmaster	Michael Slade
Buffalo Bill	John Rutherford
Thunder Cloud	Chief Thunder Cloud

Tex Houston, famous Indian scout, finds a Pony Express rider shot by Indians. He carries the rider's mailbag into town, where he meets Mary Grant and her dad, who are menaced by ruthless Bart Eaton. Bart wants to marry Mary in order to obtain her brother Tom's California gold mine. Mary flees in desperation and is aided by Buffalo Bill, who helps her escape capture by Indians. Mary's father dies in a wagon crash, and Tom is jailed on a framed murder charge. When rival outlaws spring Tom from jail in order to force him to reveal the location of the mine, Tex daringly rescues him as Indians attack the town:

While keeping the outlaws from gaining possession of the mine, Tex and Tom barely escape death from powder blasts and flaming bulidings. They save Mary from being crushed under a freight wagon, eventually clear Tom of the murder charge, and end the villainous careers of Daggett and Eaton with well-placed bullets. Tex and Mary then enjoy the luxury of contemplating the future together.

Eleanor Hansen and Johnny Mack Brown display some evidence to interested townsfolk.

Flash Gordon's Trip to Mars

15 Episodes
Universal, 1938

Directed by
Ford Beebe
and Robert Hill

CAST

Flash Gordon	—Larry "Buster" Crabbe
Dale Arden	—Jean Rogers
Emperor Ming	—Charles Middleton
Dr. Zarkov	Frank Shannon
Queen Azura	Beatrice Roberts
Prince Barin	Richard Alexander
Clay King	Montague Shaw
Happy	Donald Kerr
Tarnak	Wheeler Oakman

Flash Gordon, Dr. Zarkov, and Dale Arden zoom to Mars in a rocket ship, hoping to locate and destroy the mysterious force which is draw-ing nitrogen from the earth's atmosphere. When they land, the group is captured by the Clay People, human beings turned into clay by Azura, Queen of Magic.

Flash and Zarkov are forced by the Clay People to attempt to capture Azura's white sapphire, the source of her magic power. In the course of his many tasks, Flash, along with his friend Prince Barin who has come to Mars to convince the Martians not to ally themselves with Ming the Merciless, manages to avert a war between the Clay People and the Tree People (who also reside on Mars). Ming desired the conflict in order to increase universe tensions.

The Clay People soon become Flash's allies in the battle against Queen Azura and Ming, whose great lamp is stripping the earth of nitrogen. With the help of his friends, Flash succeeds in destroying Ming's great lamp, and the evil emperor himself is thrown into a "disintegration chamber" and presumably destroyed.

Charles Middleton relays the latest step in his plan to conquer the universe.

Anthony Warde (*seated*) carefully observes an entranced Jean Rogers.

128

Jean Rogers and Donald Kerr hide from the Tree People.

The Great Adventures of Wild Bill Hickok

15 Episodes
Columbia, 1938

Directed by
Mack V. Wright
and Sam Nelson

CAST

Wild Bill Hickok	Gordon Elliott
Cameron	Monte Blue
Ruth Cameron	Carole Wayne
Jerry	Frankie Darro
Bud	Dickie Jones
Boots	Sammy McKim
Kit Lawson	Kermit Maynard
Snake Eyes	Roscoe Ates
Danny	Monty Collins
Blakely	Reed Hadley
Gray Eagle	Chief Thunder Cloud
Little Elk	Mala
Bruce	Walter Wills
Scudder	J. P. McGowan
Stone	Eddie Waller
Metaxa	George Chesebro
Blackie	Alan Bridge

Wild Bill Hickok, U.S. marshal in Abilene, opposes the Phantom Raiders, a renegade gang seeking to balk a big cattle drive over the Chisholm Trail from Texas to Abilene. Hickok organizes the boys of the town into the "Flaming Arrows" to assist him. The Raiders launch continuing attacks against the wagon train, which is captained by army scout Kit Lawson. Finally, Hickok, Lawson, and the "Flaming Arrows" trap and destroy the marauders with the help of an army detachment. The cattle enter Abilene in a triumphant procession.

Gordon Elliott collects the guns of potential troublemakers.

Hawk of the Wilderness

12 Episodes   Directed by
(Republic, 1938)   William Witney
                   and John English

CAST

Kioga	Herman Brix
Kias	Mala
Yellow Weasel	Monte Blue
Beth	Jill Martin
Mokuyi	Noble Johnson
Solerno	William Royle
Dr. Munro	Tom Chatterton
Allen Kendall	George Eldridge
Bill Bill	Patrick J. Kelly
Dirk	Dick Wessel
George	Snowflake
Tawnee	Tuffy

Lincoln Rand, a scientist, his wife, and infant son Kioga lead an expedition to discover a lost tribe on an unknown island. As they approach the island, a violent storm erupts. As the storm worsens, Rand writes a message to his friend Dr. Munro, seals it in a bottle, and hurls it into the sea. Their ship is wrecked and all aboard lost except Mokuyi, Rand's Indian companion, who swims ashore with the baby.

Mokuyi carries the baby to the lost tribe with whom they live. But because an active volcano on the island erupted the day of the shipwreck, the natives fear the god of the volcano is angered at the presence of a white baby.

Twenty-two years later, Rand's final message, still sealed in the bottle, is discovered by a smuggler named Solerno. He takes the message to Dr. Munro who outfits an expedition to search for Rand. With him go his daughter Beth, her suitor Allen Kendall, and Professor Williams. Solerno, pretending to be a seaman, volunteers his crew to man the boat. When the expedition arrives at the island, they find Kioga grown to manhood, and discover the island conceals a rich treasure. Solerno's pirate crew immediately attempts to seize the treasure. Taking posses-sion of the ship, they leave the rest of the party at the mercy of the natives.

The Indians go on the warpath, determined to exterminate the whites. The members of the party are about to be annihilated by the savages when an earthquake shakes loose the top of a cliff, burying both whites and savages. Kioga saves the whites by drawing them into a niche at the side of the cliff. When the savages renew their attack, he rescues Beth, carrying her to the cave where he and Mokuyi live. The rest of the party is taken captive by the Indians.

Kioga enters the Indian village and, aided by Kias, a friendly Indian, rescues the prisoners. Kias, who is a childhood comrade of Kioga's, joins his group. The friends set up a campsite in the forest. Mokuyi and Tawnee, Kioga's dog, set out to hunt for food. But Mokuyi is captured by Solerno and his men who are combing the island for the treasure. As Solerno prepares to torture Mokuyi, Tawnee rushes back to Kioga and, by a series of barks, warns his master of Mokuyi's plight. Kioga follows Tawnee and, after a brief battle, succeeds in rescuing Mokuyi.

Fearful of the smoking volcano and spurred on by their witch doctor Yellow Weasel, the Indians abduct Beth and prepare to sacrifice her to the volcano god. When Kioga attempts to rescue her, he is captured also. Dr. Munro and the others realize that the only way of saving Beth and Kioga is to render the volcano inactive. Dr. Munro discovers that the volcano is active because a mountain stream, fed by recent tropical rains, has been flowing into the crater. He reasons that if he, Allan, and Kias can divert the stream by damming it, the volcano will become inactive. Professor Williams and Mokuyi are sent to the Indian's site to stall for time. They tell the Indians that the white mans' magic will overcome the volcano.

As Professor Williams performs handkerchief tricks and recites nonsense chants to preoccupy the Indians, the others manage to dam the stream with stones. The volcano suddenly becomes silent. Awestruck by the white mans' power, the Indians set Beth and Kioga free.

When the friends are reunited, Yellow Weasel is banished from the Indian village for incompetence. He then meets Solerno who tells him that the damming of the stream was what caused the volcano to become inactive. Solerno and his men begin to unblock the stream while Yellow Weasel returns to incite the Indians.

The volcano begins to erupt once again, and the Indians mount an attack. The friends flee through the forest. Desperately trying to escape the pursuing Indians they hurry through the dreaded Valley of Skulls, an ancient burial site greatly feared by the natives. Although his tribesmen will go no farther, Yellow Weasel proceeds with Solerno and his crew. Kioga and his friends enter a cave and wend their way through labyrinthine caverns until they emerge in a large, desolate valley. There they discover an airplane, which Dr. Munro and Allen recognize as having belonged to an aviator who had vanished years before during a transoceanic flight. They decide that the plane is in working condition and can carry them off the island to safety. But before they can depart, huge rocks, hurled from the volcano, block their takeoff path. They begin slowly to move the stones out of the way.

Allen, however, has begun to doubt that the plane can carry all of them safely. He believes that their chance of success would be greater if Kias didn't come along. Putting his thoughts into action, Allen rolls a boulder toward Kias. But thanks to a warning by Kioga, the Indian just barely escapes serious injury. When Allen again tries to kill Kias, Kioga catches him in the act. Mortified, Allen runs toward the caves, threatening revenge; and Kioga and Kias set off after him.

In the caves, Allen is killed by Yellow Weasel, who then attempts to kill Kioga with an arrow. But the noble Kias hurls himself in front of his friend and is hit by the arrow instead. After Kias dies, Kioga pursues Yellow Weasel and kills him. Kioga then returns to his friends, as the tremors caused by the volcano grow steadily more pronounced.

Noble Johnson watches as Herman Brix carries Jill Martin into their cave hideout.

Solerno and his men are also aware of the volcano's increased activity, and interrupt their search for Kioga in an attempt to get back to their ship. As the tremors intensify, the friends pile into the plane for an emergency takeoff. They manage to lift the craft into the air just as the island is ripped asunder by the erupting volcano.

While Dr. Munro mourns the disappearance of the island, Mokuyi reveals a small pouch he has carried with him: it contains a quantity of valuable gems, assuring future wealth for Kioga and himself.

Herman Brix faces death at the hands of Monte Blue and his tribesmen.

William Royle (*kneeling*) shows his cohorts some of the gold to be found on the island.

Jill Martin is rescued by Herman Brix from Monte Blue's murderous attack.

The Lone Ranger

15 Episodes
Republic, 1938

Directed by
William Witney
and John English

CAST

The Lone Ranger	A Man of Mystery
Silver	Silver King
Tonto	Chief Thundercloud
Allen King	Lee Powell
Bert Rogers	Herman Brix
Joan Blanchard	Lynn Roberts
Jeffries	Stanley Andrews
Father McKim	William Farnum
Blanchard	George Cleveland
Bob Stuart	Hal Taliaferro
Dick Forrest	Lane Chandler
Jim Clark	George Letz
Kester	John Merton
Sammy	Sammy McKim
Felton	Tom London
Taggart	Raphael Bennett
Snead	Maston Williams
Lincoln	Frank McGlynn, Sr.

During the lawless period of Reconstruction following the Civil War, five lawmen—Allen King, Bert Rogers, Dick Forrest, Bob Stuart, and Jim Clark—band together to combat the ruthless outlaw gang led by Jeffries. Their crusade is aided by two men who always appear in time to rescue them from danger—a mysterious masked rider known only as "The Lone Ranger" and his Indian friend Tonto.

As the pursuit of Jeffries' gang gets hotter, it becomes apparent that one of the lawmen is the Lone Ranger. But which one? As time passes, it becomes more obvious: one by one the lawmen are killed off, until only Allen King is left. He reveals his identity as the Lone Ranger and brings Jeffries to his doom.

A masked Lee Powell and Chief Thundercloud enter a cavern in pursuit of outlaw Jeffries.

Red Barry

13 Episodes
Universal, 1938

Directed by
Ford Beebe
and Alan James

CAST

Red Barry	Larry "Buster" Crabbe
Mississippi	Frances Robinson
Natacha	Edna Sedgewick
Wing Fu	Cyril Delevanti
Quong Lee	Frank Lackteen
Inspector Scott	Wade Boteler
Vane	Hugh Huntley
Cholly	Philip Ahn
Mannix	William Ruhl
Commissioner	William Gould
Weaver	Wheeler Oakman
Petrov	Stanley Price
Igor	Earle Douglas
Captain Moy	Charles Stevens

When two million dollars in bonds are stolen from a friendly Asian nation, Red Barry, famous detective, swings into action. He discovers that a prominent ballet dancer named Natacha is actually a dangerous foreign spy who is after the money, and that Quong Lee, a Eurasian underworld chieftain, heads another faction trying to lay its hands on the money. Moreover, Red comes across Vane, a mysterious criminologist who is also after the bonds.

Matters are further complicated by the fact that Mannix, the theatre manager, and Quong Lee are one and the same. But Red manages to hammer through this maze of villains and, with the help of Mississippi, a smart newspaperwoman, he recovers the bonds, nabs the espionage agents, and gets a promotion for himself.

Dick Purcell keeps his gun trained on "Buster" Crabbe, as Wheeler Oakman and Frank Lackteen state their intentions.

"Buster" Crabbe and Frances Robinson talk to a ship officer while spy Stanley Price (*right*) keeps close tabs on them.

134

The Secret of Treasure Island

15 Episodes
Columbia, 1938

Directed by
Elmer Clifton

CAST

Larry Kent	Don Terry
Toni Morrell	Gwen Gaze
Grindley	Grant Withers
Dr. X	Hobart Bosworth
Westmore	William Farnum
Collins	Walter Miller
Captain Cuttle	George Rosener
Jameson	Dave O'Brien
Dreer	Yakima Canutt
Captain Faxton	Warner Richmond
Thorndyke	Bill Boyle
Zanya	Sandra Karina
Jerry	Joe Caits
Hawkins	Colin Campbell
Professor	Patrick J. Kelly

Larry Kent, a hard-nosed reporter, is assigned by his editor to investigate the disappearance of a fellow reporter who was last seen headed for a mysterious island in the Carribean. A sea captain who owns half a map showing the location of a treasure buried on the island is killed just before he can tell the daughter of his old shipmate about the other half. The daughter, Toni Morrell, happens to be a good friend of Larry's and together they decide to solve the mysteries of the island.

Larry discovers that the island is ruled by Collins, who has mined all approaches to it in order to discourage intruders who might interfere with his treasure hunt. Collins is assisted by his henchman Grindley and by two unwilling accomplices—a nearly insane Doctor X and a professor who manufactures death bombs. Not only does Larry round up the gang, but he also discovers the treasure as well as Toni's father.

Don Terry battles a human skull as Gwen Gaze cowers behind him.

The Spider's Web

15 Episodes
Columbia, 1938

Directed by
Ray Taylor
and James W. Horne

CAST

Richard Wentworth	
Blinky McQuade	Warren Hull
The Spider	
Nita Van Sloan	Iris Meredith
Jackson	Richard Fiske
Ram Singh	Kenneth Duncan
Commissioner Kirk	Forbes Murray
Steve	Marc Lawrence
Chase	Charles Wilson
Jenkins	Donald Douglas
The Octopus	? ? ? ?

Posing as "The Spider," terror of the underworld, as well as Blinky McQuade, underworld habitué, celebrated criminologist Richard Wentworth wages a desperate battle to foil the plans of "The Octopus," whose outlaw gang is completely demoralizing the nation's transportation system.

Wentworth's activities are quickly discovered by the Octopus, who attempts to kidnap the sleuth. Escaping, Wentworth, disguised as Blinky, learns that a passenger bus loaded with explosives is to be blown up. With the aid of his faithful Sikh servant Ram Singh and disguised as the Spider, Wentworth empties the bus terminal and drives the bus from the depot. The police, however, blame him for the bombing.

The wave of terrorism continues and the Spider threads a dangerous course between the police and the Octopus. In his guise as Blinky McQuade, Wentworth finds a "deflection tube for specialized radios" in the safe of one of the men he suspects of being the Octopus. A check of tube suppliers reveals that equipment of this type was recently installed in a "technical school" located in an office building. And significantly, the office building is located in an area from which messages from the Octopus have been traced.

Arriving at the building, Wentworth finds a suspicious-looking sealed-off wing with no means of entry. Planting smoke bombs in the lobby, Wentworth waits until fire engines arrive; he then uses a fire ladder to gain access to the sixth floor. As the Spider, he leaps through an open window right into the secret headquarters of the Octopus. The startled villain is sitting with both hands on his desk, one grasping a special microphone which he has used to disguise his voice. Suddenly the Spider detects a movement beneath the robes of the Octopus, and a gun flashes into view. But before the Octopus can fire, the Spider draws his own pistol and kills the villain. The Octopus had used, as part of his deadly disguise, an artificial right hand, enabling him to get the drop on his unsuspecting enemies. The Octopus, dead, is unmasked as Chase, the banking magnate, who had hoped to dominate the nation by gaining control of its transportation, communications, and utilities. Wentworth is off at last on the long-delayed honeymoon with his fiancée, Nita.

The Spider is assaulted by one of the Octopus's henchmen.

1939

Buck Rogers

12 Episodes
Universal, 1939

Directed by
Ford Beebe
and Saul Goodkind

CAST

Buck Rogers	‒Larry "Buster" Crabbe
Wilma	Constance Moore
Buddy Wade	Jackie Moran
Captain Rankin	Jack Mulhall
Killer Kane	Anthony Warde
Dr. Huer	C. Montague Shaw
Aldar	Guy Usher
Marshall Kragg	William Gould
Prince Tallen	Philson Ahn
Captain Lasca	‒Henry Brandon
Patten	Wheeler Oakman
Lieutenant Lacy	Kenneth Duncan
Scott	Carleton Young
Roberts	Reed Howes

A giant dirigible, piloted by Buck and Buddy, crashes on an icy arctic mountain. A strange "Nirvano" gas in their gondola preserves the flyers in a state of suspended animation for five hundred years. Rescued and revived by a group of scientists, they discover that the world has been conquered by Killer Kane and a horde of supergangsters.

Taken to the scientist's Hidden City, they meet Wilma and Dr. Huer, and agree to help them resist Kane. Huer has invented spaceships, degravity belts, invisible ray machines, atom chambers, ray guns, and other strange and powerful weapons. Buck, Wilma, and Buddy go to Saturn in their spaceship to enlist the aid of the Saturnians.

Using their degravity belts, Buck, Buddy, and Wilma make a safe landing on Saturn after their ship has been bombed by Killer Kane's men who have followed them. After a pitched battle, Buck and his friends are captured by one of Kane's men, Captain Lasca. Both groups are captured in turn by the Saturnians who take them to the great council of the wise for judg-

ment and sentence. Here, Lasca convinces the rulers that Killer Kane is a just and kindly monarch. Only fast action permits Buck and his party to escape from prison and return to earth in one of Lasca's spaceships.

After resupplying themselves, Buck and Wilma return to the high tribunal of Saturn to plead their cause.

Meanwhile, Lasca discovers that the primitive Saturnian race known as "Zugg" Men, previously led by a "human robot" controlled by Lasca, have accepted an apparently new human robot, and are staging a rebellion. Lasca invades the Zugg stronghold, captures the robot, and by activating the filament-ray helmet worn by the robot, which forces it to do his bidding, once again regains control.

Buck surprises Lasca and his human robot as they are rousing the Zuggs to further warfare, and removes the robot's helmet to discover that he is a friend. The robot then orders the Zuggs to forget their rebellion and go home in peace.

Grateful because Buck has ended the war, the Saturnians agree to aid him in his battle with Killer Kane. Returning to Earth with this good news, Buck is attacked by the enemy. His ship collides with an enemy craft and goes out of control. Righting his rocket ship as it falls dizzily toward Earth, Buck makes a safe landing.

Buck and Buddy take their rocket ship to Saturn and find that Lasca is demanding the planet submit to rule by Kane. As Killer Kane's ships start to bomb the city, Buck urges them not to deal with the treacherous Lasca.

The Saturnians renew their promise to help in the war against Killer Kane, and Buck and Buddy start back to Earth. Deciding to attack from the inside, Buck lands the ship at Kane's palace airdrome. The Saturnians arrive and, in a magnificent air battle, Killer Kane's men are defeated.

As a reward, Buck is made marshal of all the nation's planes. Buddy, despite his age, is made brevet lieutenant. At last, Buck and the pretty Wilma have time to consider romance.

Larry "Buster" Crabbe and Jackie Moran spot an enemy rocket ship.

Philson Ahn looks to Buck and
Buddy for further help.

Larry "Buster" Crabbe, Jackie
Moran, and Constance Moore
reach for gas bombs to ward
off Killer Kane's men.

Buck tries to enlist the aid of
the filament-ray-helmeted human robot, as the Zugg men
look on.

Daredevils of the Red Circle

12 Episodes
(Republic,) 1939

Directed by
(William Witney
and John English)

CAST

Gene	Charles Quigley
Tiny	Herman Brix
Burt	David Sharpe
Blanche	Carole Landis
Granville (Prisoner)	Miles Mander
Granville (39013)	Charles Middleton
Dr. Malcolm	C. Montague Shaw
Dixon	Ben Taggart
Chief Landon	William Pagan
Klein	Raymond Bailey
Snowflake	Snowflake
Sheffield	George Chesebro
Jeff	Ray Miller
Sammy	Robert Winkler
Tuffie	Tuffie

After fifteen years in a federal penitentiary, convict #39013 escapes and begins a campaign of vengeance against Granville, his former partner, who is responsible for his conviction. 39013 makes Granville a prisoner, while, by means of a clever disguise, he himself takes Granville's place so successfully that no one knows of the change. He imprisons Granville in a dungeon, visits him day after day to gloat over his misery, and describes plans to destroy his loved ones and to wreck all his extensive business ventures.

The Daredevils of the Red Circle, three college athletes who are working in a sideshow on Granville's amusement pier, are enraged when 39013's plot to burn the pier results in the death of a small brother of one of them. Gene, Burt, and Tiny resolve to bring the perpetrator of this crime to justice, and make it their business to be on hand to stymie every plot 39013 attempts. In this they have an ally in Blanche, the granddaughter of the real Granville.

39013 is bent on causing Granville to lose his franchise to supply utilities to a small village. To do this, he has his cohorts attempt to wreck Granville's gas and oil holdings by devious means. But the Daredevils of the Red Circle are always on hand to foil their schemes, at great personal danger to themselves. Again and again they are trapped in burning buildings, threatened with asphyxiation, and harassed by time bombs, but they always manage to escape,

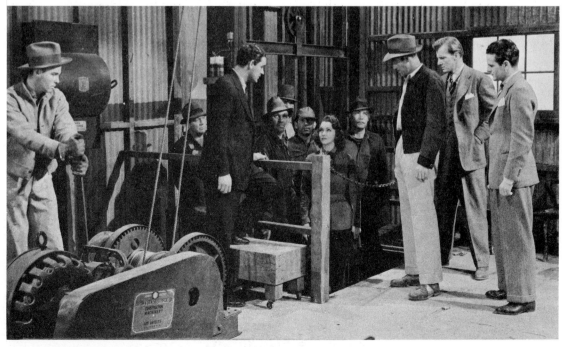

Charles Quigley bids a word of warning to Carole Landis as Herman Brix and Dave Sharpe (*far right*) show their concern.

As Charles Quigley and Carole Landis attempt to help Miles Mander, Herman Brix and Dave Sharpe discover they're *all* trapped.

usually by employing tricks used in their circus act to make aerial escapes.

The District Attorney is making an effort to bring 39013 and his gang to justice, but they mark him for death. When he goes to take his medical gamma ray treatment, the villains contrive to change the current so that he will wither away under the deadly delta rays. The Daredevils of the Red Circle, learning of this plot, hasten to rescue him at the risk of being themselves destroyed by the powerful rays.

At last the authorities learn that the real Granville is imprisoned in the basement and lay their plans to rescue him. 39013 threatens to destroy Granville with a bomb if any action is made to rescue him. Meanwhile, he arranges to escape in a high-powered car. To avoid pursuit, he has a time bomb placed in the only other car equipped to overtake it, Blanche's roadster. The bomb is to go off when the speedometer hits 70. But 39013 wrecks his own car and is knocked unconscious. One of his henchemen carries him into Blanche's parked roadster and drives off at high speed, ignorant of the bomb it carries. When the car reaches 70 miles per hour, 39013 and his men are blown to bits!

Dick Tracy's G-men

15 Episodes
Republic, 1939

Directed by
William Witney
and John English

CAST

Dick Tracy	Ralph Byrd
Zarnoff	Irving Pichel
Steve	Ted Pearson
Owen	Phylis Isley
Robal	Walter Miller
Sandoval	George Douglas
Anderson	Kenneth Harlan
Scott	Robert Carson
Foster	Julian Madison
First G-man	Ted Mapes
Second G-man	William Stahl
Third G-man	Robert Wayne
Tommy	Joe McGuinn
Ed	Kenneth Terrell
Warden Stover	Harry Humphrey
Baron	Harrison Greene

Zarnoff, the head of an international spy ring, is finally captured by Dick Tracy of the Federal Bureau of Investigation and brought to trial. He is convicted of various crimes—including murder—and is executed in a gas chamber.

After being pronounced dead, he is removed in a morgue wagon which is subsequently hijacked. Later, he is revived by powerful drugs.

Tracy and his pal Steve Lockwood get on Zarnoff's trail immediately and frustrate his attempts at sabotaging America's defenses. Tracy's G-men track Zarnoff's gang to a hidden valley in the mountains.

Fearing eventual capture, Zarnoff radios for his private plane to pick him up. Tracy knocks out the pilot, throws Zarnoff into the plane, and flies off across the desert. But, due to engine trouble, Tracy must make a forced landing. He and his prisoner begin walking across the desert. When they are nearly dying of thirst, they come to a spring. Zarnoff knocks Tracy out, ties him to a tree, and drinks his fill of the water, giving Tracy none. Tracy is rescued, after having been deserted by Zarnoff, and Zarnoff himself dies on the desert, having unwittingly poisoned himself at the arsenic spring.

Walter Miller points a pistol at Ralph Byrd as Irving Pichel (*right foreground*) watches approvingly.

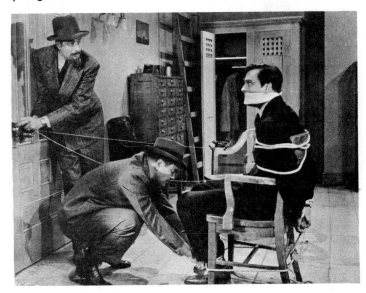

Irving Pichel explains his cunning deathtrap to a helpless Ralph Byrd.

Flying G-men

15 Episodes
Columbia, 1939

Directed by
Ray Taylor
and James W. Horne

CAST

Hal Andrews	Robert Paige
The Black Falcon	
Bart Davis	Robert Fiske
John Cummings	James Craig
Babs McKay	Lorna Gray
Billy McKay	Sammy McKim
Hamilton	Don Beddoe
Brewster	Forbes Murray
Korman	Dick Curtis
Secretary	Ann Doran
Everett	Nestor Paiva
Red	George Chesebro
Radio Man	Bud Geary
Williams	Tom Steele
Crawford	George Turner
Stokes	Hugh Prosser

Planes crash, secret plans disappear, and a reign of terror is launched as enemy spies strike at the nation's defenses. Four flying G-men—Davis, Cummings, Andrews, and Bronson—are assigned to end the crisis. Sensing the menace confronting them, the four agree that

The Black Falcon and a flying G-man get the drop on Dick Curtis and two other spies.

one of them shall assume a mysterious identity so he can strike with the swiftness of a falcon. The result is the Black Falcon.

Bronson is the spies' first victim. He is killed in an attempt to thwart their plans to capture a new-type McKay plane. McKay's sister, Babs, joins the G-men in their fight. Bob's nephew, Bill, also offers his services and that of his huge organization, the Junior Air Defenders.

In their efforts to learn the identity of the mysterious spy chief, the three remaining flying G-men discover a widespread spy net flung over every important aircraft factory, airport, steel mill, and research laboratory. In battling these murderous agents, Falcon learns enough to suspect Brewster, the owner of Brewster Airport, of being the chief spy. Through a ruse, Brewster goes aloft with Babs at his side and heads for his secret hideout. The G-man follow and close in on the spy's hideout, capture Brewster, and rescue Babs.

The Lone Ranger Rides Again

15 Episodes
Republic, 1939

Directed by
William Witney
and John English

CAST

The Lone Ranger	} Robert Livingston
Bill Andrews	}
Tonto	Chief Thunder Cloud
Silver	Silver Chief
Juan Vasquez	Duncan Renaldo
Sue	Jinx Falken
Bart Dolan	Ralph Dunn
Craig Dolan	J. Farrell MacDonald
Jed Scott	William Gould
Evans	Rex Lease
Merritt	Ted Mapes
Pa Daniels	Henry Otho
Hardin	John Beach
Thorne	Glenn Strange
Murdock	Stanley Blystone
Hank	Edwin Parker
Colt	Al Taylor
Logan	Carlton Young
Doc Grover	Ernie Adams

Craig Dolan, a powerful cattleman, is suspected of trying to rid the San Ramon valley of innocent settlers. Jed Scott, the leader of a wagon train, engages Bill Andrews to aid him in defeating the cattle baron and his henchman. Andrews, disguised as a newcomer, is actually the Lone Ranger, a fearless fighter for law and justice. He quickly discovers that Bart Dolan, Craig's nephew, is responsible for the campaign of violence.

With the help of his faithful Indian companion Tonto and his faithful Mexican companion Juan Vasquez, the Ranger is able to foil the schemes of Dolan's marauders. Finally, Dolan declares all-out war against the settlers. He orders a wagonload of explosives rolled down onto the fort where the settlers have taken refuge.

The Ranger, arriving in the nick of time, mounts the wagon and brings it to a halt before it crashes. He orders the settlers to move far away from the explosives. Bart Dolan goes to the wagon to investigate why the explosives failed to ignite. While he is investigating, the explosives go off and Dolan is killed.

Mandrake the Magician

12 Episodes
Columbia, 1939

Directed by
Sam Nelson
and Norman Deming

CAST

Mandrake	Warren Hull
Betty	Doris Weston
Lothar	Al Kikume
Tommy	Rex Downing
Andre	Edward Earle
Houston	Forbes Murray
Webster	Kenneth MacDonald
Raymond	Don Beddoe
Dorgan	Dick Curtis
Dirk	John Tyrrell
Brown	Ernie Adams
Baker	George Chesebro
Hall	George Turner

Professor Houston develops a radium-energy machine which is very much sought after by "The Wasp," the crafty head of an underworld gang. The Wasp will stop at nothing to steal the invention. In his effort to obtain the device he blows up a radio station, a power plant, and a dam. Fortunately, his explosions cause only minimum damage because of the efforts of the quick-witted Mandrake, a world-famous magician, who is on the trail of the Wasp.

Mandrake finally captures the master villain and his gang, and discovers that the Wasp is actually a scientist who has posed as a close friend of Professor Houston's. The magician is then happily reunited with Professor Houston's lovely daughter Betty and has the pleasure of seeing Professor Houston honored by the scientific world for his invention.

A rather dapper Warren Hull.

The Oregon Trail

15 Episodes
Universal, 1939

Directed by
Ford Beebe

CAST

Jeff Scott	John Mack Brown
Margaret Mason	Louis Stanley
Jimmie Clark	Bill Cody, Jr.
"Deadwood" Hawkins	Fuzzy Knight
John Mason	Ed LeSaint
Sam Morgan	James Blaine
"Bull" Bragg	Jack C. Smith
Colonel Custer	Roy Barcroft
Slade	Colin Kenny

Jeff Scott, frontier scout, is hired by Washington officials to stop outlaw and Indian raids on pioneer wagon trains crossing the plains. Strangely, only those trains bound for rich fur regions of Oregon are molested.

Keeping his identity secret, Jeff and his pal Deadwood overtake a wagon train in time to save the occupants from a massacre by the Indians. They rescue Margaret and Jimmy Clark, a youngster whose father is killed. Jeff suspects that "Bull" Bragg, wagon master, is a spy and responsible for the misfortunes. When several wagons are deliberately wrecked, Jeff has Bragg thrown out of his job.

Bragg incites the Indians to attack the train again. Colonel Custer arrives in time to rout the Indians. Jimmy overhears Slade and Bragg plotting to wipe out the wagon train by setting fire to the dry prairie grass. He races to Jeff with this news and, through fast action, Jeff leads the wagons to safety; Bragg is thrown into jail.

Sam Morgan, a rich fur syndicate manager and a scoundrel, is secretly causing the trouble. Afraid that Bragg, his chief henchman, may talk, he helps him escape from jail. Jeff follows Bragg and narrowly escapes being killed when the stagecoach in which he and Bragg are fighting hurtles over a cliff. Jeff lands in a river and is carried to shore by the current.

After many dangers, the wagon train finally reaches its destination. When the settlers prepare to stake out claims, Morgan flashes a faked land grant and demands they pay him a high price for the ground. Jeff then exposes Morgan as a crook and the settlers happily prepare to build their homes.

The enemy sneaks up from behind, as Johnny Mack Brown attends to attacking Indians.

Overland with Kit Carson

15 Episodes
Columbia, 1939

Directed by
Sam Nelson
and Norman Deming

CAST

Kit Carson	Bill Elliott
Carmelita	Iris Meredith
David Brent	Richard Fiske
Andy	Bobby Clack
Arthur Mitchell	Trevor Bardette
John Baxter	LeRoy Mason
Pierre	Olin Francis
Tennessee	James Craig
Dr. Parker	Francis Sayles
Winchester	Kenneth MacDonald
Drake	Dick Curtis
Natchez	Richard Botiller
Pegleg	? ? ? ?

A mysterious outlaw known as Pegleg dreams of an empire in the vast, rich wilderness west of the Mississippi. Lieutenant Brent is sent from Washington to persuade Kit Carson to end the reign of terror caused by Pegleg's cohorts, the Black Raiders.

Carson agrees. In the course of his assignment he meets and is attracted to Carmelita Gonzales, the daughter of a Spanish grandee who is heading west via wagon train. Escaping an avalanche started by Pegleg's men, Kit and the wagon train capture a Black Raider. Just as the prisoner is about to talk, he is slain by the mysterious Pegleg. As they seek the murderer, Kit narrowly escapes an Indian ambush and hurries to warn the unsuspecting trappers at the Trapper's Rendezvous that Pegleg intends to massacre them.

The Black Raiders attack the post and Pegleg attempts to lure Carmelita to "safety." Kit pursues him as his men capture the Black Raiders. Carson finally catches up with Pegleg when the villain's horse is recognized as belonging to Mitchell, a post trader. In his struggle to escape, the outlaw slips and is trampled to death by his horse.

Bill Elliott is temporarily subdued by two of Pegleg's thugs.

TO BE CONTINUED

The Phantom Creeps

12 Episodes
Universal, 1939

Directed by
Ford Beebe
and Saul A. Goodkind

CAST

Dr. Alex Zorka	—Bela Lugosi
Captain Bob West	Robert Kent
Jim Daly	—Regis Toomey
Jean Drew	Dorothy Arnold
Chief Jarvis	Edward Van Sloan
"Mac"	Eddie Acuff
Rankin	Anthony Averill
Monk	Jack C. Smith
Parker	Roy Barcroft
Black	Forrest Taylor

Dr. Alex Zorka, eccentric scientist, carries on mysterious experiments in his secret laboratory with the aid of Monk, an ex-convict. Zorka has invented many strange and powerful weapons of warfare, including a terrifying mechanical eight-foot-tall robot and a divisualizer belt which allows him to operate without being seen. He also has a deadly meteorite fragment from which he extracts a strange element that can induce suspended animation in an entire army.

Foreign spies trying to buy or steal some of the marvelous element operate under the guise of a foreign language school. Because Zorka will not turn over his inventions to the U.S. government, his former partner Dr. Mallory reports the matter to Captain Bob West of the Military Intelligence Department. Zorka moves his laboratory and, when his wife is accidentally killed, he swears eternal vengeance against society.

Drunk with the power of his inventions, he decides to use them to make himself world dictator. With the meteorite element, the devisualizer belt, and the giant robot, he is a menace to world peace and disrupts national progress as spies and government agents trail him. Jean Drew, pretty girl reporter, aids police while covering the story for her newspaper.

Directed by Bob West, army planes finally bomb Zorka's laboratory, but he attempts to escape in a plane. Trapped, he dumps the meteorite element overboard, hoping to destroy the world with himself. An earthquake results, but civilization is saved. West is rewarded by the government and Jean writes the greatest news story of the age.

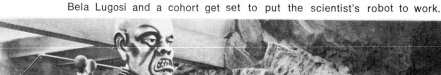

Bela Lugosi and a cohort get set to put the scientist's robot to work.

Scouts to the Rescue

12 Episodes
Universal, 1939

Directed by
Ray Taylor
and Alan James

CAST

Bruce Scott	Jackie Cooper
Mary Scanlon	Vondell Darr
Pat Scanlon	Edwin Stanley
Hal Marvin	William Ruhl
Skeets Scanlon	Bill Cody, Jr.
Rip Dawson	David Durand
Pug O'Toole	Ralph Dunn
Doc	Jason Robards
Ken	Frank Coghlan, Jr.
Turk Mortenson	Ivan Miller
Hurst	Victor Adams
Hermie	Sidney Miller
Leeka	Richard Botiller

Eagle Scout Bruce Scott leads a troop to the deserted village of Ghost Town, where they find a buried treasure. G-man Hal Marvin, whom the scouts rescue from a plane crash, tells them that the "treasure" is counterfeit money. He has been on the trail of a counterfeiting gang headed by Turk Mortenson. Implicated with the gang is Pat Scanlon, father of Scout Skeets Scanlon.

Mortenson imprisons the father and son but Skeets escapes, only to be caught by a marauding band of Indians. Scanlon and Skeets both manage to get free and help fight off the Indian attack. In Ghost Town, Marvin finds evidence that clears Scanlon from suspicion and proves Mortenson to be the gang leader.

Scout Frank Coghlan, Jr. (*center*), stands prepared for danger.

Zorro's Fighting Legion

12 Episodes
Republic, 1939

Directed by
William Witney
and John English

CAST

Zorro	Reed Hadley
Volita	Sheila Darcy
Ramon	William Corson
Felipe	Leander de Cordova
Gonzalez	Edmund Cobb
Pablo	C. Montague Shaw
Manuel	John Merton
Juan	Budd Buster
Juarez	Carleton Young
Francisco	Guy D'Ennery
Kala	Paul Marian
Tarmac	Joe Molina
Moreno	Jim Pierce
Donna Maria	Helen Mitchel
Tomas	Curley Dresden
Valdez	Charles King
Rico	Al Taylor
Pepito	Charles B. Murphy

In 1824, Benito Juarez, first president of the newly formed Republic of Mexico, attempts to put the republic's treasury in order by forwarding gold shipments from the rich San Mendolita Mines.

Three of the mine officials conspire to defeat his purpose. One, donning a suit of gold armor, makes the native Yaqui Indian tribes believe that he is one of their gods, and enlists their aid in blocking gold shipments. Don Francisco organizes a fighting legion to aid Juarez. Don Diego, alias Zorro, arrives on a visit the day Francisco is killed. Aided by his friend Ramon and his servant Juan, he takes over the legion and succeeds in getting the first gold shipment through to Juarez. But Juarez warns him that he can give no legal standing to the legion.

Back in San Mendolita, Don-del-oro, the armored god, locates the mission headquarters of Zorro and plants dynamite in the cellar. Zorro's men are trapped, but he returns in time to free them and defeat the outlaws. Juan trails the outlaws to their hideout in an abandoned mine. Zorro, as Don Diego, receives a message from Juan and goes to inspect the mine. The renegades trap him in the mine's depths. As he attempts to climb out, they loosen the brake of a huge ore carrier, and it hurtles down upon Zorro. He escapes death by clinging close to the walls.

Zorro's men capture one of the outlaws. Zorro attempts to question the captive when a mysterious golden arrow takes the captive's life. Don-del-oro plans to sidetrack a munitions train on its way to Juarez, and to arm his Yaquis. Zorro learns of this plan and rides off to warn the driver of the train but is trapped by the outlaws on the brink of a deep gorge. He dismounts and attempts to cross a fragile suspension bridge. The outlaws shoot the ropes loose, and Zorro barely manages to escape death. He warns the munitions train by lighting a huge "Z" on the mountainside, but the train guards are slain when they offer resistance to the bandits.

Zorro trails the captured train to a cave concealed beneath a waterfall and sends a note to the Council promising to recapture the train. He is discovered, and his enemies ignite a wagon loaded with powder which they roll down the hill toward Zorro's hiding place. Zorro deflects the wagon's course, preventing the disaster, and his legions recapture the train.

Ramon and his sister are captured by the outlaws. Zorro goes to their rescue and captures Manuel, a local military official whom he suspects of masquerading as Don-del-oro. Manuel escapes, however, and Zorro recaptures him after many perilous adventures. He disguises Ramon as Manuel and places him in jail. The outlaws burn the jail and Ramon is captured. Zorro rescues him, and the two trail Manuel who had escaped to the cave. Outlaws kill Manuel as he begins to talk.

Don Diego tells the Council that he knows the identity of Don-del-oro and is shot at by Tarmac, a Yaqui outlaw. Kala, hereditary leader of the Yaqui, attempts to convince Zorro of his story of the false Don-del-oro. The two go in search of the empty suit of armor, only to find that the false god has returned and donned it. The Indian tribe turns on the two men but they manage to escape. Zorro trails Don-del-oro to the Indian village where the outlaw is arming the Yaquis for an immediate attack on the San Mendolita Mines. Zorro rushes in and succeeds in unmasking the supposed god, who turns out to be Pablo, chief magistrate of the mines. The Indians kill Pablo, and Zorro arranges a treaty between the Indians and the white men.

Reed Hadley and members of the council appear alarmed at an apparent gap in their security system.

Reed Hadley and Sheila Darcy during a lull in the action.

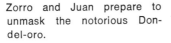

Zorro and Juan prepare to unmask the notorious Don-del-oro.

1940

Don "Red" Barry delivers a smashing right and floors an outlaw.

Adventures of Red Ryder

12 Episodes
Republic, 1940

Directed by
William Witney
and John English

CAST

Red Ryder	Don "Red" Barry
Ace Hanlon	Noah Beery
Little Beaver	Tommy Cook
One-Eye	Bob Kortman
Colonel Tom Ryder	William Farnum
Duchess	Maude Pierce Allen
Beth	Vivian Coe
Cherokee	Hal Taliaferro
Calvin Drake	Harry Worth
Sheriff Dade	Carleton Young
Shark	Ray Teal
Deputy Lawson	Gene Alsace
Harrison	Gayne Whitman
Treadway	Hooper Atchley
Hale	John Dilson
Sheriff Andrews	Lloyd Ingraham
Rancher Brown	Charles Hutchison
Barnett	Gardner James
Boswell	Wheaton Chambers
Clark	Lynton Brent

When Calvin Drake, banker of Mesquite, learns that the Santa Fe will build its railroad through this territory, he makes plans to gain control of all the land. In the ensuing war of intimidation, Ira Withers, a rancher, is killed, and Red Ryder, together with his dad, Colonel

Red gets a little unfriendly advice from Noah Beery.

Ryder, forms an organization to drive the gun-fighters out of the territory. Before Colonel Ryder can carry out his plans to arrest an outlaw for Withers's murder, he is slain by Drake's henchmen. Another victim is Sheriff Andrews, whose daughter Beth is a horrified witness. Red, vowing vengeance, captures Shark, one of the Drake outlaws, and plans to turn him over to the new sheriff, Dade.

Unaware of the fact that Drake and Sheriff Dade are crooks, and that Shark is one of their henchmen, Red sends word that he is bringing the prisoner to town. Dade instructs his henchman Hanlon to intercept them. Red and his young Indian companion Little Beaver manage to escape with their prisoner and turn him over to Dade who is amazed at the hitch in his plans.

Hanlon orders Pecos Bates to make sure that Shark does not talk. Just as he is about to divulge his relationship with Hanlon, Shark is shot down by Bates, who fires through the jail window. Red is hot on Bates's trail. The two grapple right in the path of the oncoming posse. Bates is trampled to death but Red luckily escapes serious injury.

Back in Mesquite, Drake convinces the ranchers that the raids are all over, and Red and the others arrange for a large sum to be brought in via stagecoach, to help the ranchers repair the damage to their property. Drake and Hanlon, to prevent the money from reaching Mesquite, order a couple of outlaws to rob the coach, with Sheriff Dade putting up a half-hearted defense. Red and Cherokee ride to the

Red takes on Drake's gang in a burning room.

rescue, tie up the would-be bandits, and order the coach to continue to Mesquite. Here the heavies attack again and escape with the money, while Red is busy fighting two of their number.

To raise money, Red enters the Wells-Fargo stagecoach race. To keep him from competing in the race, Hanlon's men capture Red and hold him prisoner. Little Beaver helps him make his escape by dropping cartridges down the chimney so that their explosion surprises Red's guards and permits him to catch them off guard. Red escapes and dashes to the race, which has already started, and beats the outlaw's coach across the finish line, netting the first prize of $5,000. When Grimes, one of Drake's men, attempts to grab the money there is a battle in which a bystander is shot. Sheriff Dade seizes this opportunity to accuse Red and jail him for the murder. To prevent the real killer from getting away, Red escapes with Dade and his posse in hot pursuit. Red eludes

the posse and, with the aid of Little Beaver, arranges a trap that leads them to Grimes's hiding place. Sheriff Dade, meanwhile, sends a group of men out with orders to shoot Red on sight.

Grimes, in a last minute effort to escape, is killed by the bullets intended for Red. But Red has secured from Grimes, before his death, a confession written in charcoal on a tabletop, and when Dade seeks to press his charges against Red for murder, Red reveals the fact that Grimes's written confession is still in the shack where he died. Dade is trapped by Red and Cherokee in the act of destroying this evidence and thus reveals himself for the first time as being in league with the outlaws.

This leads Red directly to Drake's trail and he faces him in a last desperate battle. As fate would have it, during this encounter Drake falls upon his own sword blade, killing himself instantly.

Deadwood Dick

15 Episodes
Columbia, 1940

Directed by
James W. Horne

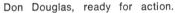

CAST

Deadwood Dick — Don Douglas
Ann Butler — Lorna Gray
Dave — Harry Harvey
Calamity Jane — Marin Sais
Wild Bill Hickok — Lane Chandler
Buzz — Jack Ingram
Tex — Charles King
Drew — Ed Cassidy
Ashton — Robert Fiske
Bentley — Lee Shumway

A renegade band led by a mysterious masked character known as "The Skull" is terrorizing the countryside around the town of Deadwood, South Dakota. Dick Stanley, editor of the *Dakota Pioneer Press* and a leading member of the Statehood for Dakota Committee, is, unknown to his fellow townsmen, the equally mysterious Deadwood Dick—the Robin Hood of the plains—who is fighting the Skull and his gang.

One by one, Deadwood Dick smashes the schemes devised by the Skull to gain control of the Dakota Territory's communications, banks, and other vital interests. But it is not until Deadwood Dick has triumphantly fought his way into and out of burning buildings, dynamited mines, and stampeding cattle that he finally unmasks the Skull—who turns out to be Drew, the town banker! After he has smashed the gang, Deadwood Dick reveals his own identity.

Don Douglas, ready for action.

Drums of Fu Manchu

15 Episodes
Republic, 1940

Directed by
William Witney
and John English

CAST

Fu Manchu	—Henry Brandon
Sir Dennis Nayland Smith	William Royle
Allen Parker	Robert Kellard
Fah Lo Suee	Gloria Franklin
Dr. Petrie	Olaf Hytten
Professor Randolph	Tom Chatterton
Mary Randolph	Luana Walters
Sirdar Prahin	Lal Chend Mehra
Professor Parker	George Cleveland
Howard	John Dilson
Loki	John Merton
Anderson	Dwight Frye
Dr. Humphrey	Wheaton Chambers

Fu Manchu, a sinister Oriental, heads a secret organization known as Si Fan, whose purpose is to foment war in Central Asia and secure world domination during the subsequent upheaval. In order to stage his revolution successfully, he must secure the long-lost scepter of Genghis Khan, which the Himalayan hillmen will accept as identification of his authenticity as a new world conqueror. To secure the scepter, he must find its traditional hiding place, the long-lost tomb of the Great Khan.

Fu Manchu's efforts to uncover the secret of the Great Khan's tomb lead him to America where he is involved in the abduction and murder of various individuals who stand in his way. Among his henchmen are the "Dacoits"—eerie, bald men who bear a forehead scar indicating where Dr. Fu Manchu has operated on them and removed a portion of the frontal lobe of their brains so that they are bereft of willpower and become slaves to his diabolical will.

Active in the campaign to suppress Fu Manchu is Sir Dennis Nayland Smith, a special representative of the British Foreign Office, who allies himself with James Parker, an eminent archaeologist, who possesses clues to the Lost Tomb for which Fu Manchu is searching. When Parker is mysteriously killed, his young son Allen, joins forces with Smith in order to avenge his father's death.

Fu Manchu's chief accomplice is his daughter Fah Lo Suee, who exercises a mysterious power over the hapless persons who come under her spell. She subjects them to the Incense of Obedience so that they are compelled to do her bidding.

The deceased Dr. Parker had written a manuscript known as the Dalai Plaque. This manuscript reveals the hiding place of the Great Khan's scepter, and is the object of a desperate search on the part of Fu Manchu and his henchmen, as well as Sir Dennis Nayland Smith, Allen, and Mary Randolph, daughter of the curator of the museum which had sheltered the Dalai Plaque. The hiding place of Genghis Khan's scepter is revealed at last when Dr. Fu Manchu and his men obtain the plaque and translate the message.

The quest for the scepter leads all parties to the Himalayan country, where, after numerous hairbreadth escapes from Fu Manchu's wrath, Allen finally recovers the scepter, proves to the Himalayan hillmen that Fu Manchu's power is false, and destroys for all time the threat of his aggression.

Startled guests cower behind Robert Kellard as Henry Brandon makes a mysterious appearance.

Henry Brandon supervises John Merton (*center*) and another Dacoit, as they plant some dynamite.

Robert Kellard and William Royle are attacked from behind by a Dacoit.

William Royle (*right*) offers the Dalai Plaque, held by Luana Walters, to Robert Kellard.

At the tomb of the Great Khan, William Royle prepares to piece some clues together.

A robed and capped Henry Brandon conspires with two cohorts.

Robert Kellard comes across another artifact leading to the scepter of Genghis Khan.

Flash Gordon Conquers the Universe

12 Episodes	Directed by
Universal, 1940	Ford Beebe
	and Ray Taylor

CAST

Flash Gordon	— Larry "Buster" Crabbe
Dale Arden	Carol Hughes
Ming	—Charles Middleton
Dr. Zarkov	Frank Shannon
Sonja	Nancy Gwynne
Prince Barin	Roland Drew
Princess Aura	Shirley Deane
Thong	Victor Zimmerman
Torch	Don Rowan
Karm	Michael Mark
Korro	Sigmund Nilssen
Roka	Lee Powell
Turan	Edgar Edwards
Lupi	Ben Taggart
Keedish	Harry C. Bradley

When the earth is visited by a deadly epidemic known as the Plague of the Purple Death, Flash Gordon, Dale Arden, and Dr. Zarkov set out into the stratosphere in Zarkov's rocket ship and discover that Ming the Merciless, ruler of the Planet Mongo, is spreading death dust in Earth's atmosphere as part of his vicious plan to conquer the universe.

Flash and his friends—the friendly ruler of Arboria, Prince Barin, and his wife Aura, Ming's daughter—invade Ming's palace and partially wreck the power rooms and machinery. Flash then leads an expedition to the frozen land of Frigia where he mines for Polante, the only known antidote for the Purple Death.

But Ming's spaceship, operated by Sonja, Torch, and Thong, attack Dale and Dr. Zarkov and take them prisoner. Flash, Barin, and a few followers avoid an electrical death ray to rescue Dale and the scientist. They then attack Ming. Flash resets the controls of a solarite ship aimed at the earth and bales out just before the spacecraft crashes into Ming's stronghold and kills the evil emperor. The terrific explosion marks the end of Ming's dream of absolute omnipotence, and Flash is acclaimed the conqueror of the universe.

Charles Middleton, every inch the ruler of the universe.

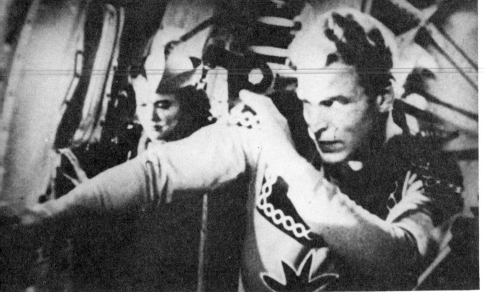

Carol Hughes and Buster Crabbe react to an exploding missile just outside their spaceship.

A rocket ship circles for a landing.

The Grand Chamber of Ming, the Merciless.

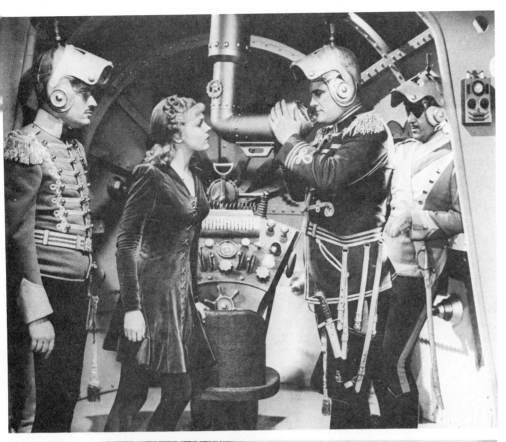

Nancy Gwynne listens carefully as Don Rowan puts in a call to Ming.

Charles Middleton, Don Rowan, and Nancy Gwynne have the regal Shirley Deane in a tight spot.

The Green Archer

15 Episodes
Columbia, 1940

Directed by
James W. Horne

CAST

Spike Holland	Victor Jory
Valerie Howett	Iris Meredith
Abel Bellamy	James Craven
Savini	Robert Fiske
Elaine Bellamy	Dorothy Fay
Howett	Forrest Taylor
Brad	Jack Ingram
Inspector Ross	Joseph W. Girard
Captain Thompson	Fred Kelsey
Dinky	Kit Guard

Michael Bellamy inherits Garr Castle but his brother Abel has him imprisoned unjustly and moves into the castle himself. When Michael's wife, Elaine, fails to return after visiting Abel, her sister Valerie Howett, accompanied by Mr. Howett and Spike Holland, a detective, rent an adjoining estate, determined to investigate the case.

After learning that Valerie, her husband, and Spike are in the vicinity, Abel is afraid that they will discover his association with a gang of jewel thieves and desperately tries to have them all killed. Each attempt, however, is thwarted by the Green Archer, who mysteriously appears with his deadly bow and arrows whenever needed. It isn't until Abel succeeds in capturing Mr. Howett, Holland, and Valerie that the Green Archer reveals his identity. After a fierce struggle he defeats Abel, releases the prisoners, and unmasks himself as Michael Bellamy.

Iris Meredith and Victor Jory, under the protective shadow of the Green Archer.

The Green Hornet

13 Episodes
Universal, 1940

Directed by
Ford Beebe
and Ray Taylor

CAST

Brett Reid	Gordon Jones
Michael Oxford	Wade Boteler
Kato	Keye Luke
Lenore Case	Anne Nagel
Jasper Jenks	Philip Trent
Dean	Walter McGrail
Hawks	John Kelly
Carney	Gene Rizzi
Mortinson	Douglas Evans
Andy	Ralph Dunn
Joe Ogden	Arthur Loft
Felix Grant	Edward Earle
Monroe	Cy Kendall

Crusading publisher Britt Reid finds out that a crooked insurance ring has profited from accidents at a tunnel-construction site. He also uncovers a flying school scandal and an auto-stealing ring. In addition, he comes across a contraband munitions ring and a transportation racket.

In the guise of the Green Hornet and accompanied by his servant Kato, Reid pursues each of these criminal gangs. He soon discovers that all of the gangs are masterminded by one person. The Green Hornet eventually tracks the archcrook down, despite the interference from the police and concerned citizens who believe he himself is a criminal. Although the ringleader is brought to justice, the Hornet is still looked upon with suspicion by the police, and realizes that he will have to continue working outside of the law.

Gordon Jones watches as Keye Luke does some engine work on the Black Beauty.

The Hornet gets the drop on an outlaw with his gas bomb gun, while Keye Luke applies a little physical pressure.

Wade Boteler tells Anne Nagel, Gordon Jones, and Phillip Trent that he'll capture the Green Hornet and win the reward offered.

165

The Green Hornet Strikes Again

13 Episodes	Directed by
Universal, 1940	Ford Beebe
	and John Rawlins

CAST

Britt Reid/	
The Green Hornet	Warren Hull
Kato	Keye Luke
Michael Oxford	Wade Boteler
Lenore Case	Anne Nagel
Lowery	Eddie Acuff
Grogan	Pierre Watkins
Dolan	Joe A. Devlin
Don DeLuca	William Hall
Frances Grayson	Dorothy Lovett
Foranti	Jay Michael
Weaver	Montague Shaw

Britt Reid, crusading newspaper publisher, finds that a racketeering organization has extended its activities into virtually every industry in the city. With the aid of his Japanese servant Kato, his secretary Lenore Case, his bodyguard Michael Oxford, and ace reporter Lowery, Britt learns that the racketeers are controlled by a sinister undercover boss.

Disguised as the Green Hornet, Britt makes forays against the underworld establishment. Each attack brings him closer to the identity of the syndicate mastermind, an archcrook named Grogan. Grogan is finally cornered by the Hornet, whom the outlaw has tried to bribe. The Hornet names his price: a full confession of the organization's activities. Grogan is forced to sign and the remaining racketeers are exposed and easily rounded up.

Keye Luke and the Green Hornet keep tabs on the racketeers.

Keye Luke is about to fell an outlaw with a karate chop as the Hornet watches.

Keye Luke to the rescue amidst the debris of an explosion which has stunned the Hornet and an injured prisoner.

Junior G-men

12 Episodes	Directed by
Universal, 1940	Ford Beebe
	and John Rawlins

CAST

Billy Barton	Billy Halop
Gyp	Huntz Hall
Terry	Gabriel Dell
Lug	Bernard Punsley
Midge	Roger Daniels
Jim Bradford	Phillip Terry
Buck	Kenneth Lundy
Colonel Barton	Russell Hicks
Brand	Cy Kendall
Harry Trent	Kenneth Howell

Following the mysterious disappearance of certain military and scientific leaders including Colonel Barton, inventor of a deadly new explosive of great value in the War Department, Jim Bradford, famed G-man, is assigned to investigate.

Barton's son Billy, who ran away from home five years earlier and now leads a band of juvenile street fighters, distrusts Bradford's invitation to help in the search for his missing father. But, when his life is saved by the federal agent, Billy joins forces with a group of Junior G-men headed by Harry Trent. They find that an anarchist band called the "Order of the Flaming Torch," led by Brand, is bent on destruction of national military projects.

The boys play detective and keep hot on the trail of the traitor suspects.

Captured during a fight with enemy agents, Billy and Harry are imprisoned in a tenement building. Billy cuts his wrist bonds with a piece of glass and flashes a signal to friends on the street, who race to the rescue. During the battle that ensues, Billy falls against a window railing and hurtles toward the pavement below. Fortunately, he lands on a broad awning and rushes to join his gang. Brand's men have escaped, but Lug finds a wallet dropped by one of them. Notes in the wallet reveal a plan to kidnap the inventor of a new aerial torpedo.

In Billy's shack Gabriel Dell, Kenneth Lundy, Kenneth Howell, Bernard Punsley, Billy Halop, Roger Daniels, and (*foreground*) Huntz Hall discuss their next move.

Billy and Harry race to an airfield and hide in the inventor's plane. One of Brand's men blackjacks the pilot and takes his place at the ship's controls. Harry, a licensed pilot, tries with Billy's help to overpower the outlaw but, as the trio struggles, the plane goes into a spin and screams toward earth. At the last moment the boys succeed in knocking out the enemy pilot and Harry gains control of the plane, stopping it from crashing.

Billy takes the captured pilot to his shack where the police place the agent under arrest. Acting on a clue, Billy and Harry find the gang's headquarters in an old warehouse, where Colonel Barton is being held prisoner. Brand captures the two boys and tries to force Barton to

yield the formula for the new explosive, but he steadfastly refuses. Locked in a dungeon, Billy and Harry climb through a ventilator and into an elevator shaft just as the elevator drops upon them.

Rolling to safety past the elevator gate, Billy and Harry make their way to the radio room of the gang's headquarters where they barricade themselves and wire their location to the police. The enemy agents are about to break through to the boys when the G-men, led by Jim, dash in and capture the entire band of anarchists.

Barton is reunited with his son, now a full-fledged member of the Junior G-men, and the valuable explosive formula is delivered intact to the War Department.

King of the Royal Mounted

12 Episodes
Republic, 1940

Directed by
William Witney
and John English

CAST

Sergeant King — Allan Lane
Kettler — Robert Strange

Corporal Tom
 Merritt, Jr. — Robert Kellard
Linda Merritt — Lita Conway
Inspector King — Herbert Rawlinson
Wade Garson — Harry Cording
Crandall — Bryant Washburn

Vinegar Smith — Budd Buster
Merritt, Sr. — Stanley Andrews
Dr. Shelton — John Davidson
Dr. Wall — John Dilson
Excellency Zarnoff — Paul McVey
Admiral Johnson — Lucien Prival
Captain Tarner — Norman Willis
Le Couteau — Tony Paton

Merritt, a Canadian, has invented what he calls "Compound X," a substance that will cure infantile paralysis. He extracts this substance from a mine at Caribou, Canada. A country at war with Canada discovers that Compound X has certain magnetic properties which would make their mines effective against the British fleet. Accordingly, they dispatch one of their intelligence officers, Juan Kettler, to insure a steady stream of Compound X from the Caribou Mine.

From this point on, there is a continuous battle between the Canadian Royal Mounties, who want to preserve the Compound X for the paralysis victims, and the foreign agents, who want to use it for purposes of destruction. Sergeant King's father is killed in one of the battles with the enemy agents, and King continues on in his place, in command of a Mountie Post. He works tirelessly, to thwart the efforts of Kettler and his men to steal the precious substance.

On one occasion, the foreign agents open a fake "sanitarium" hoping to gain quantities of Compound X allegedly for paralysis victims, and ship it abroad to their country. King uncovers their plan and exposes "Dr. Shelton," the head of their hospital, as a foreign agent. In their raid on the hospital, the Mounties succeed in securing some fuse caps, which will provide undeniable proof that Kettler and his men are saboteurs. In an effort to recover the telltale fuse caps, the agents kidnap Linda Merritt, the sister of Sergeant King's friend Mountie Tom Merritt. King rescues her at great personal risk, a feat greatly appreciated by Tom.

It is discovered that one of the key men in the agent's plot is Crandall, part owner of the Caribou Mine and supposedly an honest man. King exposes him, and a special officer, Sir Bolton, is sent up from Ottawa to take him into custody. Kettler disguises himself as Sir Bolton, makes the arrest, and later frees his prisoner. King, however, arrives in time to stop the prisoner from making good his escape.

In a final effort to secure a supply of Compound X, the agents manage to have it loaded on a submarine. They imprison King and Tom Merritt in the torpedo room. King decides to shoot Tom to safety through the torpedo tube and then blow up the submarine, sacrificing himself in a heroic effort to thwart the enemy. But Tom anticipates his plan; he slugs King, shoots him to safety through the torpedo tube, and then blows up the ship. Tom sacrifices himself so that his best friend will be able to marry his sister, and Compound X will forever be out of the hands of the enemy.

Allan Lane radios an urgent message to Mountie headquarters.

An enemy agent prepares to toss a helpless victim off a high dam.

Allan Lane uses hands and feet to ward off two assailants.

Ted Mapes (*far left*) seems peeved as a cohort loads bombs into a crate and John Davidson (*far right*) carefully mixes some Compound X.

Mysterious Dr. Satan

15 Episodes
Republic, 1940

Directed by
William Witney
and John English

CAST

Doctor Satan	Eduardo Cianelli
Bob Wayne	Robert Wilcox
Speed Martin	William Newell
Professor Scott	C. Montague Shaw
Lois Scott	Ella Neal
Alice Brent	Dorothy Herbert
Governor Bronson	Charles Trowbridge
Chief of Police	Jack Mulhall
Colonel Bevans	Edwin Stanley
Stoner	Walter McGrail
Gort	Joe McGuinn
Hallett	Bud Geary
The Stranger	Paul Marion
Airport Radio Announcer	Archie Twitchell
Scarlett	Lynton Brent
Corwin	Kenneth Terrell
Joe	Al Taylor
Red	Alan Gregg

Robert Wilcox is caught in the clutches of the robot belonging to Eduardo Cianelli as Montague Shaw looks on helplessly.

The Copperhead leaps after one of Dr. Satan's men. (That's stuntman David Sharpe doubling as the Copperhead.)

Dr. Satan, mysterious master criminal, has invented a mechanical man with which he plans to rob and terrorize the nation. To perfect this robot, he needs a remote control device recently developed by an eminent scientist, Thomas Scott. His attempts to obtain it, however, are thwarted by the appearance of a man in a copper mask. This "Copperhead" is Bob Wayne, who has adopted the disguise worn by his father when the latter was a fugitive from crooked justice in the old West. Bob is determined to protect society from the machinations of Dr. Satan, and, at the same time, wipe out the stigma attached to the name Copperhead.

Dr. Satan makes various attempts to secure the remote control device by threatening the death of Scott's daughter Lois. The Copperhead comes to Lois's rescue when she appears doomed on a sinking yacht which carries the secret of the device to a watery grave.

Subsequently, Dr. Satan and his men salvage the remote control device. But the Copper-

As the walls of a room close in on him, the Copperhead avoids being crushed by executing a masterful "mirror shot" into the control panel being operated by Dr. Satan.

A well-placed bottle of acid stops the metal robot and saves the Copperhead from certain capture.

head risks death again and again to prevent the inhuman scientist from using it for the destruction of mankind.

On one occasion, Dr. Satan demonstrates the power of his robot by having it crush one of his henchmen; not long after, the Copperhead himself comes to death grips with the robot, saving himself only when, at the eleventh hour, he is able to shut off the mechanism that propels the mechanical monster.

Learning that Dr. Satan, in order to forstall police action, plans to destroy a passenger plane by remote control, the Copperhead takes off in his own plane. Although he is able to save the transport from destruction, his own plane crashes into a high mountain peak. He is saved by bailing out in the nick of time.

After kidnapping Scott, Satan threatens to turn the robot on him unless he installs the control device. After watching Scarlett, one of Satan's men, crushed to death by the robot because he had tried to help him escape, Scott gives in.

However, Scott manages to get a radio message to the Copperhead. After fighting his way inside, the Copperhead is about to free Scott when Dr. Satan sets his robot upon him. Before the robot can crush the Copperhead, Scott reaches the controls, halts the monster, and enables the Copperhead to escape.

In order to penetrate Dr. Satan's headquarters, the Copperhead hides himself in a box which is supposed to hold the robot. Once inside the headquarters, Copperhead locates Professor Scott, but, as the two discuss their plans to escape, they are interupted by Dr. Satan. They knock him unconscious and, hearing some of the doctor's henchmen approaching, Copperhead removes his mask, places it on Dr. Satan, and hides in another room. Scott tells Satan's thugs that he had discovered the Copperhead prowling about and knocked him out. Satan's men know just what to do. They take the supposed Copperhead into another room and set a robot upon him. Dr. Satan regains consciousness just as the robot grips him, and, in his death throes, Dr. Satan, still clutched by the robot, crashes through a window, falling several stories to his doom.

The Shadow

15 Episodes
Columbia, 1940

Directed by
James W. Horne

CAST

Lamont Cranston ⎫
Lin Chang ⎬ Victor Jory
The Shadow ⎭
Margot Lane   Veda Ann Borg
Vincent   Robert Moore
Turner   Robert Fiske
Marshall   J. Paul Jones
Flint   Jack Ingram
Roberts   Charles Hamilton
Inspector Cardona Edward Peil, Sr.
Commissioner Weston Frank La Rue
The Black Tiger   ? ? ? ? ?

Railroads are dynamited, airplanes wrecked, and industrial plants blown up. No institution in the nation is safe from the machinations of the secret mastermind of the underworld, known only as The Black Tiger. While the police theorize and make futile arrests, Lamont Cranston, scientist and criminologist, acts. Assuming the guise of the Shadow, a black-garbed, masked figure, he risks his life to warn citizens of the impending attacks and frustrate the plans of Black Tiger.

As The Tiger persists in his efforts to rob chemicals and electrical equipment needed for his sophisticated death-dealing devices (including a mysterious death ray), Cranston works with Commissioner Weston and a group of solid citizens consisting of Rand, Connor, Marshall, Hill, and Prescott, to track the master villain down.

Disguised as Lin Chang, a Chinese merchant, the Shadow gains the temporary confidence of the Black Tiger, and manages to discover the secret lair of the criminal. Trapped by the Shadow, the Black Tiger proves to be the man Cranston had suspected—Stanford Marshall, one of the supposedly reputable community leaders. Attempting to escape, Marshall stumbles and falls back against an electrical control panel. There is a flash and a shower of sparks; the Black Tiger is no more.

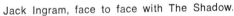

Jack Ingram, face to face with The Shadow.

Terry and the Pirates

15 Episodes
Columbia, 1940

Directed by
James W. Horne

CAST

Terry Lee	William Tracy
Pat Ryan	Granville Owen
Normandie Drake	Joyce Bryant
Connie	Allen Jung
Big Stoop	Victor De Camp
Dragon Lady	Sheila Darcy
Fang	Dick Curtis
Dr. Lee	J. Paul Jones
Drake	Forrest Taylor
Stanton	Jack Ingram

Dr. Herbert Lee, an American archaeologist, leads an expedition into Asia to discover a lost civilization. Terry, Dr. Lee's son, and Pat Ryan, his father's assistant, come to the trading post town of Wingpoo with documents required by the doctor. They are befriended by trader Allen Drake and his daughter Normandie.

Fang, a half-caste warlord of considerable power, convinces a band of white renegades in the area to ambush Dr. Lee's party, and the doctor is captured. Fang intends to seize the treasures hidden beneath the temple of the God Mara, deep in the jungle. From Dr. Lee, Fang learns that the natives believe an era of great happiness will begin when the great stone idol Mara speaks.

Accompanied by their Chinese servant Connie, and Big Stoop, a giant street magician who has taken a liking to them, the two Americans set out to find Dr. Lee. First they visit the headquarters of the Dragon Lady, the leader of the followers of Mara and a sworn enemy of Fang. During their meeting with the Dragon Lady, the Tiger Men, a terrorist group led by Stanton, one of Fang's henchmen, attack the Dragon Lady's Temple of the Dawn. During the attack, Fang's men succeed in stealing the stone idol Mara. Terry and Pat decide to track down the stolen idol and return it to the Dragon Lady.

Normandie is captured by Gori, one of Fang's men, and his pet gorilla. In an attempt to rescue the girl, Pat and Terry are also captured and taken to Fang's headquarters. As the villains leave with their captives, they are observed by Connie and Big Stoop, who pursue them.

In order to persuade Dr. Lee to translate an inscription found on the idol, Fang decides to torture Terry. But the enormous Big Stoop single-handedly attacks the torturers, allowing Terry, Pat, and the doctor to escape.

The threesome goes to the Dragon Lady to offer their services to recover the idol. The Dragon Lady sends Dr. Lee off on his mission with a party of her followers. But Dr. Lee is ambushed by the renegades and is captured. Fang discovers a scroll hidden inside the idol. Dr. Lee, aware of its importance, grabs it and attempts to flee. Unfortunately, he is captured.

While combing the jungle, Terry and Pat find their way to Fang's lair, discover the hidden idol, and examine it carefully. They find that Fang has placed a hidden phonograph in the idol to fool the natives into believing it speaks. Having made this important discovery, the two Americans stealthily reach Dr. Lee and attempt to rescue him. The doctor, however, refuses to leave until he can recover the Mara scroll.

Fang, accompanied by his Tiger Men, brings the idol to the Temple of the Dawn. By using a hidden microphone, Fang fools the natives into believing the idol has spoken and assumes control over the Dragon Lady's temple. But Terry and Pat have disguised themselves as Tiger Men, and escape with the Dragon Lady through a secret door known only to her.

The boys escort the Dragon Lady to safety, rejoin Connie, Big Stoop, and Normandie, and head for the trading post. They find Mr. Drake in Wingpoo under attack by Fang's renegades. Terry and Pat rout the assailants.

The two Americans then set out for the temple of Mara to find Dr. Lee. They are unaware that the doctor has escaped and is carrying the key to the Mara manuscript.

Terry and Pat disguise themselves as Tiger

William Tracy battles one of Fang's assailants.

The dreaded "Tiger Men."

Men and make their way into the Temple of the Dawn. When they find the idol Mara, Terry removes the record that Fang has placed inside it. They are discovered by Fang's men and flee into an ammunition shed. When a bullet hits a keg of powder, the boys escape through a hole in the wall.

Meanwhile Dr. Lee has been reunited with Connie, Big Stoop, and Normandie, and all four join the Dragon Lady at her villa. But Dr. Lee learns from jungle drums that Fang's men are preparing to attack Terry and Pat; he leaves with Connie and Big Stoop to help them. Left alone, the Dragon Lady and Normandie are captured by the renegades.

On their way to help Terry and Pat, the doctor, Connie, and Big Stoop are ambushed by Fang's renegades and also taken prisoner. When they are brought before Fang in the jungle temple, Dr. Lee pushes the warlord into the hands of Gori's gorilla. As Gori rushes to subdue his murderous pet, the Dragon Lady escapes through a secret passage. She joins Terry and Pat at her villa, and takes the scroll from its hiding place. The threesome then make their way to where their friends are being held prisoner. In a daring raid, they free Dr. Lee and Normandie.

The friends then decide to remove the treasure themselves for safekeeping. But Fang and his men have followed and attack them before they can escape. Terry alone flees. The others are tied to a funeral pyre which is ignited. Terry suddenly appears, seizes a flaming powder keg, and hurls it at the natives, scattering them. He frees Pat and the others. Pat, speaking in the name of Mara through a loudspeaker that he and Terry had rigged in the temple, exposes Fang's trickery.

As they flee through the temple's scroll library, two of Fang's men find the huge diamond that is the treasure of Mara. Realizing that he is beaten, Fang kills his henchmen to keep the diamond for himself. But when he shoots Gori, Gori's infuriated gorilla breaks its chains, leaps upon Fang, and kills him.

Pat returns the diamond to the Dragon Lady, and she is restored to her throne. In turn, she promises full cooperation to Dr. Lee in his archaeological quest.

Granville Owen, Allen Jung, and William Tracy study a possible clue.

Victor De Camp makes an auspicious entrance, to the amazement of two traders and the amusement of William Tracy, Granville Owen, and Allen Jung.

Forrest Taylor tells Joyce Bryant, Granville Owen, and William Tracy about an attack by Fang's men.

Winners of the West

13 Episodes
Universal, 1940

Directed by
Ford Beebe
and Ray Taylor

CAST

Jeff Ramsay	Dick Foran
Claire Hartford	Anne Nagel
Jim Jackson	James Craig
Tex Houston	Tom Fadden
Snakeye	Charles Stevens
Raven	Trevor Bardette
King Carter	Harry Woods
Chief War Eagle	Chief Yowlatchie
John Hartford	Edward Keane
Brine	William Desmond
Maddox	Edmund Cobb

Fighting to advance the great Hartford Transcontinental Railroad through Hellgate Pass, Jeff Ramsay, assistant to John Hartford, the president of the line, is blocked by King Carter, self-styled ruler of the prairie domain beyond the pass.

Determined to prevent completion of railway construction, Carter hires Snakeye, a renegade half-breed, to lead local Indians in raids on the construction camps. Spurred on by Carter, the Indians rob stagecoaches, pirate wagon supply trains, drive surveying men to shelter, and burn down the telegraph station. At one point, John Hartford's daughter Claire is captured by Carter's henchmen and held as a hostage until Jeff and his sidekick Tex Houston discover her whereabouts and come to her rescue.

Finally, in a battle at Blackhawk, the outlaw's lair, Carter's headquarters is wiped out by Jeff and his friend Jim Jackson. Carter is captured and turned over to the government, and a peace treaty is signed with Chief War Eagle, the Indian tribe's leader. Hartford, his daughter Claire, and her new husband Jeff Ramsay beam with happiness as pioneers welcome the arrival of the first transcontinental train.

Dick Foran, James Craig, and Tom Fadden, set to combat Carter's men.

1941

Adventures of Captain Marvel

12 Episodes
Republic, 1941

Directed by
William Witney
and John English

CAST

Captain Marvel	Tom Tyler
Billy Batson	Frank Coghlan, Jr.
Murphy	William Benedict
Betty Wallace	Louise Currie
The Scorpion	? ? ? ? ?
John Malcolm	Robert Strange
Professor Bentley	Harry Worth
Henry Carlyle	Bryant Washburn
Tal Chotali	John Davidson
Dr. Stephen Lang	George Pembroke
Dwight Fisher	Peter George Lynn
Rahman Bar	Reed Hadley
Howell	Jack Mulhall
Barnett	Kenneth Duncan
Shazam	Nigel de Brulier
Cowan	John Bagni
Martin	Carleton Young
Major Rawley	Leland Hodgson
Owens	Stanley Price
Akbar	Ernest Sarracino
Chan Lai	Tetsu Komai

To a remote section of Siam, zealously guarded by an unconquered native tribe, comes the unwelcome Malcolm Scientific Expedition, seeking knowledge of the ancient Scorpion Dynasty. Billy Batson, assistant to the radio operator, is the only one of the party who does not enter a forbidden chamber inside an ancient underground tomb.

An erupting volcano causes part of the tomb to collapse, and Billy finds himself confronted by Shazam, the tomb's guardian. Because he has heeded the sacred chamber's warning, Billy is endowed with the magic power to transform himself into Captain Marvel, merely by uttering the word Shazam. Before he vanishes, the old man tells Billy that this power will last only as long as the Golden Scorpion is threatened.

Meanwhile, the scientists who have entered the sacred temple have discovered the Scorpion, a powerful golden weapon the full potency of which is released by focusing five highly polished lenses. The scientists divide the lenses among themselves so that no one of them will have complete power. There is a pitched battle between the native tribesmen and the scientists during which Betty, the expedition's secretary, appears to meet her death by falling into a gorge.

Billy, as Captain Marvel, rescues her and transforms himself back to Billy Batson before she regains consciousness. The party returns to America but is pursued by a sinister gang headed by a human Scorpion who wants to wrest from them the secret of the places they have hidden their lenses.

The scientific group, at the home of Malcolm, its leader, has assigned Betty the task of getting one of the lenses, Carlyle's, from the safe at his mountain lodge. Billy insists that she use his car, which is equipped with a two-way radio system. The gangsters abduct Betty, forcing her to drive her car into their moving van. When they attempt to make her reveal the combination of Carlyle's safe, she throws the switch of the radio so that Billy overhears. He transforms himself into Captain Marvel and rescues Betty.

It is apparent that one of the scientists is the mysterious Scorpion, but all of them, of course, indignantly deny any complicity.

The scientists receive a message from the Scorpion, warning them that he has acquired all the lenses but one, and that death will befall anyone who stands in his way in securing the last. Each scientist races for home to see who has the remaining lens, which is exactly what the Scorpion intended in order to make them reveal their hiding places.

Marvel learns that the Scorpion's men have made off with the last lens. Meanwhile, since Billy and Captain Marvel always seem to be on the spot whenever the Scorpion's various plottings take place, Malcolm suggests that perhaps they are in league with the Scorpion. The Scorpion decides to capture Captain Marvel,

Frank Coghlan, Jr., is bestowed marvelous powers by Nigel de Brulier.

Tom Tyler prepares to put an end to the myth of the Scorpion, as John Davidson, Louise Currie, William Benedict, and Reed Hadley look on.

once and for all, using Billy and Betty as bait. Betty is captured and Billy pursues, assuming the character of Captain Marvel.

The Scorpion observes Billy in the act of transforming himself into Captain Marvel, but is not certain of how this phenomenon is accomplished. Billy is captured by the Scorpion's henchmen, along with Betty and the other members of the party. The Scorpion now has all of the lenses fitted into the golden Scorpion, which makes it the most powerful instrument in the world. He threatens to use it on Billy and his friends, causing their immediate annihila-

tion, unless Billy will reveal the secret of how he transforms himself into a superman. Billy nods agreement, tricking the Scorpion into removing the gag. Billy utters the magic word, becomes Captain Marvel, rescues his friends, and slips the hood from the Scorpion, revealing him as none other than Professor Bentley, one of the original members of the expedition. When he tries to escape, Bentley falls in front of the ray from the Golden Scorpion's lenses and is *disintegrated*. Captain Marvel throws the deadly device into a pit of molten lava and becomes Billy Batson again as his magic powers vanish.

Dick Tracy vs. Crime, Inc.

15 Episodes
(Republic, 1941)

Directed by
William Witney
and John English

CAST

Dick Tracy	—Ralph Byrd
The Ghost	? ? ? ? ?
Billy Carr	Michael Owen
June Chandler	Jan Wiley
Lucifer	John Davidson
Morton	Ralph Morgan
Lieutenant Cosgrave	Kenneth Harlan
Weldon	John Dilson
Chandler	Howard Hickman
Brewster	Robert Frazer
Cabot	Robert Fiske
Wilson	Jack Mulhall
Trent	Hooper Atchley
Corey	Anthony Warde
Trask	Chuck Morrison

Dick Tracy is summoned from Washington to halt the activities of a master criminal known only as "the Ghost." Unknown to all, the Ghost is a member of the Council of Eight, a body of influential citizens organized to rid the city of a reign of crime. Through the inventive genius of a mad fanatic known as Lucifer, the Ghost is able to make himself invisible and has murdered three council members without revealing his own identity.

Tracy quickly goes to work and prevents the Ghost's men from dynamiting the city's harbor and robbing vital scientific devices and gold shipments. After one crime, Tracy discovers a medal presented only to Council of Eight mem-

bers and suspects that one of the members is the Ghost.

But the Ghost maintains his efforts to destroy the city and responds to Tracy's heightened pursuit by disappearing in thin air right before the astonished detective. Tracy uses bloodhounds to track the Ghost. With Tracy in hot pursuit, The Ghost tries to cross some high-tension wires and is electrocuted. When he becomes visible, he is revealed as Council member Morton. Tracy deduces that Morton was gaining revenge on society for the death of his gangster brother.

Holt of the Secret Service

15 Episodes
Columbia, 1941

Directed by
James W. Horne

CAST

Jack Holt Nick Farrel	} Jack Holt
Kay	Evelyn Brent
Malloy	Montague Shaw
Valden	Tristram Coffin
Arnold	John Ward
Quist	Ted Adams
Crimp	Joe McGuinn
Jim	Edward Hearn
Severn	Ray Parsons
Frank	Jack Cheatham

Jack Holt, U.S. Secret Service agent, is assigned to track down counterfeiters who are flooding the country with bogus money. Getting pretty Kay Drew, another operative, to help, he plans to join the gang by posing as a desperate criminal, Nick Farrel.

Learning that one member of the gang, Crimp Evans, is in a police hospital, Holt has himself checked in as a patient. Kay, posing as

Jack Holt studies a bottle of acid used by a gang of counterfeiters.

his wife, calls the next day with a plan for escape. Crimp begs to go along, telling Holt he will lead him to his boses' hideout.

That night, Crimp and Holt escape. Crimp leads the detective to a canoe he has hidden nearby, and the men start for the mountains via the river. While Holt is paddling, a note from Kay falls out of his pocket and Crimp, reading it, learns his companion's true identity. They start fighting. Suddenly, the canoe plunges over the rapids, dashing itself to pieces on the rocks far below!

Miraculously, Holt is unhurt, but Crimp has disappeared. Kay, who has followed the men, helps Holt out of the water and the two of them, after searching the woods, stumble upon the outlaw camp where they are accepted by the counterfeiters who believe that Holt is a criminal.

The head of the counterfeiters is Lucky Arnold and, in the ensuing action, Holt manages to gain possession of the printing plates vital to the gang and to pass them on to Kay who hides them. Holt and Kay are both captured and Holt is tortured so badly that Kay breaks down in order to save the detective and reveals where the plates are hidden. But Holt breaks away and a fight begins. During the struggle a fire starts and Lucky is killed. The fire attracts other people with whose help the gang is rounded up. With the plates recovered, Holt and Kay plan to make their vacation a honeymoon.

The Iron Claw

15 Episodes	Directed by
Columbia, 1941	James W. Horne

CAST

Bob Lane	Charles Quigley
Jack Strong	Walter Sande
Patricia Benson	Joyce Bryant
Anton Benson	Forrest Taylor
James Benson	Alex Callam
Roy Benson	Norman Willis
Culver Benson	James Metcalfe
Simon Leach	Allen Doone
Milly Leach	Edythe Elliot
Gyves	John Beck
Silk	Charles King
Casey	James Morton
O'Malley	Hal Price

The dreaded "Iron Claw."

Culver Benson, after quarreling with his two brothers Anton and Roy over the division of a huge fortune in hidden gold, is murdered by the mysterious "Iron Claw." Newspaper reporter Bob Lane and Patricia Benson, Anton's niece, investigate.

The Claw makes several attempts on Pat's life for reasons that Bob can't quite understand. To add to the confusion, two other outlaw gangs as well as the greedy Benson brothers are also after the gold. In the end, however, Bob unmasks the Claw, locks up the crooks, and reveals that Pat is the heiress to the entire hidden fortune.

Charles Quigley, Walter Sande, Forrest Taylor, and Joyce Bryant try to anticipate the Iron Claw's next move.

Joyce Bryant, being abducted by the Iron Claw.

Jungle Girl

15 Episodes	Directed by
Republic, 1941	William Witney
	and John English

CAST

Nyoka	Frances Gifford
Jack Stanton	Tom Neal
Meredith-Bradley	Trevor Bardette
Slick Latimer	Gerald Mohr
Curly Rogers	Eddie Acuff
Shamba	Frank Lackteen
Wakimbu	Tommy Cook
Bombo	Robert Barron
Lutembi	Al Kikume
Brock	Bud Geary
Claggett	Al Taylor
Bone	Joe McGuinn
The Lion Chief	Jerry Frank
Mananga	Kenneth Terrell

Dr. Meredith, driven from society by the criminal activities of his twin brother, takes his young daughter Nyoka into the African jungle. She grows up with the natives and wins their confidence.

Because Dr. Meredith is able to cure the natives of many diseases, they regard him as a superman. But all of the natives are not happy with him; he incurs the disfavor of the native witch doctor Shamba.

Dr. Meredith's wicked twin brother learns of a vast store of diamonds to which the doctor has access and is determined to gain possession of the fabulous gems. He joins forces with Shamba and a group of criminals to stir unrest among the natives. They lure Dr. Meredith away from the jungle and he is murdered by their cohort, "Slick" Latimer. Dr. Meredith's evil brother assumes his identity, and the resemblance is so close that even Nyoka does not suspect that her father is dead.

Jack Stanton and Curly Rogers, two aviators, come to the jungle and champion the cause of Nyoka.

The trio meet a native who is carrying little Kimbu, a native boy who has been wounded in an animal trap. Nyoka first becomes suspicious of her "father" when the child is taken to him for treatment and he is obviously unfamiliar with the surgical instruments. Her suspicions are confirmed when she compares the fingerprints on the real Dr. Meredith's passport. Latimer sees her making the comparison, and bluntly tells her that the man posing as her father is indeed a fake, but that she will be killed before she can reveal the truth. Kimbu, sizing up the situation, loosens a suspension device for the central lamp in the room; it falls and knocks Latimer to his knees and Nyoka escapes to warn the boys.

By now Meredith has the diamonds and plans to escape, leaving Nyoka and the boys stranded in the jungle. But he learns that Stanton and Curly have in their possession a small engine part without which his plane cannot run. To obtain the part, the false Meredith, whose true identity is still unknown to the natives, exhorts them to capture the two boys, professing to them that the latter have kidnapped Nyoka. The boys elude the natives, capture the diamonds from Meredith and, with Nyoka and Kimbu, enter the plane to escape. As the engine starts, a hidden gun previously planted by Meredith to thwart any escape attempt goes off, apparently killing Stanton, who is at the controls.

Curly shuts off the ignition and stops the plane. With the wounded Stanton in their arms, he and Nyoka run into the jungle. Kimbu attempts to retrieve the diamonds, but, seeing that he is surrounded, stuffs them into a flashlight. This very flashlight is used by the heavies as they follow Latimer's orders to "Comb the jungle and find those diamonds"! Stanton's wounds are only superficial; the amulet he was carrying in his shirt pocket deflected the bullet which is now lodged in his shoulder. Nyoka sends Kimbu's pet monkey to her father's rooms for medical supplies; the animal is seen by Meredith and Latimer, who set out in hot pursuit.

Nyoka eludes them, but is captured by Shamba and his natives. They tie her to a stake in front of a spear-discharging machine.

Curly arrives in time to knock the post over just as the spears hurtle past the spot where Nyoka had stood. Curly is taken prisoner, and in order to save Nyoka's life, reveals that the diamonds are hidden in the flashlight. Latimer immediately sets out to retrieve the flashlight, which was left in camp. Meanwhile, Meredith has opened the flashlight, found the diamonds, and removed most of them. When Latimer arrives and finds only a few of the gems left, he suspects he has been double-crossed and kills Meredith. Stanton invokes the loyalty of the natives to help him save Nyoka and, with their aid, he is successful in killing Shamba. Latimer attempts to escape in the plane, but Stanton seizes him and hurls him from the plane after a desperate fight.

Natives prepare to roast Eddie Acuff.

✗ King of the Texas Rangers

12 Episodes	Directed by
Republic, 1941	William Witney
	and John English

CAST

Sergeant King	"Slingin' Sammy" Baugh
Barton	Neil Hamilton
Sally Crane	Pauline Moore
Pedro Garcia	Duncan Renaldo
Crawford	Charles Trowbridge
Colonel Avery	Herbert Rawlinson
Evans	Frank Darien
His Excellency	Robert O. Davis
Captain King	Monte Blue
Lynch	Stanley Blystone
Wichita	Kermit Maynard
Ross	Roy Barcroft
Nick	Kenneth Duncan
Shorty	Jack Ingram
Blake	Robert Barron
Cole	Frank Bruno
Dade	Monte Montague
Professor Nelson	Joseph Forte
Captain	Lucien Prival

Captain King of the Texas Rangers is murdered after he has learned that John Barton, supposedly a respectable citizen, and "His Excellency," a mysterious alien, are the leaders of a sabotage gang engaged in destroying the Bordertown oil fields. His son Tom King, a famous football player, joins the Rangers, eager to avenge his father's death.

Tom does not have long to wait for action. He goes to Mexico with Pedro Garcia of the famous Mexican police—the Rurales—to burn one of the gang's hideouts. There he finds that his sweetheart Sally Crane, a newspaper editor, has been trapped in a blaze in the oil fields. King rescues Sally and has the fire extinguished before it can do much harm.

The saboteurs then decide to liquidate Professor Nelson, the inventor of an important new aviation gasoline. Their attempt to wreck the train on which Nelson is riding to Bordertown is foiled when King himself acts as the professor's bodyguard. An attempt to kidnap Nelson also fails. Then Barton hits upon a more successful scheme—he spreads a rumor that the aviation gasoline is dangerous to fly with. King decides to disprove the rumor by flying in an airplane powered by the fuel. After he and Sally take off, it is learned that a time bomb has been placed on board. Pedro, however, goes up in a second plane and warns them of the danger. They escape just before the bomb goes off.

The saboteurs' next project is to ruin the oil in the storage tanks by putting a destructive chemical in them. After several brushes with the saboteurs, King finds the pumping station where the chemicals are being added to the oil. While he is in the station, members of the gang try to kill him by driving a truck into the building. He escapes by jumping through a window seconds before the collision occurs.

In the meantime, Sally Crane has been doing some detective work. She finds the tin shop where the counterfeit license plates for the saboteurs' cars have been made and is about to get valuable information when she is caught by Lynch, Barton's lieutenant. When King comes to Sally's rescue, Lynch sets the building on fire and tries to sneak her out the back way. King is slightly injured in the fire but he and Pedro do away with Lynch in a gun battle and rescue the girl.

The next night, King learns that the saboteurs are planning to blow up Whitney Dam and flood the oil fields. To prevent this, he and Pedro identify Barton as one of the fifth-column leaders. They go to Barton's house, but he traps them in a tunnel filled with poison gas. Sally rescues the two men and tells them that Barton has stolen the aviation gasoline formula and is escaping by plane to the zeppelin operated by "His Excellency." King and Pedro follow in their own plane and crash it into the dirigible. All the saboteurs are killed, but King and Pedro parachute safely to earth. They are subsequently honored by the Texas Rangers for their bravery and courage.

Neil Hamilton, Charles Trowbridge, "Slingin' Sammy" Baugh, and Pauline Moore are told of a new oil formula that can benefit the war effort.

Duncan Renaldo and Sammy Baugh take to the air to attack an enemy dirigible.

Riders of Death Valley

15 Episodes
Universal, 1941

Directed by
Ford Beebe
and Ray Taylor

CAST

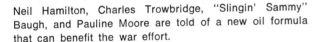

Jim Benton	Dick Foran
Pancho	Leo Carrillo
Tombstone	Buck Jones
Wolf Reade	Charles Bickford
Butch	Lon Chaney, Jr.
Smokey	Noah Beery, Jr.
Borax Bill	"Big Boy" Williams
Mary Morgan	Jeanne Kelly
Joseph Kirby	James Blaine
Rance Davis	Monte Blue
Tex	Glenn Strange

During the days of the California gold strike, a group of vigilantes, called the "Riders of Death Valley," organized to protect the miners against raiders and confidence men. The leaders of the vigilantes are Jim Benton and his sidekick Tombstone. The Riders set out to break up a fake "protection" league that is trying to gain control of the big mining claims. After their successful action, they return to town and the nearest saloon. Chuckowalla, an old desert rat, is carried into the saloon and reveals that he has found the Lost Aztec Mine, a fabulous bonanza.

The miner is dying, but first asks that his share of the claim be given to his niece Mary Morgan. She is in serious danger, for the stage on which she is riding is also carrying a large shipment of gold, and Wolf Reade, a notorious bad man of the territory, has plans for robbing it. Thanks to fast action by the Riders, Mary and the gold are saved, but not before the stagecoach itself is demolished.

Wolf Reade, however, is determined to obtain not only the gold, but also to lay claim to all of the mines that might exist in the Panamint district. After a number of attempts at harassment, which are foiled by the Riders, Wolf sends for every cutthroat in the region and daringly takes possession of Panamint itself, capturing Mary, who is visiting there, and holding her as a hostage.

Benton hides in a stagecoach in order to enter the town secretly, sending the Riders to attack. They shoot two of Reade's henchmen, Butch and Kirby, but Reade himself escapes. Benton goes after him, finally trapping the outlaw on the top of a high cliff. Wolf is about to drop a huge rock upon Benton, sweeping him into the river depths below, but a shot rings out, from Tombstone, that hurtles Reade to his death. With this accomplished, the Riders set off for new conquests.

"Big Boy" Williams in the lead, as the wagon train tries to elude outlaws.

Sea Raiders

12 Episodes
Universal, 1941

Directed by
Ford Beebe
and John Rawlins

CAST

Billy Adams	Billy Halop
Toby Nelson	Huntz Hall
Bilge	Gabriel Dell
Butch	Bernard Punsley
Swab	Hally Chester
Lug	Joe Recht
Brack Warren	William Hall
Tom Adams	John McGuire
Aggie Nelson	Mary Field
Elliott Carlton	Edward Keane
Leah Carlton	Marcia Ralston
Carl Tonjes	Reed Hadley
Captain Olaf Nelson	Stanley Blystone
Jenkins	Richard Alexander
Zeke	Ernie Adams
Anderson	Jack Clifford
Krans	Richard Bond
Captain Lester	Morgan Wallace
Captain Meredith	Eddie Dunn

Elliott Carlton and Carl Tonjes order their band of foreign agents, the Sea Raiders, to blow up a freighter on which Billy Adams and Toby Nelson are stowaways. The boys are seeking to escape the wrath of Brack Warren, harbor police officer detailed to guard a new type of torpedo boat built by Billy's brother Tom for the Navy.

The boys are trapped on the doomed freighter but are rescued by their courageous pals. Together they find the Sea Raiders' island hideout and set out to investigate the saboteurs' underground arsenal on the seacoast. The chief of the Sea Raiders ruthlessly detonates the explosives stored in the arsenal.

Imprisoned by the explosion of the underground arsenal, Billy and Toby are rescued by Brack Warren. Brack and Billy don the uniforms of captured Sea Raiders and board a yacht that serves as headquarters for the Raiders. They set off a secret bomb device which destroys Tonjes and his henchmen.

The evil, gun-wielding Reed Hadley (*second from right*) seems to have harbor officials well in hand.

Sky Raiders

12 Episodes
Universal, 1941

Directed by
Ford Beebe
and Ray Taylor

CAST

Captain Robert Dayton	Donald Woods
Tim Bryant	Billy Halop
Lieutenant Ed Carey	Robert Armstrong
Felix Lynx	Edward Ciannelli
Mary Blake	Kathryn Adams
Innis Clair	Jacqueline Dalya
The Countess Irene	Jean Fenwick
Caddens	Reed Hadley
Hinchfield	Irving Mitchell
Teal	Edgar Edwards
Hess	John Holland
Major General Fletcher	Roy Gordon
Captain Long	Alex Callam
Jack Hurd	Bill Cody, Jr.

Former World War ace Captain Bob Dayton, with his buddy Lieutenant Ed Carey, operates Sky Raiders, Inc., an airplane manufacturing concern. Dayton has perfected a fast pursuit plane for the U.S. Army. Felix Lynx, agent for a foreign government, is kept informed of the Sky Raiders' plane by a spy in Dayton's office.

During a test flight, Lynx's men force the plane to crash. When Dayton shows up unharmed, Mary Blake, the captain's attractive secretary, insists the flyer has a charmed life. Dayton hires Tim Bryant, member of the Air Youth of America and an expert model plane builder, to do experimental work for him.

After several vain attempts either to steal or wreck the Sky Raider plane, Lynx turns his attention to the new bombsight Dayton has invented and is preparing for tests in Honolulu. The spy chief, in a fast fighter plane, machine-guns a Honolulu-bound clipper. The passengers —Dayton, Mary, and a group of army officers— are rescued from the sea by a government cutter.

Returning to the mainland, Dayton and Mary are met by Carey and Tim. A powerful automobile, containing Lynx and his henchmen, tries to force Carey's car off the road, but the foreign agents crash head on into a big truck.

Mary tells Tim and Carey that in Hawaii she became Mrs. Bob Dayton.

Donald Woods does his best to block enemy agents from seizing the secret pursuit plane.

Dave O'Brien and Mary Ainslee huddle under the protection of The Spider.

The Spider Returns

15 Episodes
Columbia, 1941

Directed by
James W. Horne

CAST

Richard Wentworth	
Blinky McQuade	Warren Hull
The Spider	
Nina Van Sloan	Mary Ainslee
Jackson	Dave O'Brien
Commander Kirk	Joe Girard
Ram Singh	Kenneth Duncan
McLeod	Corbet Harris
Westfall	Bryant Washburn
Van Sloan	Charles Miller
Trigger	Anthony Warck
Stephen	Harry Harvey
The Gargoyle	? ? ? ? ?

When a gang of saboteurs led by the Gargoyle, a mysterious foreign agent, threatens national defense projects, socialite Richard Wentworth, alias the Spider, returns to his war with the underworld.

Wentworth calls a meeting of the country's biggest businessmen, but the Gargoyle's gang disrupts it with a tear-gas bomb. Wentworth is captured by the gang and taken away in an airplane. The pilot then sets the plane afire and bails out, leaving Wentworth unconscious in the spinning plane. Fortunately, Wentworth recovers in time and parachutes to safety. Disguised as Blinky McQuade, underworld habitué, Wentworth joins the gang of saboteurs in an effort to learn the Gargoyle's identity; but he is unable to obtain the information.

After a number of successful attempts to circumvent the Gargoyle's many schemes to sabotage the nation's leading defense industries, the Spider discovers the foreign agent's hideaway and crashes into the torture room. After a furious struggle, he routs the gunmen and unmasks the arch fiend as McLeod, one of the industrialists!

White Eagle

15 Episodes
Columbia, 1941

Directed by
James W. Horne

CAST

White Eagle	Buck Jones
Grizzly	Raymond Hatton
Janet	Dorothy Fay
Darnell	James Craven
Running Deer	Chief Yowlachie
Cantro	Jack Ingram
Brace	Charles King
Ronimo	John Merton

Bart Darnell, a sinister character, fights with the Indian brave White Eagle, a pony express rider, and is discharged from government service. He vows vengeance. Bart is in league with Gregory Cantro, a crook who gives forged federal government warrants in payment for horses.

Knowing that a letter soon due from Washington will expose them, Bart and Gregory disguise their gang as Indians, hold up the stage, and murder several of the passengers. Janet Rand, sister of White Eagle's boss, escapes. White Eagle defends the Indians, claiming their innocence. But Bart and Gregory follow up the stage outrage with other murders, making it appear that the Indians have done the deeds.

Ignoring White Eagle's efforts to keep the peace, the town settlers attack a village of the Bannock tribe. White Eagle, who has been made a prisoner, escapes and joins his father Gray Wolf in the war on the whites. Captain Blake of the government post finally makes peace through White Eagle. White Eagle then discovers that Janet and her brother, victims of a ruse, have gone with Gregory and Bart. He follows them to Gregory's outlaw camp and rescues Janet and her brother. The Indians manage to capture Gregory's band of outlaws and return all the stolen horses. White Eagle gets the girl he loves—Janet.

Pony Express rider Buck Jones.

1942

TO BE CONTINUED

Captain Midnight

15 Episodes
Columbia, 1942

Directed by
James W. Horne

CAST

Captain Midnight	Dave O'Brien
Joyce	Dorothy Short
Ivan Shark	James Craven
Chuck	Sam Edwards
Ichabod Mudd	Guy Wilkerson
Edwards	Bryant Washburn
Fury	Luana Walters
Major Steel	Joe Girard
Borgman	Ray Teal
Dr. Jordan	George Pembroke
Martel	Charles Hamilton
Gardo	Al Ferguson

When enemy bombing planes, directed by Ivan Shark, begin terrifying the nation, Major Steele sends for Captain Albright. A famous aviator, Albright is even more famous under the alias of Captain Midnight. In the meantime, Shark orders Martel, his assistant, to steal a range finder which has been invented by John Edwards. Anticipating such a move, Edwards gives the model to his daughter Joyce and instructs her to give it to Albright. Soon afterward, Edwards is kidnapped by the Shark's men. When Albright learns of the kidnapping, he dresses as Midnight, locates the cabin where Edwards is being held prisoner, and rushes off to save him.

As the gangsters drive away from the cabin with Edwards in their car, Midnight tries to stop them, but is unsuccessful. That afternoon, Shark orders Martel to get the model of the range finder from Albright's mountain laboratory. Edward relays this information to Joyce; Joyce, in turn, conveys it to Midnight who quickly flies home. But the gangsters have beaten him to the punch and have already overpowered Chuck and Mudd, the captain's two assistants. As Midnight lands, the crooks race a truck onto the field and, as Midnight's plane taxis to a halt, the huge truck smashes into it head on.

Midnight's plane is only slightly damaged in the crash and he leaps out with guns blazing. When the gangsters see that he is still alive, they beat a hasty retreat.

Luckily for Midnight, Edwards gets away by himself. In the meantime, Fury, Shark's daughter, has captured Joyce and driven off with her. Midnight and the police follow in separate cars. Martel takes off in his plane and bombs the police car. Then he bombs the road immediately in front of Midnight. The daring aviator's car careens off the road into a ditch.

Miraculously, Midnight is unhurt. When Fury turns back to see what has happened, Midnight rescues Joyce and captures Shark's daughter. Some time later, Midnight notices one of Shark's men hanging around and loudly announces to his friends that he is taking Fury to the mountain hideout. When Shark gets the report, he flies to the cabin and instructs his men to bail out and surround it. In reality, Midnight has led Shark into a trap and speedily captures all of the gunmen.

After capturing Joyce and her father, the archvillain imprisons his two newly captured prisoners in an underground vault along with Major Steele. Meanwhile he has gained possession of Edward's range finder and busily arranges a method by which to electrocute all of his prisoners before getting away. But Midnight, accompanied by the police, bursts into the house before Shark can escape. During the struggle, Shark accidentally touches a crowbar to some of the wires in the prison cell. The sizzling electricity shoots through his body and the mastermind falls dead. Meanwhile, his gang has been broken up and the vast enemy sabotage ring is successfully smashed by Captain Midnight.

196

Peter Leeds, Walter Sande, Don Terry, Ben Taggert, Anne Nagel, and Claire Dodd watch one of the Scorpion's men escape.

Enemy agent John Litel and a cohort get set to release a torpedo.

Don Winslow of the Navy

15 Episodes
Universal, 1942

Directed by
Ford Beebe
and Ray Taylor

CAST

Don Winslow	Don Terry
Lt. Red Pennington	Walter Sande
Mike Splendor	Wade Boteler
Captain Fairfield	Paul Scott
Menlin	John Litel
Chapman	Peter Leeds
Misty	Anne Nagel
Mercedes	Claire Dodd
Koloki	Frank Lackteen

The unscrupulous Scorpion has a field day against U.S. military forces in the Pacific until Don Winslow is assigned to Navy intelligence. Winslow traces the evil genius to the island of Tongita, the home of a harassed naval installation and a crucial chemical plant.

From his headquarters in an undersea cave, the Scorpion conducts a three ring circus of espionage and intrigue. He tries to steal Navy codes, hijack ships, and create havoc at the chemical plant's reduction chamber.

Winslow tenaciously fights off a seemingly endless stream of Scorpion henchmen and a tribe of easily confused natives. Eventually he succeeds in blowing the whistle on the Scorpion and sealing the lid on his entire operation.

Walter Sande comes to the rescue of Don Terry.

Not much of a ship left, but Don Terry ploughs determinedly on.

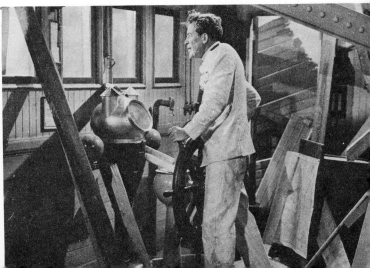

Detectives Kent Taylor and Robert Armstrong question one of Professor Mortis's men.

Gang Busters

13 Episodes
Universal, 1942

Directed by
Ray Taylor
and Noel Smith

CAST

Bill Bannister	Kent Taylor
Vicky Logan	Irene Hervey
Professor Mortis	Ralph Morgan
Tim Nolan	Robert Armstrong
Happy Haskins	Richard Davies
Chief O'Brien	Joseph Crehan
Mayor Hansen	George Watts
Halliger	Ralph Harolde
Wilkinson	John Gallaudet
Barnard	Victor Zimmerman
Mason	George Lewis

Detective Lieutenant Bill Bannister is assigned to run down an unknown gang of terrorists who have spread a net of crime over the city. Aiding him is Detective Tim Nolan; following his investigations closely are Vicki Logan, a news photographer in whom Bill is interested romantically, and her reporter teammate Happy Haskins.

After investigating a rapid sequence of daring crimes, including attempts at his life, Bill finds that the gang's ringleader is a mysterious Professor Mortis. Bill recognizes some of Mortis's men and, by checking police records, discovers the amazing fact that Mortis's gang is made up of known criminals officially listed in police records as dead. Each has become a member of Mortis's "League of Murdered Men" after supposedly having hanged himself while awaiting the death penalty.

Professor Mortis has a pistol planted in Vicki's camera as she goes to cover a new chase of the mob. Seizing an opportunity to get a candid shot of Bill, she focuses on him and presses the shutter release, firing the pistol. Fortunately, the bullet narrowly misses Bill. It now seems clear to Bill and Vicki that there is a traitor in their midst. All signs point to Happy, for only he has had access to Vicki's camera.

Happy is kept under close surveillance and is arrested when he is caught attempting to dynamite police headquarters. In prison, Happy apparently commits suicide and Bill, suspecting that Professor Mortis will try to retrieve Happy's body, takes his place in the coffin. Sure enough, Professor Mortis's men, disguised as morgue attendants, arrive to pick up the corpse and deliver it to their leader's underground hideout.

Once in Mortis's headquarters, Bill learns that Mortis has a death-simulating drug and an antideath treatment that he has used to recruit his gang of criminals. Bill places Mortis under arrest, but the lights are suddenly doused and the professor makes his escape through the subterranean chambers beneath the city's subways. As he makes his way into a subway tunnel, a train roars down the track and crushes Mortis, killing him instantly. Bill, having rounded up the gang, is given a promotion to captain of detectives.

Huntz Hall and Billy Halop collar an enemy agent as Gabriel Dell stands by.

Junior G-men of the Air

13 Episodes
Universal, 1942

Directed by
Ray Taylor
and Lewis D. Collins

CAST

"Ace" Holden	Billy Halop
Eddie Holden	Gene Reynolds
The Baron	Lionel Atwill
Jerry Markham	Frank Albertson
Don Ames	Richard Lane
"Bolts" Larson	Huntz Hall
"Stick" Munsey	Gabriel Dell
"Greaseball" Plunkett	Bernard Punsley
Jack	Frankie Darro
Araka	Turhan Bey
Beal	John Bleifer
Monk	Noel Cravat
Comora	Edward Foster

Ace Holden, Bolts Larson, Stick Munsey, and Greaseball Plunkett work as a wrecking crew for Ace's father, the owner of an auto and airplane junkyard. One day while the youths are fighting with another street gang, several members of a fifth column organization, the "Order of the Black Dragonfly," steal the boy's wrecking truck.

Later, as Ace and the others are working in the junkyard on a plane they have assembled from wreckage parts, the truck is returned by Don Ames, state bureau of investigation official. Ace, who is distrustful of "cops," refuses to give Don a description of the men who stole the truck.

Meanwhile, the Axis agents—Araka, Augar, Beal, Monk, and Comora—report to the Baron, the Japanese leader of the organization, who has his headquarters in a cleverly camouflaged farm several miles from the city.

Don Ames decides to let Jerry Markham, young leader of the Junior G-men try to gain Ace's cooperation. Jerry knows Ace and Ace's brother Eddie through their mutual interest in planes and flying.

Eddie and Ace join with Ames and Jerry's Junior G-men in a campaign to round up the enemy agents.

In their attempt to track down the saboteurs, Ace and his friends drive their truck near the headquarters of the Order of the Black Dragonfly and are spotted by the agents. Instructions are given to Monk, the enemy pilot, to bomb the boy's truck. The boys swerve frantically to avoid the falling bombs and manage to escape destruction.

Working on information provided by Ames, Ace and Bolts trail the saboteurs to an oil field and hide in an ambulance used by the enemy agents for transporting nitroglycerin. As the axis henchmen set about their task of destroying the oil wells, Ace and Bolts try to escape in the ambulance. But they are spotted by Comora, who struggles with them as the ambulance careens crazily through the refinery. Comora succeeds in knocking Ace out but, as the car heads for one of the burning oil wells, he

199

leaps from the vehicle. Bolts manages to pull Ace from the car just before it plunges into the roaring inferno.

Ace and Eddie are captured by the Baron's men and brought to the spy chief's secret farm headquarters, which also serves as the agent's airplane landing field. The boys make a desperate dash for freedom and leap into a nearby plane. During their hurried takeoff, the plane's landing gear hits a fence—the gas line breaks and the plane is set on fire. Out of range of the enemy, the boys parachute to safety and make it back to government headquarters.

Ace leads his friends and a contingent of State Guards back to the enemy's hideout. A gun battle ensues and the government forces break through just as the Baron tries to escape through an underground tunnel. But Ace and Jerry spot the Baron and personally capture him. The boys receive the thanks of the government for bringing the sabotage ring to justice.

King of the Mounties

12 Episodes	Directed by
Republic, 1942	William Witney

CAST

Sergeant King	Allan Lane
Commissioner	Gilbert Emery
Marshal Carleton	Russell Hicks
Carol Brent	Peggy Drake
Professor Brent	George Irving
Admiral Yamata	Abner Biberman
Marshal Von Horst	William Vaughn
Count Baroni	Nestor Paiva
Blake	Bradley Page
Harper	Douglas Dumbrille
Ross	William Blakewell
Pierre	Duncan Renaldo
Collins	Francis Ford
Lewis	Jay Novello
Stark	Anthony Warde
Radio Announcer	Norman Nesbitt
Lane	John Hiestand
Sato	Allen Jung
Jap Bombardier	Paul Fung
Craig	Arvon Dale

Under the supervision of Admiral Yamata, Count Baroni, and Marshal Von Horst, chiefs of the Axis Fifth Column in Canada, that country is bombed mercilessly by a mysterious enemy plane called the Falcon. No one can identify the plane until an American inventor, Professor Brent, and his daughter Carol arrive with a new type of plane detector. Since the detector is a threat to their work in preparing western Canada for an invasion, the enemy agents have Brent kidnapped by Gil Harper, the local quisling. While on patrol, Sergeant King of the Mounties attempts to rescue Brent, but the inventor is killed when a plane in which he is held captive crashes into a riverboat.

Carol determines to carry on her father's work. With King's aid, she prevents the enemy agents from capturing the plane detector. When the enemy agents make a last desperate attack on the cabin in which the plane detector is hidden, Carol destroys the device. But in the process she is captured and taken to the crater of a volcano, where the spy ring makes its headquarters.

King trails Harper to his hideout and, in the ensuing fight, Harper accidentally shoots himself. King takes the Falcon plane to the volcano, rescues Carol, and blows the volcano to bits.

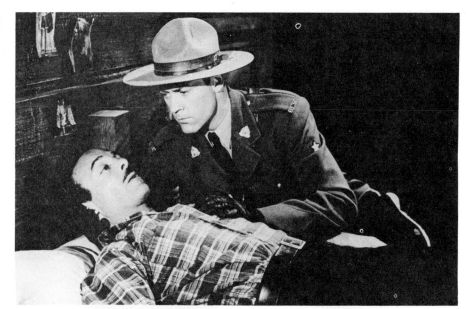

Allan Lane listens intently to a dying Jay Novello.

An Axis agent about to plant a knife in the back of an Indian.

Anthony Warde attempts to polish off Allan Lane.

201

Overland Mail

15 Episodes
Universal, 1942

Directed by
Ford Beebe
and John Rawlins

CAST

Jim Lane	Lon Chaney, Jr.
Barbara Gilbert	Helen Parrish
Sierra Pete	Noah Beery, Jr.
Buckskin Billy Burke	Don Terry
Young Bill Cody	Bob Baker
Frank Chadwick	Noah Beery
Tom Gilbert	Tom Chatterton
Puma	Charles Stevens
Charles Darson	Robert Barron
Sam Gregg	Harry Cording

Jim Lane, frontiersman, and his sidekick Sierra Pete are detailed to investigate a breakdown of U.S. Mail delivery, in the La Paz country. The mail is carried by the Overland Company operated by Tom Gilbert. Stages are being looted, equipment destroyed, and pony express riders ambushed in attacks by Indians and renegades.

On their way to La Paz, Jim and Sierra rescue Gilbert's daughter Barbara and undercover renegade chief Chadwick from a holdup. Jim and Sierra find their pal Buckskin Bill, a scout working with Gregg and Darson, Chadwick's henchmen. Bill immediately joins up with Jim and the trio discover that the attacks are led by gunmen disguised as Indians.

In tracking down the renegades the friends learn that Chadwick is causing the trouble because he wants to take over the mail delivery franchise owned by Barbara's father.

His gang overpowered, Chadwick is killed trying to make his getaway. Jim becomes manager of operations for the Overland Company. Sierra and Bill enlist as his aides, and Barbara looks forward to becoming Mrs. Jim Lane.

Lon Chaney, Jr., and Noah Beery, Jr., are overpowered by renegades.

Forbes Murray, Kay Aldridge William Benedict, and Clayton Moore attend to an ailing Robert Strange.

✗ **Perils of Nyoka**

15 Episodes
Republic, 1942

Directed by
William Witney

CAST

Nyoka	Kay Aldridge
Larry	Clayton Moore
Red	William Benedict
Vultura	Lorna Gray
Cassib	Charles Middleton
Torrini	Tristram Coffin
Professor Campbell	Forbes Murray
Professor Gordon	Robert Strange
John Spencer	George Pembroke
Maghreb	George Renavent
Lhoba	John Davidson
Batan	George Lewis
Ahmed	Ken Terrell
Ben Ali	John Bagni
Abou	Kenneth Duncan
Bedouin	Arvon Dale

Professor Campbell, an archaeologist, and his assistant Dr. Larry Grayson discover an ancient papyrus giving instructions for finding the long-lost Tablets of Hippocrates, which record the medical knowledge of the ancient Greeks. They lead an expedition to the Arabian Desert to find Nyoka Gordon, the only person capable of deciphering it.

Nyoka is hunting for her lost father, Henry Gordon, and living with a tribe of Bedouins. But Campbell's plans become known to Vultura, the exotic ruler of a band of vicious Arabs. Vultura, determined to obtain the tablets and the treasure hidden with them, steals the papyrus before Nyoka joins the expedition. Nyoka and Larry break into Vultura's temple, but are attacked by Vultura's gorilla Satan. Satan tears out the supporting pillars of the temple and brings the

Kay Aldridge and Clayton Moore face the savage gorilla Satan.

Vultura's pet, Satan, examines a former victim.

stone roof crashing down—Larry and Nyoka manage a split-second escape through the broken walls.

Vultura realizes that even though she has the papyrus, it can be translated only by Nyoka, and plots to seize the girl. Nyoka is lured into a trap set by Cassib, a follower of Vultura, and is captured after a desperate chase. Brought be-fore Vultura at Cassib's camp, she is tortured until she agrees to make the translation. Larry, who has been trailing her, attacks the camp and, in the confusion which follows, Nyoka gets the papyrus and tries to escape in Vultura's chariot.

Nyoka and Larry alternately flee from and pursue the avaricious Vultura, and finally bring her to justice.

Perils of the Royal Mounted

15 Episodes
Columbia, 1942

Directed by
James W. Horne

CAST

Sergeant MacLane	Robert Stevens
Ransome	Kenneth MacDonald
Winton	Herbert Rawlinson
Diana	Nell O'Day
Blake	John Elliott
Black Bear	Nick Thompson
Flying Cloud	Art Miles
Brady	Richard Fiske
Little Wolf	Richard Vallin
Hinsdale	Forrest Taylor
Collins	Kermit Maynard
Gaspard	George Chesebro
Baptiste	Jack Ingram

The Sitkawan trading post learns that In-dians have massacred settlers aboard a wagon train. When Sergeant MacLane of the Royal Canadian Mounted Police investigates, he finds

204

proof that the attackers were really renegade white men led by Mort Ransome. Ransome has conspired with Black Bear, medicine man of a friendly Indian tribe, and the Indian follows orders by persuading a number of rebellious braves to take the warpath.

The renegade uses every trick imaginable to kill Mounties MacLane and Blake, but they survive savage Indian attacks, a death-defying leap off a burning bridge, a terrific dynamite blast in a deserted mine shaft and a raging forest fire. In a final Indian attack, Black Bear is killed and MacLane follows one of Ransome's men who is making a getaway. The Mountie trails him to the outlaw's hideout located behind a waterfall. In the fight that follows Ransome is killed and the entire gang rounded up.

Mounties Robert Stevens and John Elliott return outlaw fire.

Anne Nagel about to clobber Paul Kelly.

The Secret Code

15 Episodes	Directed by
Columbia, 1942	Spencer G. Bennet

CAST

Dan Barton	Paul Kelly
Jean Ashley	Anne Nagel
Pat	Clancy Cooper
Hogan	Alex Callam
Jensen	Trevor Bardette
Thyssen	Robert O. Davis
Feldon	Gregory Gay
Metzger	Louis Donath
Quito	Beal Wong
Stahl	Lester Dorr
Linda	Jacqueline Dalya

Assigned to smash an enemy sabotage ring, Police Lieutenant Dan Barton arranges to have himself thrown off the force in disgrace. When he assaults a high government official while trying to "steal" a secret synthetic rubber formula, the saboteurs invite him to join them. Dan learns they have been ordered to obtain the formula by a secret code. Disguised in a Black Commando suit, Dan plays a grim game of life and death, becoming the hunted prey of the police and the federal government as a spy and, as the Black Commando, hunted and hunter of the sabotage ring. Finally, with the aid of lovely Jean Ashley, a reporter, and Pat Flannagan, his patrolman partner, Barton manages to round up the ring, locate the secret code, and expose the respected Jensen as the mastermind behind the enemy agents.

Marguerite Chapman and Kane Richmond face the Mask.

Spy Smasher

12 Episodes	Directed by
Republic, 1942	William Witney

CAST

Spy Smasher	Kane Richmond
Admiral Corby	Sam Flint
Eve Corby	Marguerite Chapman
The Mask	Hans Schumm
Drake	Tristram Coffin
Durand	Frank Corsaro
Captain Gerhardt	Hans Von Morhart
The Governor	Georges Renavent
Colonel Von Kohr	Robert O. Davis
Lazar	Henry Zynda
Lawlor	Paul Bryar
Crane	Tom London
Hayes	Richard Bond
Dr. Hauser	Crane Whitley
Steve	John James

Spy Smasher, American free-lance agent in occupied France, is captured by the Germans while trying to get information about the Mask, head of the German spy ring in America, and sentenced to death before a firing squad. But Pierre Durand, a Free Frenchman, saves him and helps him escape to America.

In America, he contacts his twin brother Jack and enlists his aid. The brothers learn that the Mask is planning an attack on Admiral

Kane Richmond and Marguerite Chapman kneel over the body of Spy Smasher's brother.

Corby, head of the United States Foreign Service and father of Jack's fiancée, Eve. While protecting the admiral, they uncover a counterfeiting plot hatched by the Mask. Tracing the counterfeiters to an underground hideout, Spy Smasher is threatened with sudden death from a flood of burning oil which the spies have released into a conduit. He leaps on a handcar and tries to outrun the torrent. Just before the flames reach him, Spy Smasher hurls a hand grenade which caves in the conduit and snuffs out the fire.

Admiral Corby and Jack examine the counterfeit money and learn that it is being made on the French island of Martinidad, just off the coast of the United States. Spy Smasher, acting on his own, flies to this island where he has arranged to meet Durand. They report their suspicions to the island's administrator, who voices disbelief at the possibility of Nazi operations on his island. When Spy Smasher and Durand insist and cite evidence, the administrator presses a button and sends the two allies falling through a trapdoor into a subterranean chamber. The administrator, really a Nazi agent, soon appears on a balcony high above the two friends and informs them that they are doomed. But while he is speaking, Spy Smasher reaches for a nearby rope and, using it as a whip, winds it around the Nazi's wrist and pulls him from the balcony. Forcing the agent to reveal the location of the counterfeit printing facilities, Spy Smasher and Durand attack the Nazi base and destroy it.

After returning to the United States and working with Jack and Admiral Corby, Spy Smasher is successful in thwarting the Mask's attempts to steal a new bombsight and a weapon capable of melting plane engines while in flight. But, despite these setbacks, the Mask remains an elusive and dangerous foe. While Eve is working one evening, an agent of the Mask enters and kidnaps her. Spy Smasher and Jack arrive shortly after, in time to receive a phone call from the Mask offering to return Eve if the Spy Smasher will give himself up to the spies, the exchange to take place at a building located nearby.

Certain it's a trap, Jack volunteers to go as Spy Smasher, but Allan insists it's his job. However, Jack is determined not to let Allan be sacrificed: he knocks Allan out, dons a Spy Smasher outfit, and leaves to confront the spies. Allan recovers a few minutes later and sets out after his brother. Jack reaches the building, busts in on the Nazis and manages to free Eve. But he himself is pursued to the roof of the building and is shot; he plummets ten stories to the pavement.

Allan arrives, finds his dead brother and, vowing revenge, follows a fleeing Nazi to the waterfront. There he boards a motorboat in order to meet the Mask, who is aboard a submarine just off the coast. Spy Smasher leaps onto the motorboat and battles with the Nazi as the U-boat surfaces. Spy Smasher knocks the Nazi unconscious and, steering the small boat right at the submarine, jumps from the craft as it rams into the U-boat, capsizing it and sending the Mask and his crew to a well-deserved, watery death.

Hans Schumm watches as the U-boat captain observes coastline defense plants.

The Valley of Vanishing Men

15 Episodes
Columbia, 1942

Directed by
Spencer G. Bennet

CAST

Bill	Bill Elliott
Missouri	Slim Summerville
Consuelo	Carmen Morales
Kincaid	Kenneth MacDonald
Butler	Jack Ingram
Taggert	George Chesebro
Mullins	John Shay
Slater	Tom London
Engler	Arno Frey
Jose	Julian Rivero
Luke	Roy Barcroft

Bill Tolliver and Missouri Benson ride into the Territory of New Mexico to search for Bill's father, who disappeared while prospecting. In the course of their travels, they discover that a ruthless outlaw named Kincaid has joined forces with Carl Engler, a renegade European general. Kincaid controls a giant gold mine and uses captured Mexican patriots to work as slaves on his property. Bill and Missouri become friendly with Consuelo Ramirez, an attractive government agent, and the trio eventually learn that Bill's father is being forced to work as a slave in the mine.

After freeing his father, Bill sets out to smash both the slave mine and Engler's attempts to defeat Benito Juarez, the legal president of Mexico. He convinces U.S. Army authorities that Engler actually is aiding a European government in its attempt to stir up trouble on this continent, and they agree to aid him. The army forces then attack Engler's men at the same time as Bill and the Army of Juarez attack Kincaid's gang. After a furious fight to the finish, the battlers for liberty are completely victorious and Bill quietly rides off with his bride-to-be, Consuelo.

I. Stanford Jolley takes to the trail with Bill Elliott.

1943

Adventures of the Flying Cadets

13 Episodes
Universal, 1943

Directed by
Ray Taylor
and Lewis D. Collins

CAST

Danny Collins	Johnny Downs
Jinx Roberts	Bobby Jordan
Scrapper Mackay	Ward Wood
Zombie Parker	Billy Benedict
Karl Von Heiger	Eduardo Cianelli
Captain Ralph	
Carson	Regis Toomey
Arthur Galt	Robert Armstrong
Professor Mason	Selmer Jackson
Andre Mason	Jennifer Holt

Flying students Danny Collins, Jinx Roberts, Scrapper Mackay, and Zombie Parker are suspected of a series of murders perpetrated by the mysterious Black Hangman. The Hangman, pretending to be a Nazi agent, is actually an engineer named Arthur Galt, who has disposed of several friends who accompanied him on an expedition which successfully located lost helium deposits in Africa. To keep the helium a secret, Galt has also imprisoned the remaining members of the expedition, Professor Mason and Mason's daughter Andre.

Galt plots to sell the helium to Germany through a Gestapo ring headed by Karl Von Heiger. Meanwhile, the four air cadets, thinking that Galt is their friend, fly with him to Africa, to clear their own names of the murder charges. But when Galt leads them into a Nazi trap and they are imprisoned with Andre, they discover his true intentions. While captured, Danny manages to make his way to a radio and notifies Allied headquarters of the Nazi's location. Allied planes are sent to bomb the area and, as the bombs begin to fall, the friends make good their escape—all except Danny and Jinx, who fall through a trapdoor and find themselves once again Galt's prisoners.

When Galt proposes that the boys fly helium to Nazi bases or face instant death, the boys agree, planning to fly instead to Allied headquarters. While in flight, however, the plane goes into a tailspin and Danny is just barely able to land. Upon landing, Danny overpowers Galt and takes him to Allied headquarters, but Galt convinces the authorities that he has merely been a victim of Nazi activities. Allowed to go free, Galt, observed by the boys, makes the mistake of trying to contact enemy agents and is finally brought back to the authorities with unarguable evidence against him.

Completely vindicated, the cadets receive their Air Force wings and prepare to join the Allied pilots at the front.

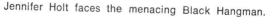
Jennifer Holt faces the menacing Black Hangman.

210

A villainous quartet plot their next move: William Haade, George Lewis, Robert Frazer, and Ted Adams.

Allan Lane aids a wounded Eddie Acuff.

William Haade is down but not out, as Allan Lane is about to get clobbered by George Lewis.

G-men vs. the Black Dragon

15 Episodes	Directed by
Republic, 1943	William Witney

CAST

Rex	Rod Cameron
Chang	Roland Got
Vivian	Constance Worth
Haruchi	Nino Pipitone
Ranga	Noel Cravat
Lugo	George J. Lewis
Marie	Maxine Doyle
Muller	Donald Kirke
Inspector	Ivan Miller
Williams	Walter Fenner
Nicholson	C. Montague Shaw
Tony	Harry Burns
Kennedy	Forbes Murray
Caldwell	Hooper Atchley
Captain Gorman	Robert Homans
Fugi	Allen Jung

During World War II, Vivian Marsh, British secret agent, joins American Rex Bennett, special investigator, and Chang of the Chinese secret service, to search out and destroy the nefarious Black Dragon Society, led by Haruchi, who has been smuggled into the United States from Tokyo.

When Haruchi and his henchmen successfully stage a series of ship sinkings by secretly putting an incendiary ingredient into the ship's paint, the G-men realize the power and ingenuity of their opponent.

Chang pretends to be a Japanese prisoner recently escaped from Manzanar and infiltrates the Black Dragon Society, enabling him and his friends to gain possession of an enemy submarine locator. They take it to Professor Nicholson, who describes it as the most powerful locator he has ever seen; he then uses it to detect and destroy an enemy submarine laying along the coastline.

Haruchi sends some of his men to recover the locator at any cost, but Chang and Rex destroy the device before it can be taken from them. However, Black Dragon agents, hearing that Professor Nicholson is able to reproduce the locator, kidnap him and torture him into revealing the whereabouts of his blueprints. Attempting to escape, Nicholson is shot down.

While attempting to steal the blueprints, Lugo, one of Haruchi's men, is captured by Vivian and Chang who arrange to fly him to Washington for questioning. Haruchi secretly disposes of the plane's pilot and substitutes his own, who frees Lugo and engages Rex in a fistfight midair. Lugo knocks Rex out and parachutes from the plane, but Rex recovers and parachutes to safety just before the plane crashes.

Haruchi receives a report that American Representative James Kennedy is flying to the Coast with valuable television camera plans for a conference with the Chinese envoy Wong Kei. Haruchi kills Wong Kei, disguises himself as the envoy and meets Kennedy, who is guarded by Rex and Chang. As soon as Kennedy shows the plans, which are photographed on microfilm, Haruchi, as Wong Kei, gives the men a drugged drink, attaches the plans to a raven's leg, and releases the bird through a window. He then takes a suspended-animation drug and collapses. The other men come to, but cannot revive the bogus Wong Kei, who is pronounced dead and taken away in an ambulance driven by his own men. Rex finds the real Wong Kei murdered and pursues Haruchi, but to no avail. With incredible powers of observation, he detects the raven bearing the plans to a remote point, and retrieves them. When the raven arrives at headquarters minus the plans, Lugo and Ranga are sent to investigate. Rex is overtaken at a dock and knocked unconscious by a grappling hook thrown by Ranga. He apparently lies helpless in the bottom of a boat which is swept over the spillway of a dam and splintered on the rocks below.

Rex recovers and jumps from the boat before it goes over the falls, but Lugo and Ranga believe he was carried over with the plans of the television camera still in his pocket. Rex then arranges for a newspaper story to be printed saying he was picked up unconscious below the falls and taken to a certain hospital. Just as Rex expected, Lugo and Ranga go to Rex's room in the hospital and take the cylinder which they believe contains the plans. In the fistfight that follows, Rex is knocked unconscious and taken along as hostage for the spies' escape. Vivian and Chang trail Rex and his captors and, in the ensuing fight, Ranga escapes in a truck. By running downslope, Rex is able to intercept the paint truck Ranga is driving and hop onto the rear. Ranga drives directly to Black Dragon headquarters; Chang and Vivian

trail him by following paint which has leaked on the roadway from his truck. Rex confronts the Japanese agents but is knocked unconscious. He is about to be beheaded by Haruchi when Chang and Vivian arrive. Haruchi escapes in an explosive-laden speedboat and heads for an offshore Japanese submarine. Rex follows in another boat, leaps onto Haruchi's boat, and struggles with him. He knocks Haruchi overboard just as the submarine surfaces, dead ahead. Rex jumps overboard as the explosive-loaded boat hits the submarine; both are blown up. With Haruchi dead, the Black Dragon menace is ended.

Rod Cameron boards the enemy submarine.

Black Dragon agents George J. Lewis, Nino Pipitone, and Noel Cravat listen as British agent Constance Worth tries to convince them that she can be trusted.

George J. Lewis and Noel Cravat smuggling in explosives from a Black Dragon submarine.

217

The Masked Marvel

12 Episodes   Directed by
Republic, 1943   Spencer Bennet

CAST

Crane	William Forrest
Alice Hamilton	Louise Currie
Sakima	Johnny Arthur
Jim Arnold	Rod Bacon
Frank Jeffers	Richard Clarke
Mace	Anthony Warde
Bob Barton	David Bacon
Terry Morton	Bill Healy
Warren Hamilton	Howard Hickman
Officer	Kenneth Harlan
Matthews	Thomas Louden
Meggs	Eddie Parker
Spike	Duke Green
Kline	Dale Van Sickel
Newscaster	Wendell Niles
Reporter	Lester Dorr

Warren Hamilton and Martin Crane, chief executives of the World-Wide Insurance Company, enlist the aid of the Masked Marvel to ferret out Sakima, a former Japanese envoy, whom they suspect is responsible for extensive sabotage of war industries. Crane is secretly in league with Sakima and together they arrange for Hamilton's murder. The murdered man's daughter Alice joins a stranger called the Masked Marvel who comes to her aid and leads a campaign to expose and apprehend Sakima. The Masked Marvel is one of four insurance company special agents—Bob Barton, Frank Jeffers, Terry Morton, and Jim Arnold. He hides his identity beneath a black mask, and only Alice knows that he is one of the four investigators.

Sakima lays plans to intercept a valuable shipment of industrial diamonds, loss of which will seriously cripple defense plants. In spite of the heroic opposition put up by the Masked Marvel and his men, Sakima gets the diamonds; but, finding himself unable to smuggle them out of the country, he attempts to use them as a trap to get the Marvel into his power. The Marvel is momentarily overpowered, but he manages to escape.

Learning that Sakima's men plan to steal the plans of the city drainage system so that they can plant a bomb in the storm drain under an aircraft plant, the Masked Marvel and his men hasten to the city engineer's office and overpower Sakima's henchman Mace while he is in the act of stealing the plans. The bomb almost explodes, but the boys escape in the nick of time.

In an attempt to learn how secret information regarding truck shipments leaks out, Alice disguises herself and takes a job as a waitress at the Seaside Cafe, a truck drivers' hangout. She learns of the enemy's plan to plant a bomb in a truck which is to be delivered aboard a ship. When she phones this information to the Marvel, she is overheard, captured, and enclosed in a wooden crate which is loaded on the truck with the bomb. But the Marvel arrives in time to rescue her.

The Masked Marvel finally confronts Sakima in his lair and a gun battle ensues. Sakima uses a large desk for cover; the Marvel hides behind a heavily upholstered chair. After the Masked Marvel fires off six shots, Sakima, realizing that the Masked Marvel's gun is empty, leaves his hiding place and approaches him. Gloating over his apparent victory, Sakima prepares to dispose of his enemy. But, suddenly, a shot rings out and Sakima slumps to the floor, wounded. The Masked Marvel emerges from his hiding place, his pistol, which he had *reloaded,* still smoking in his hand.

While the Masked Marvel is phoning for an ambulance, the injured Sakima sets a timing device to blow up his hideout along with himself and the Masked Marvel. At the last moment, however, the Masked Marvel notices this and leaps out of a window to safety, just as Sakima's hideout explodes.

The Marvel unmasks and reveals himself to be Bob Barton, but refuses any newspaper publicity, preferring to keep his identity secret so that he may resume the role again when needed.

Evil William Forrest signals an all-clear to accomplice Anthony Warde.

The Masked Marvel and Louise Currie rescue a proposed victim of Sakima.

The Phantom

15 Episodes   Directed by
Columbia, 1943   B. Reeves Eason

CAST

Godfrey Prescott ⎫	
The Phantom ⎭	Tom Tyler
Dr. Bremmer	Kenneth MacDonald
Professor Davidson	Frank Shannon
Diana	Jeanne Bates
Devil	Ace, the Wonder Dog
Byron Andrews	Guy Kingsford
Singapore Smith	Joe Devlin
Rusty	Ernie Adams
Moku	John S. Bagni

Professor Davidson and his daughter Diana search Africa for the Lost City of Zoloz, reputed to be the source of a vast hidden treasure. Their efforts are complicated by Singapore Smith, a local crook, who wants the treasure for himself. Villainy comes from another source as well. Dr. Bremmer, an international crook, plans to destroy the peace in which the native tribes have been living for many years and build a secret air base at Zoloz.

Fortunately, the Phantom, who is also Diana's fiancé, is more than a match for the two villains. He exercises considerable influence over the natives and possesses superhuman strength. The Phantom circumvents each enemy move, escaping from one death trap after another: avalanches, poison gas, flaming pyres, and explosions fail to fluster his dauntless spirit. With the help of his four-footed pal Devil, he finally overpowers all the enemy factions, convinces the natives to kill Dr. Bremmer, and brings peace to the jungle once again.

Frank Shannon and Jeanne Bates watch as natives lay Kenneth MacDonald at the feet of Tom Tyler.

Secret Service in Darkest Africa

15 Episodes   Directed by
Republic, 1943   Spencer Bennet

CAST

Rex Bennett	Rod Cameron
Janet Blake	Joan Marsh
Pierre LaSalle	Duncan Renaldo
Sultan Abou Ben Ali ⟩	
Baron Von Rommler ⟩	Lionel Royce
Ernst Muller	Kurt Kreuger
Wolfe	Frederic Brunn
Luger	Sigurd Tor
Armand	George Renavent
Hauptmann	Kurt Katch
Riverboat Captain	Ralf Harolde
Captain Beschert	William Vaughn
Commandant	William Yetter
First Officer	Hans Von Morhart
Colonel Von Raeder	Erwin Goldi
Sir James Langley	Frederick Worlock

Rex Bennett, American undercover agent posing as a member of the Gestapo in Berlin, learns of the Nazis' plan to swing the African Arabs to the Axis cause, using as persuasion the Dagger of Solomon and a forged Scroll purporting to be the words of an ancient Moslem leader.

Outwitting the Gestapo, Rex escapes with these symbols and joins forces in Casablanca with Janet Blake, an American correspondent working secretly as a United Nations agent, and Pierre LaSalle, a French officer. Rex agrees to turn over the Dagger and Scroll to the great

Arab leader, Sultan Abou Ben Ali, ignorant of the fact that the real sultan has been kidnapped and a Nazi officer, Baron Siegfried Von Rommler, has assumed his identity. Von Rommler arranges for the Dagger and Scroll to be "stolen" and placed aboard a munitions-laden riverboat.

Rex follows and regains the Dagger and Scroll, but a Nazi hurls a keg of explosives into the boat's boiler and it is blown up. Rex returns the Dagger and forged Scroll to Von Rommler, believing him to be the sultan. Rex is captured and, under threat of torture, pretends to give his captors the address of United Nations secret agents in Berlin.

Rex escapes and reports back to headquarters to continue in his efforts to gain the allegiance of the Arabs to the Allied cause. But because he still does not realize that Sultan Ben Ali is in reality Von Rommler, each of his plans meets Nazi interference.

Von Rommler decides to kill the real sultan, burn down his home, and move on, in order to obtain the secret war plans of the United Nations. The underling assigned to this task is not very competent, however, and the real sultan is discovered by Rex and Pierre, alive, though seriously injured. He explains Von Rommler's masquerade and reveals the Nazi's mission to steal the war plans from the headquarters of Sir James Langley.

Rex hurries to the scene and arrives just as Sir James is being bound and gagged. He engages Von Rommler in a sword fight, vanquishes him, and puts to an end the Nazi spy complex in North Africa.

Duncan Renaldo reports in to Lionel Royce as Rod Cameron and John Davidson observe.

1944

Black Arrow

15 Episodes   Directed by
Columbia, 1944   B. Reeves Eason

CAST

Black Arrow   Robert Scott
Mary   Adele Jergens
Jake Jackson   Kenneth MacDonald
Buck Sherman   Robert Williams
Tom Whitney   Charles Middleton
Pancho   Martin Garralaga
Snake-That-Walks   George J. Lewis

Carpetbaggers Jake Jackson and Buck Sherman arrive in Big Mesa in search of gold. Refused permission by Tom Whitney, the Indian agent, to enter the Navajo reservation, they enter illegally. Meanwhile, Black Arrow, son of Aranho the Navajo chief, wins a place on the Council of Elders, nosing out Snake-That-Walks. Jackson and Sherman are intercepted by Aranho and Running Water, both of whom they shoot fatally. Before dying, however, Aranho tells Whitney that his son, believed killed years before in an Indian raid, is alive. Under Indian law, the white man's chief must also be killed in retribution. When Black Arrow refuses to kill Whitney, he is driven off the reservation, narrowly escaping death in a stampede.

On Big Mesa, Black Arrow finds his friends Pancho, Mary, and Whitney are eager to prevent trouble with the Indians by helping discover who killed Aranho.

Snake-That-Walks captures Sherman but agrees to free him if he can capture Black Arrow. Jackson and Sherman attempt to do this, but in the attempt, Sherman is captured by Black Arrow. Black Arrow turns Sherman over to the Navajos. Under threat of torture, he is about to name Aranho's murderer when he is shot by Wade.

Wade is hit by a shot by Snake-That-Walks, who in turn is slain by one of his own braves. Wade crawls to Pancho's ranch and dies after first writing an accusatory note. Jackson finds the note and changes it so that it accuses Black Arrow of Sherman's murder. At Big Mesa, Jackson incites the populace to "get" Black Arrow. He is tried and sentenced to death. Mary finds the rest of the note, exonerating Black Arrow.

Realizing that the game is up, Jackson prepares to leave Big Mesa. But before leaving, Jackson decides to try once more for the Zuñi treasure. Meanwhile, Black Arrow tells Whitney that Jackson is Aranho's murderer. They catch up with Jackson at the Zuñi pueblo and he is killed when a ladder topples under his weight during the chase. The Navajos assemble to name Black Arrow as their new chief but it is disclosed that he is, in reality, Whitney's long-lost son.

Captain America

15 Episodes
Republic, 1944

Directed by
John English
and Elmer Clifton

CAST

Captain America)	
Grant Gardner }	Dick Purcell
Gail Richards	Lorna Gray
Dr. Maldor	Lionel Atwill
Commissioner Dryden	Charles Trowbridge
Mayor Randolph	Russell Hicks
Matson	George J. Lewis
Gruber	John Davidson
Newscaster	Norman Nesbitt
Professor Lyman	Frank Reicher
Professor Dodge	Hugh Sothern
Henley	Tom Chatterton
Dr. Clinton Lyman	Robert Frazer
Hillman	John Hamilton
Dirk	Crane Whitley
Dr. Baracs	Edward Keane
Monk	John Bagni
Simms	Jay Novello

Dr. Maldor, the curator of the Drummond Museum, feels that he has been cheated out of his share of the wealth and fame accruing from an archaeological expedition he headed. For revenge, he is systematically murdering every member of the expedition, one by one, and securing their wealth and scientific treasures for himself. Calling himself "The Scarab," he eliminates his enemies by means of a poison known as "The Purple Death." From his most recent victim he has secured plans for a dynamic vibrator, a machine that harnesses light and sound waves and converts them into a weapon of terrific destructive power. But Captain America (who is in reality District Attorney Grant Gardner) intervenes and, with the aid of his assistant Gail Richards, robs Maldor and his henchman Matson of their Purple Death weapon.

Maldor then concentrates on eliminating Captain America with his new dynamic vibrator.

Grant learns that Dr. Lyman, brother of the murdered professor, has invited all the members of the Mayan expedition to view a demonstration of his new invention, a machine that will bring a dead animal back to life. Maldor, who has been invited to the party, arranges to have two of his men impersonate the Humane Society attendants who bring out the body of a dog for the experiment. Although Grant manages to kill one of the imposters, the other gets away with the Life-Restoring Machine.

Grant learns that Hillman, another member of the Mayan expedition, has just discovered a plaque hidden in a clay tile which, when deciphered, proves to be half of a map that locates a fabulous Mayan treasure. Maldor has the other half in his museum and is eager to retrieve the missing half. He goes to Grant's office, ostensibly to report the "theft" of half the plaque, and secretly hides a dictograph. Later, Kane, one of his men, breaks into the office, listens to the dictograph, and discovers where Grant has taken Hillman for safe keeping. Matson and Gordon, disguised as waiters, gain entrance to Hillman's apartment and force him to turn over his half of the map.

Maldor, now in possession of both sections of the map, tortures Hillman, attempting to force him to decipher the ancient symbols on the map. Grant, who has learned of the location of the farmhouse, is hot in pursuit. But Matson has been so brutal with Hillman that he and Maldor are forced to go to town to get a doctor. Before they leave, however, Maldor is warned that Grant is on his way to rescue Hillman. Knowing that Hillman can identify him as the Scarab, Maldor sets off with Matson in a plane to bomb the farmhouse. Captain America arrives, discovers Hillman, and carries him from the house. Maldor, frantic to keep Hillman from revealing his true identity, sends Matson to seize Gail and bring her to his office. Gail tells Matson that a famous brain surgeon is being sent direct to the hospital where Hillman is secreted, know-

225

ing that the Scarab will send one of his men there, disguised as the doctor. Grant immediately gives orders for the arrest of the "doctor" as soon as he arrives at the hospital. Grant knows Maldor is the Scarab because the name Gail fabricated for the phony doctor—Rodlam Baracs—is Maldor Scarab spelled backward. Maldor is warned of the danger and starts to collect his valuables for a quick getaway, while his assistant puts Gail in a glass case and starts to connect it to a supply of gas which will turn her into a mummy. Captain America arrives in the nick of time to save Gail, and Maldor and Matson die in the electric chair.

George J. Lewis listens attentively to his cohort Tom Steele as they seek to empty a safe.

The Desert Hawk

15 Episodes	Directed by
Columbia, 1944	B. Reeves Eason

CAST

The Hawk } Hassan }	—Gilbert Roland
Princess Azala	Mona Maris
Omar	Ben Welden
Akbar	Kenneth MacDonald
Faud	Frank Lackteen
Saladin	I. Stanford Jolley
Koda Bey	Charles Middleton
Grey Wizard	Egan Brecher

Evil Hassan slips back into his native land of Ahad and plots to overthrow his twin brother Kasim, who has just been crowned caliph. Enlisting the aid of Faud, the chief chamberlain, Hassan and several of his henchmen steal into the royal palace and knock the young caliph

Gilbert Roland is up against the wall as he holds off two assailants.

226

unconscious. Then, while Faud and Hassan remain in the palace, two of their hirelings carry their victim to a lonely part of town, planning to murder him. Before they can do him in, however, he regains consciousness and, after a furious fight, succeeds in breaking away, but not before he is seriously wounded. Several weeks later, Kasim, who has been nursed back to health by Omar, a beggar, goes to the public square and denounces his brother Hassan as an imposter. But no one believes him, and the authorities chase him from the scene.

In an old storeroom, Kasim finds and dons a coat of mail with a great hawk emblazoned across the chest. He then assumes the identity of the Desert Hawk in order to fight his way back to his rightful place on the throne. However, further complications arise when the emir of the neighboring land of Talez brings his gorgeous daughter Azala to marry Kasim. She, of course, does not realize that the man who welcomes her to the palace is an imposter. However, the Hawk, in spite of the fact that he cannot prove to her that he is not an outlaw, wins her confidence.

Aided by Azala, Kasim succeeds in foiling Hassan's attempts to victimize the people while gathering evidence that exposes the identity of the false caliph.

The Great Alaskan Mystery

13 Episodes
Universal, 1944

Directed by
Ray Taylor
and Lewis D. Collins

CAST

Jim Hudson	Milburn Stone
Ruth Miller	Marjorie Weaver
Bosun	Edgar Kennedy
Herman Brock	Samuel S. Hinds
Dr. Hauss	Martin Kosleck
Dr. Miller	Ralph Morgan
Bill Hudson	Joseph Crehan
"Grit" Hartman	Fuzzy Knight
Captain Greeder	Harry Cording
Brandon	Anthony Warde

Dr. Miller, an American scientist, his daughter, Ruth, Jim Hudson, and Bosun go to Alaska in hopes that the ore in an old mine found by Jim's father Bill Hudson will supply the element necessary to make Miller's invention the Pera-

Milburn Stone, Ralph Morgan, and Marjorie Weaver behind the deadly Peratron.

.ron a successful defense weapon. Accompanying them is Miller's assistant, Dr. Hauss who is actually in league with a ring of fascists headed by Captain Greeder and Brock, seemingly a responsible businessman.

After surviving a shipwreck and a flaming plane crash, the party reaches the mine. There, Jim, Ruth, and Bosun narrowly escape death in a series of "accidents" engineered by Brock's gang which is led by Brandon. Brandon makes repeated attempts to steal the Peratron. During one such attempt Greeder is killed by the rays of the deadly machine used by Grit, an aide of Miller's. Frustrated by his failure to wipe out the Americans, Brock orders Brandon to attack the Hudson mine. Hauss shows his hand, slugs Miller, and escapes with the Peratron. In the melee, Brandon is shot down by Bill Hudson.

Jim, Ruth, and Bosun trail Hauss to Brock's office where Brock, to protect himself, accuses Hauss of stealing Miller's invention. Hauss retaliates by shooting Brock and in turn is arrested. With the entire subversive band either dead or in custody, Ruth and Jim face a happier future together.

Haunted Harbor

15 Episodes
Republic, 1944

Directed by
Spencer Bennet
and Wallace Grissell

CAST

Jim Marsden	Kane Richmond
Patricia Harding	Kay Aldridge
Kane	Roy Barcroft
Yank	Clancy Cooper
Tommy	Marshall J. Reed
Galbraith	Oscar O'Shea
Dr. Harding	Forrest Taylor
Lawson	Hal Taliaferro
Vorhees	Edward Keane
Dranga	George J. Lewis
Gregg	Kenne Duncan
Snell	Bud Geary
Port Captain	Robert Homans
Neville	Duke Green
Duff	Dale Van Sickel
Mead	Tom Steele
Teamil	Rico de Montez

Jim Marsden, owner of the schooner *Dolphin,* reported lost at sea with a million in gold bullion aboard, is arrested for the murder of an island banker, Vorhees. Vorhees was, in reality, the victim of his partner Kane, alias Carter, with whom Vorhees was in a criminal, secret enterprise. Vorhees's dying words are "Carter—Haunted Harbor." Convicted of the crime, Marsden escapes from prison with the aid of sailor friends, Yank and Tommy, in a boat furnished by another friend, Galbraith. In order to track down the real murderer, Marsden plans to operate from Galbraith's trading post and investigate suspicious native stories of sea monsters in a local harbor. At sea, the trio sight a sloop in distress and rescue Dr. Harding and his daughter Patricia.

Jim learns that the doctor and Patricia travel from island to island treating ill natives. Jim takes them to Galbraith's trading post where they meet the man in charge Dranga, who is supposed to operate a nearby gold mine and is secretly a henchman of Kane's. In reality, Kane is in possession of the gold bullion stolen from Marsden's schooner and keeps it hidden in the gold mine. Dranga warns Kane of Jim's arrival. In an effort to learn why the natives fear Haunted Harbor, Patricia arranges a meeting between Kassim, son of a chieftain, and Jim. Kane, told of the planned meeting by Dranga, sends two men, Gregg and Snell, to ambush and kill Kassim. Kassim is wounded but reaches Jim and Patricia.

Kane, seeking to learn Jim's plans, visits his bungalow and finds Dr. Harding there. Harding feels he has seen Kane before; Kane denies this. Later, when he consults his records, the doctor identifies Kane as Carter, the criminal. Not wanting to take any chances, Kane sends Gregg to kill Harding. Patricia arrives just after her father has been shot, but in time to identify Gregg as the killer.

Determined to avenge her father's death, she and Jim set out for Haunted Harbor. As they enter the harbor, wild piercing screams are heard, the water boils up furiously, and an unearthly sea monster emerges and attacks their boat. Before serious damage is done, the sea monster submerges, and vanishes as mysteriously as it appeared.

Later, Jim decides to explore the mysteries of Haunted Harbor in a diving outfit but, before he can do this, Carter's men attack him and destroy the diving gear. Jim and Patricia fly to nearby Amoa to obtain new diving equipment. With this new outfit, Jim explores the harbor bottom and finds the "sea monster"—a fake attached to wires leading to shore.

In the meanwhile, Kane and Gregg have decided to melt the *Dolphin*'s gold to avoid its identification. Jim and Patricia, tracing the wires, arrive in time to capture Gregg as he enters the mine; they tie him up in a mine shaft. Jim believes that Gregg is Carter, and leaves Gregg with Kane while he goes to talk with other miners. Kane realizes Jim doesn't suspect him and kills Gregg to protect his secret. Jim and Patricia hear the shot and return to where Kane says Gregg tried to escape. Jim, now suspicious, pretends to leave but slips back to trail Kane through the mine tunnels to the *Dolphin*'s gold. A fight takes place and Kane is scalded to death when he trips over a crucible of molten gold. Jim returns with Patricia to Amoa, where he is cleared of the murder charge.

Kane Richmond comforts Kay Aldridge as villainous George J. Lewis looks on.

Jim and Patricia face the mysterious sea monster of Haunted Harbor.

Kane Richmond rescues Kay Aldridge from Kane's native henchmen.

Mystery of the River Boat

13 Episodes
Universal, 1944

Directed by
Ray Taylor
and Lewis D. Collins

CAST

Steve Langtry	Robert Lowery
Jug Jenks	Eddie Quillan
Celeste Eltree	Marion Martin
Jenny Perrin	Marjory Clements
Rudolph Toller	Lyle Talbot
Clayton (Paul Duval)	Arthur Hohl
Captain Perrin	Oscar O'Shea
Napoleon	Mantan Moreland
Herman Einreich	Ian Wolfe
Pierre	Jay Novello
Batiste	Francis McDonald

Lyle Talbot, Marion Martin, and Anthony Warde conspire on the river boat.

Three old Louisiana families—the Langtrys, the Perrins and the Duvals—are coowners of swampland in the bayou country. Unaware that the property contains oil deposits, they are considering an offer from speculator Herman Einreich. Einreich knows the secret of the swamps since he has killed the scientist who discovered it and stolen his geological maps and notes. Einreich boards the *Morning Glory,* a steamboat, for Duval's Landing.

Among others on the steamer, skippered by Captain Ethan Perrin, are the captain's daughter Jenny; Steve Langtry, who's been away at college; Toller (a crooked gang-leader); and a bearded man named Clayton, who is really Paul Duval the disinherited renegade son of the Duvals. Paul believes his younger brother Jean has cheated him out of his share of the estate and is going home to get even.

With the aid of an ally, Batiste, Clayton murders Einreich, steals his maps, and almost kills Steve and Jenny. They are saved by Napoleon, a steward and a friend of Steve's.

The Toller faction, assisted by Celeste Eltree, an entertainer aboard ship, reaches an agreement with Clayton and tries to pin Einreich's murder on Steve. Meanwhile, Clayton kills his brother and claims his "rights" to the Duval estate.

To avoid capture by the conspirators Steve jumps ship, hides in the swamps, and then gives himself up. The police, however, release him to track down the real criminals, which with the aid of his friends he proceeds to do.

When Napoleon leads Steve to an oil hole he has discovered on the Langtry property, Steve decides to drill immediately. He quickly rounds up a work crew and equipment and begins drilling. But just as Steve's crew is about to strike oil, the henchmen of Clayton and Toller attack the site and wreck the drilling equipment. Steve decides that his only hope is to dynamite the well, on the chance that the blast will cause a strike. Steve drops a stick of dynamite into the well, narrowly missing death as the blast rips the earth and the oil comes gushing skyward.

Determined to gain possession of the oil lands, Clayton produces an old court record indicating that his family, the Duvals, are the owners of the well and the surrounding Langtry land.

Steve counters by insisting Clayton's document was obtained fraudulently. He also introduces a surprise witness, Batiste, who has decided to betray Clayton. He begins to testify and is shot by Clayton, who in turn is killed by the police.

Now desperate, Toller and his gang blow up the oil well, but Steve and his friends shoot Toller, and the rest of the gang are either killed or rounded up.

The story ends with Captain Perrin announcing the engagement of Jenny and Steve.

Raiders of Ghost City

13 Episodes
Universal, 1944

Directed by
Ray Taylor
and Lewis D. Collins

CAST

Captain Steve Clark	Dennis Moore
Cathy Haines	Wanda McKay
Alex Morel	Lionel Atwill
Idaho Jones	Joe Sawyer
Captain Clay Randolph	Regis Toomey
Trina Dessard	Virginia Christine
Doc Blair	Eddy C. Waller
Carl Lawton	Emmett Vogan
Colonel Sewell	Addison Richards
Abel Rackerby	Charles Wagerheim

During the latter part of the Civil War, a gang of supposed Confederates headed by Alex Morel raid all the gold shipments coming from Oro Grande, California, and destined for Union headquarters in Washington.

On the train to Oro Grande, Captain Steve Clark is recognized as a Union Secret Service agent by Morel's attractive accomplice Trina Dessard. Consequently, Clark, together with his friend Idaho Jones, is lured into the baggage car, knocked unconscious, and sent to almost certain death when the car is uncoupled and plunges down the mountainside.

But Idaho and Steve leap to safety from the train and continue to Oro Grande where Steve joins his brother Jim and reports to Colonel Sewell. Idaho introduces himself as the company's detective to pretty Cathy Haines, a Wells Fargo agent.

Steve and Idaho discover that the Morel gold raiders are not Confederates but hard-riding Westerners with headquarters at Morel's saloon, the Golden Eagle. In their first raid on the hideout, Steve's brother is killed by the gang.

The raiders' second victim is Confederate captain Clay Randolph, who has accidentally discovered that Morel is connected with a group of Prussian spies. Before his death, Clay gives Steve a clue to the activities of the spy ring.

The clue leads Steve to a San Francisco dive owned by Rackerby, who captures Steve, and, believing he has him in his power, exposes the ring's activities and methods of operation.

With the help of the San Francisco Secret Service, Steve once again eludes his enemies, returns to Oro Grande, and, with Idaho at his side, finally rounds up the spies. Cathy retires from her job to marry Steve, and Idaho moves into the Wells Fargo spot she vacates.

Regis Toomey (*foreground, right*) and his men hold some outlaws at bay.

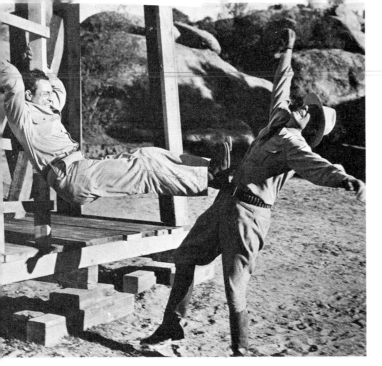
Allan Lane uses some fancy footwork to combat an attacker.

The Tiger Woman

12 Episodes
Republic, 1944

Directed by
Spencer Bennet
and Wallace Grissell

CAST

Allen Saunders	Allan Lane
Tiger Woman	Linda Stirling
Jose	Duncan Renaldo
Morgan	George J. Lewis
Walton	LeRoy Mason
Dagget	Crane Whitley
High Priest	Robert Frazer
Tegula	Rico de Montez
Slim	Stanley Price
Captain Scott	Nolan Leary
Gentry	Kenne Duncan
Tunnel Heavy	Tom Steele
Flint	Duke Green
Travis	Eddie Parker
Depot Heavy	Ken Terrell
Rand	Cliff Lyons

Allen Saunders, ace engineer for the Inter-Ocean Oil Company, is sent to the jungle town of Alta Vista to investigate the cause for the delay in developing a new oil field. The company has a government franchise on its new field and a set time limit in which a well must be brought in. The company is very anxious to clear up any trouble that will hamper the work.

Between the town and the oil land is a strip of jungle inhabited by a race of brown-skinned people ruled by a mysterious white queen known as "The Tiger Woman." While the company was negotiating a pact with the tribe to pass through the jungle, there was much disruption. The Tiger Woman is blamed.

Dagget, proprietor of a general store and secretly the agent for a rival oil company, attempts to murder Saunders when he arrives. Thanks to the Tiger Woman's intervention, the plan fails. Saunders immediately realizes that the Tiger Woman is innocent of the attacks upon the oil workers and equipment that have slowed down the work.

Dagget and an unscrupulous attorney, Walton, believe the Tiger Woman to be Rita Arnold, the heiress to a vast fortune, who was lost as a child in a plane crash over the jungle. They plan to smash the oil project, secure proof of the girl's identity, kill her, and substitute another girl in her place. This way they can collect the fortune.

Saunders discovers that a sacred urn kept in the Tiger Woman's temple contains the secret to her identity. He arrives at the temple just in time to kill Walton and Dagget who are threatening the life of the Tiger Woman. The contents of the urn prove that the Tiger Woman is indeed Rita Arnold. But, in the final scene, she remains undecided whether to claim her fortune or stay on in the jungle to take care of her people.

Zorro's Black Whip

12 Episodes
Republic, 1944

Directed by
Spencer Bennet
and Wallace Grissell

CAST

Vic Gordon	George J. Lewis
Barbara Meredith	Linda Stirling
Tenpoint	Lucien Littlefield
Hammond	Francis McDonald
Baxter	Hal Taliaferro
Harris	John Merton
The Banker	John Hamilton
The Merchant	Tom Chatterton
The Commissioner	Tom London
The Marshal	Jack Kirk
Randolph Meredith	Jay Kirby
Zeke Haydon	Si Jenks
Hedges	Stanley Price
Hull	Tom Steele
Evans	Duke Green
Danley	Dale Van Sickel

It is 1889, and law-abiding citizens of the Territory of Idaho are in favor of holding an election to determine whether their territory should become a state and enter the Union. But sinister forces, opposed to the coming of law and order, begin a reign of terror against the lives and property of all who favor statehood. The head of the outlaws is Hammond who is apparently one of the leading citizens of Crescent City and the owner of the stage line.

Randolph Meredith, the owner and operator of a newspaper campaigning for statehood, is killed in a battle between the lawless elements of Crescent City and those who want order in the Territory. But only his sister Barbara and Tenpoint, their printer, knew that Meredith was also the mysterious Black Whip, a masked avenger expert with cattle whip and gun. After her brother's death, Barbara takes over the management of the paper, and becomes the Whip. Whenever the Whip arrives at the scene of a fight, the outlaws are defeated. The Black Whip becomes synonymous with justice and no one in the town suspects that Barbara is the masked avenger.

At the paper, Barbara is aided by Vic Gordon, a secret government agent sent to investigate the trouble. He too is unaware that Barbara is the Whip, and she manages successfully to conceal the truth from him. When the outlaw gang attempts to prevent the arrival of a wagon carrying new presses for the newspaper, Gordon fights to protect the driver but is knocked unconscious and thrown into the runaway wagon. The Whip arrives on the scene and attempts to overtake the driverless team, but she is too late—the wagon crashes over a cliff.

Fortunately, the wagon falls into a river and remains afloat just long enough for the Whip to rescue Vic. Vic offers $10,000 reward for clues to the identity of the leader of the outlaw gang. Hammond plots to have the money stolen from his own stage company vault, and then to have the safe blown up so that Vic will be suspected. The scheme works, and the angry townspeople have Vic jailed. As the Whip, Barbara recovers the money and captures one of the culprits, Harris, just in time to save Vic from mob violence.

The outlaw gang notices that Barbara's ranch is very close to where the Whip disappears and concludes that she knows the Whip's identity. They take her to their hideout and force her to write a note to be printed in her own newspaper. The note tells the Whip to appear at a rendezvous in order to save Barbara's life. Barbara words the note so Vic and Tenpoint can locate the hideout. When Vic rides to the hideout, he finds that Barbara has already escaped. As he battles the outlaws, Barbara appears as the Whip and lashes a gun from an outlaw's hand just in time to save Vic from being shot.

But the outlaws capture Vic anyhow and imprison him, hoping to get him to reveal some vital information. Hammond decides that Barbara knows the identity of the Whip and threatens to kill Vic unless she produces him. Barbara agrees. She rides to her cave, dons the Whip disguise, and returns to the outlaw's hideout where she frees Vic and leaves her boots exposed under a curtain as a decoy. The outlaws rush toward the room where Vic has been held captive and spot the Whip's boots under the curtain. By the boots she has left, the outlaws surmise that Barbara is the Whip. They capture her and take her back to their shack. Vic, who also suspects that Barbara is the Whip, finds her costume and puts it on. He rides to the shack and rescues her. The outlaws, now totally confused, are convinced that Barbara is *not* the Whip.

Election day arrives. When Hammond learns that the votes will carry the statehood proposal, he orders his men to destroy the ballots. Vic learns of the plot and enlists the aid of government agents who defeat Hammond and his men. Hammond follows the Whip into a cave and is about to kill her when her horse rears up and knocks him to the ground—dead. His death signals the end of the reign of terror; the election is won by the statehood forces and Idaho is proudly admitted to the Union.

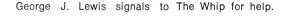

George J. Lewis signals to The Whip for help.

Jack Kirk (*left*) and angry townsfolk accuse George J. Lewis of stealing stage company money.

An imprisoned George J. Lewis is visited by Linda Stirling.

Vic attempts to ward off outlaws bent on robbing the stage.

235

1945

A bound and gagged victim sits helplessly as Joan Woodbury is threatened by Wheeler Oakman.

Brenda Starr, Reporter

13 Episodes
Columbia, 1945

Directed by
Wallace W. Fox

CAST

Brenda Starr	Joan Woodbury
Lieutenant Larry Farrel	Kane Richmond
Chuck Allen	Syd Saylor
Tim	Joe Devlin
Frank Smith	George Meeker
Joe Heller } Lew Heller }	Wheeler Oakman
Vera Harvey	Cay Forester
Zelda	Marion Burns
Abretha	Lottie Harrison
Charlie	Ernie Adams
Kruger	Jack Ingram
Muller	Anthony Warde
Schultz	John Merton
Pesky	Billy Benedict

Assigned to cover a fire in an old house, Brenda Starr and her photographer Chuck discover the wounded body of Joe Heller, a gangster suspected of stealing a quarter-million-dollar payroll. In his dying words Heller tells Brenda that someone took his satchel of stolen money and gives her a coded message.

Kruger, the mobster who shot Heller, escapes to his gang's hideout with the bag, but finds that it is filled with paper instead of money.

The gang, knowing of Heller's dying declaration to Brenda, tries to get the star reporter to tell them where the crook hid his money. Thanks to her photographer and police Lieutenant Larry Farrel, she is able to withstand the gang's efforts.

In the end, an office boy decodes Heller's message, and the money and the gang of hoodlums are captured.

Marten Lamont comes to the rescue and gets the drop on George J. Lewis and one of his henchmen.

Federal Operator 99

12 Episodes
Republic, 1945

Directed by
Spencer Bennet
and Wallace Grissell

CAST

Jerry Blake	Marten Lamont
Joyce Kingston	Helen Talbot
Jim Belmont	George J. Lewis
Rita Parker	Lorna Gray
Matt Farrell	Hal Taliaferro
Morton	LeRoy Mason
Martin	Bill Stevens
Morello	Maurice Cass
Jeffries	Kernan Cripps
The Countess	Elaine Lange
Hunter	Frank Jaquet
Wolfe	Forrest Taylor
Heinrick	Jay Novello
Crawford	Tom London
Riggs	Jack Ingram

Federal Officer Jeffries is making the train trip to the West Coast with prisoner Jim Belmont, leader of a powerful underworld gang. During the night, an airplane drops a man on to the train who rescues Belmont.

Belmont makes plans with his chief aide Farrell; Rita, a beautiful adventuress; and Morton, his crafty secretary, to steal Princess Cornelia's crown jewels. The jewels are in the vault of a local bank, but are to be transferred back to Europe by Countess Delremy.

Rita and a gunman force Joyce, Jeffries's secretary, to tell of the countess's arrival by plane that afternoon. Before they leave, Jerry Blake, Operator 99, drops in. There is a fight, the gunman is killed, but Rita escapes. The gang kidnaps the countess and gets the vault key. Belmont drops a smoke bomb in the bank, causing a fire alarm. Two gangsters, disguised as firemen, break into the vault and grab the jewels. Jerry sees them drive away and pursues them, but he is forced to crash into a service

Marten Lamont helps the treacherous Lorna Gray out of a trapdoor.

station which explodes and goes up in flame. Jerry manages to escape only seconds before the explosion.

Belmont offers to return the jewels to the countess for a huge ransom payment and she agrees to pay through Jerry. Jerry makes an agreement with Belmont to send Joyce with the money. Joyce plans to radio Jerry when she gets the jewels and he will take up the trail. Belmont double-crosses Jerry by sending Farrell on a motorcycle to meet Joyce. He takes the money from her and refuses to turn over the jewels. Farrell also destroys the car radio so she can't summon Jerry. Jerry, however, has expected a trick and is in a plane overhead. He follows the cyclist across country and when he goes into a cafe, Jerry parachutes to the ground and captures him.

But Belmont soon kidnaps Joyce and offers to trade her for Farrell. Jerry discovers a bugging device in his office, planted there by Belmont. He traces the wires to a nearby theatre and finds a secret passageway leading to Belmont's lair. Jerry barges in on the criminal, chases him and, during a fight on a high catwalk, sends Belmont hurtling to his doom.

Jungle Queen

13 Episodes
Universal, 1945

Directed by
Ray Taylor
and Lewis D. Collins

CAST

Bob Elliott	Edward Norris
Chuck Kelly	Eddie Quillan
Lang	Douglass Dumbrille
Pamela Courtney	Lois Collier
Lothel	Ruth Roman
Dr. Elise Bork	Tala Birell
Kyba	Clarence Muse
Maati	Napoleon Simpson
Tambosa Tim	Cy Kendall
Godac	Clinton Rosemond

During World War II, the Nazi High Command sends agents into the African jungle to stir up the Tongghili tribes against the Allies. Nazi Commander Elise Bork, posing as a scientist with the Tambosa Experimental Farm, and her subordinate Lang infiltrate the area and locate a few native tribesmen who are willing to help them.

All of the Tongghili are in awe of their leader and adviser Lothel, the Mysterious Queen of the Jungle who can walk through flames and appear or vanish at will. Two young Americans, Bob Elliott and his pal Chuck Kelly, arrive to help the Allied cause. En route they meet Pam Courtney who is searching for her father, an explorer who has disappeared while on safari. While feigning friendship for the three newcomers, the erstwhile scientists Bork and Lang do everything within their power to obstruct the trio, including attempts at murder.

But the three friends have a powerful ally in Lothel, who makes frequent well-timed appearances to save them from a variety of dangers, including raging jungle infernos, ferocious lions, and mobs of angry natives. In desperation, the Nazis attempt to murder Lothel.

But the mysterious Jungle Queen easily thwarts their efforts and takes the initiative in helping Bob, Chuck, and Pam to gather evidence against the Nazis. With the evidence in hand, the local British Commissioner raids the Nazi headquarters and rounds up the entire crew of spies. With the threat to her people gone, Lothel vanishes in a sheet of flame as mysteriously as she had appeared.

Jungle Queen, Ruth Roman.

Jungle Raiders

15 Episodes
Columbia, 1945

Directed by
Lesley Selander

CAST

Bob Moore	Kane Richmond
Joe	Eddie Quillan
Cora	Veda Ann Borg
Zara	Carol Hughes
Ann	Janet Shaw
Dr. Moore	John Elliott
Tom	Jack Ingram
Jake Rayne	Charles King
Charley	Ernie Adams
Brent	I. Stanford Jolley
Cragg	Kermit Maynard
Dr. Reed	Bud Buster
Carter	George Turner
The Chief	Nick Thompson
Mark	Jim Aubrey

Kane Richmond and Eddie Quillan on the alert.

Dr. Moore, carrying a cure-all healing powder, stops off at Jake Rayne's trading post for supplies before proceeding into the jungle in search of his colleague Dr. Reed, who has vanished in the wild country of the Arzecs. He departs accompanied by a few of Rayne's men, sent along to find out if there is anything of value to be gained from the expedition. When Dr. Moore and Rayne's men arrive at the Hidden Village of the Arzecs, they are seized. The natives prepare, to sacrifice them to the Gods in an attempt to appease the angry Gods and save the life of their chief, who is dying of an unknown malady.

Meanwhile, Dr. Reed's daughter Ann and Dr. Moore's son Bob meet at Rayne's post and team up in an attempt to rescue their parents. Rayne, entranced by rumors of a fabulous Arzec treasure, decides to make his own bid for the village and endeavors to murder Bob and Ann. For Rayne has held Dr. Reed prisoner for many months, because the doctor had inadvertently mentioned the treasure.

Dr. Moore cures the chief by using his wondrous medicine. But in the process, he rouses the enmity of Zara, the Priestess of the Hidden Village, who subsequently allies herself with Rayne's group. In combating this double-barreled threat, Bob and Ann survive a number of deadly obstacles, including a landslide in the Valley of Sounds, a crocodile-infested swamp, the Fire Test, and the Dagger Pit. Eventually, the villains fall into the Dagger Pit and Bob and Ann find the treasure. They are reunited with their parents, and prepare to return to civilization to cure humanity's ills with the wonder medicine.

Manhunt of Mystery Island

15 Episodes
Republic, 1945

Directed by
Spencer Bennet,
Wallace Grissell,
and Yakima Canutt

CAST

Lance	Richard Bailey
Claire	Linda Stirling
Mephisto	Roy Barcroft
Brand	Kenne Duncan
Professor Forrest	Forrest Taylor
Hargraves	Forbes Murray
Armstrong	Jack Ingram
Braley	Harry Strang
Melton	Edward Cassidy
Raymond	Frank Alten
Reed	Lane Chandler
Ruga	Russ Vincent
Barker	Dale Van Sickel
Lyons	Tom Steele
Harvey	Duke Green

While on an expedition in search of new radium fields, Dr. Forrest, inventor of the radiatomic power transmitter, a device designed to revolutionize the traffic of the world by supplying power from widely separated points, disappeared with his aide.

His daughter Claire searches for him and enlists the aid of Lance Reardon, famous criminologist. From the dust found on the clothing of a murdered man known to have been on the expedition, Lance learns that the professor was on Mystery Island, a tiny dot of land in the Pacific.

Claire and Lance go to Mystery Island and discover that it is owned by four men—Professor Hargraves, Edward Armstrong, Frederick Braley, and Paul Melton—all descendants of a Captain Mephisto, who governed the island more than two hundred years before. Each of the men pledges aid in finding Dr. Forrest, but what Claire and Lance do not know is that one of the owners is holding Dr. Forrest prisoner.

By using a strange device known as the "Transformation Chair," one of these men is able to change the molecular structure of the blood and can become, at will, the exact counterpart of the original Captain Mephisto. As the mysterious and sinister captain, he circumvents at every turn the efforts of Claire and Lance to locate Dr. Forrest and hopes to gain control of the power transmitter himself. When Melton indicates to Lance and Claire that he has information as to Forrest's whereabouts, he is murdered by Mephisto.

In their search, Lance and Claire employ a powerful radium detector in the hope that it will lead them to Dr. Forrest. Mephisto and Brand, his henchman, take the radium from the power transmitter into a cave. Lance and Claire, by using the detector, track Mephisto to the cave tunnels. But the nefarious Mephisto opens floodgates that unleash a torrent of rushing water. The water sweeps Lance and Claire through the tunnel and out of a hole in the mountainside to their apparent doom. But, luckily, they land in a lake and swim to safety.

Because their whereabouts are constantly known, Lance and Claire begin to suspect that one of the island owners is Captain Mephisto. At first they suspect Armstrong, but when he is found murdered their suspicions shift to Braley

Later, while Claire is apparently safe in her room, a secret panel slides open and Mephisto grabs her. Claire's screams attract Lance, who rushes to the room. Although Mephisto escapes with Claire, Brand is captured by Lance. Lance announces that he is willing to trade Brand for Claire. Mephisto seemingly agrees and sets up a rendezvous at a cabin across a foot suspension bridge. Lance encounters Mephisto and Claire on the suspension bridge and a fight ensues. Wounded by Lance, Mephisto reaches the end of the bridge and cuts the supporting ropes. Lance and Claire plunge earthward, but both manage to grab hold of the ropes and escape by swinging across the canyon.

After her escape, Claire pilots a plane and scouts for clues as to Mephisto's hideout; she keeps in constant radio contact with Lance. When she spots Brand's car in front of a cave, Lance quickly rushes to investigate. He enters the cave and, after a short battle during which Mephisto and Brand flee, succeeds in rescuing Dr. Forrest.

Returning to the island mansion, Lance and Claire plan a trap for Mephisto. They leave Dr. Forrest alone in the mansion with Braley and Hargraves, one of whom they are certain is the evil captain. In his pocket Forrest has a television tube, and Claire watches the action on a "scanning screen." After Braley and Hargraves leave the room, Forrest is alone only for a moment. A wall painting swings open and Brand steps out, forcing Forrest to go with him through a secret passage to Mephisto's quarters. Claire radios this information to Lance who bursts into the secret headquarters and is quickly knocked unconscious by Mephisto.

Now the captain plots the perfect crime. He will place Lance in the transformation chair, turn him into Mephisto, and leave him to be hanged by the authorities while he escapes scot-free with the transmitter. But Claire arrives and shoots Mephisto, ending his greedy schemes. The dead Mephisto is revealed to be Braley. Lance, Claire, and Dr. Forrest return to the mainland.

Linda Stirling faces a watery grave unless she reveals the location of the transmitter control unit to Roy Barcroft.

Richard Bailey defends himself against Roy Barcroft.

Roy Barcroft discusses his next scheme with cohort Kenne Duncan.

The Master Key

13 Episodes	Directed by
Universal, 1945	Ray Taylor
	and Lewis D. Collins

CAST

Tom Brant	—Milburn Stone
Janet Lowe	Jan Wiley
Jack Ryan	Dennis Moore
Garret Donohue	Addison Richards
Professor Henderson	Byron Foulger
Dorothy Newton	Maria Wrixon
Aggie	Sarah Padden
Chief O'Brien	Russell Hicks
Migsy	Alfred La Rue
Herman	George Lynn

Plotting to create a financial panic in the United States, Nazi agents kidnap mineralogical scientist Elwood Henderson and utilize his Orotron machine to extract gold from the ocean. Operating under the secret leadership of "The Master Key," the gang is trailed by Federal Investigator Tom Brant, aided by detective Jack Ryan and reporter Janet Lowe.

Through clues obtained from Police Chief O'Brien and his secretary Dorothy Newton, the trail leads to a warehouse where gold produced by the Orotron machine is being stored. Brant overhears the enemy agents plotting to ship out large quantities of the metal by plane and relays this information to his aides before following the agents to the plane. As the craft carrying the gold takes off and heads out to sea, Brant's men arrive with guns blazing, causing the plane and its cargo to crash.

Meanwhile, Professor Henderson escapes from his captors and makes his way to Janet, who takes him to her apartment. When Brant and Ryan arrive at Janet's apartment they find it wrecked and abandoned. A dictagraph machine, however, reveals that Janet and Henderson have been kidnapped by a Nazi agent, Herman, and taken to a secret location. The kidnapped pair is trailed to a Nazi hideaway and rescued, but Herman escapes.

Brant announces that Professor Henderson has been injured and is under care at a certain hospital. Herman and some cohorts, disguised as interns, enter the hospital and kidnap the patient—who turns out to be Brant. Followed

245

Alfred La Rue, Jan Wiley, Dennis Moore, and Milburn
Stone try to anticipate the Master Key's next move.

by Ryan, who was aware of the plant, Brant is brought to Nazi headquarters and sentenced to be executed by a firing squad. Before this can be carried out, however, Ryan arrives and saves Brant. Professor Henderson identifies many of the captured Nazis, and also reveals various formulas in the Orotron gold-making process.

Checking fingerprints found in the headquarters, Brant and Janet discover that Dorothy Newton is "The Master Key." She had been directing her agents through a microphone device which changes her voice. The Master Key tries to escape with one of her henchmen, but their plane is blasted from the air.

The Monster and the Ape

15 Episodes
Columbia, 1945

Directed by
Howard Bretherton

CAST

Ken Morgan	Robert Lowery
Ernst	George Macready
Professor Arnold	Ralph Morgan
Babs Arnold	Carole Mathews
Flash	Willie Best
Nordik	Jack Ingram
Flint	Anthony Warde
Butler	Ted Mapes
Blake	Eddie Parker
Mead	Stanley Price

At the Bainbridge Research Foundation, Professor Ernst is proudly shown the Metalogen Man, a robot built by Professor Arnold for Ken Morgan and the large company he represents. Professor Ernst, however, is no casual admirer of Arnold's accomplishment—he is an enemy agent out to get the robot and the metalogen metal that makes it run.

Ernst's underhanded schemes are aided by both human henchmen and a trained ape named Thor. After many confrontations, Arnold finally kills Thor before the ape can kill Morgan. Morgan, in turn, sees to it that Ernst's thugs meet their end in a plane crash. Both Morgan and Arnold then turn their attention to Ernst who falls to his death from a high embankment while trying to escape.

The Purple Monster Strikes

15 Episodes
Republic, 1945

Directed by
Spencer Bennet
and Fred Brannon

CAST

Craig Foster	Dennis Moore
Sheila Layton	Linda Stirling
Purple Monster	Roy Barcroft
Dr. Cyrus Layton	James Craven
Garrett	Bud Geary
Marcia	Mary Moore
Emperor of Mars	John Davidson
Stewart	Joe Whitehead
Saunders	Emmett Vogan
Meredith	George Carleton
Mitchell	Kenne Duncan
Helen	Rosemonde James
Harvey	Monte Hale
Benjamin	Wheaton Chambers
Crandall	Frederick Howard
Tony	Anthony Warde
Andy	Ken Terrell

Roy Barcroft prepares to take on the identity of James Craven.

Dr. Cyrus Layton, celebrated astronomer and inventor of the Scientific Foundation, notices a strange meteor from outer space landing near his observatory. Investigating, he discovers a mysterious being who introduces himself as an inhabitant of Mars sent to contact Dr. Layton concerning his inventions, most notably a spaceship capable of flying to other planets.

Flattered, Dr. Layton brings the stranger into the observatory and shows him the construction plans for the spacecraft, stating that "this is the proudest day of my life." "Unfortunately," remarks the Martian, "this is also the last day of your life." He tells the bewildered Layton that he is the scout of an invasion force from Mars bent on conquering Earth. All the Martians need to bring off the invasion is a spaceship capable of making round trips from Earth to Mars. The Martian kills Dr. Layton and, through an advanced scientific process, enters the doctor's body and assumes his physical characteristics.

Craig Foster, legal counsel for the Scientific Foundation, and Layton's niece Sheila arrive just as the Martian assumes the doctor's identity. Unsuspecting, they believe him when he says a Martian known as the Purple Monster stole his plans for the spaceship. As Craig and Sheila pursue clues to the whereabouts of the Purple Monster, the Martian aided by an American hoodlum named Garrett whom he has coerced into cooperating, proceeds to build the spacecraft in a hidden wing of the observatory.

In order to complete the rocketship, the Purple Monster must obtain a number of items being developed by other members of the Scientific Foundation: a special rocket fuel, an electroannihilator (a beam that destroys anything in its path), and a multitude of other complex devices. But Craig and Sheila anticipate the Martian's needs and attempt to thwart his efforts to obtain the other materials.

One Foundation scientist, Dr. Benjamin, is in the process of completing a stabilizer essential to space flight. To aid him in stealing Benjamin's plans, the Purple Monster, via a televisionlike "distance eliminator," contacts the Emperor of Mars and asks for Marcia, a female Martian, to be sent to assist him. Marcia lands on Earth, enters Dr. Benjamin's laboratory, kills his secretary, and takes on her physical characteristics. From this position, Marcia keeps the Purple Monster informed of the scientist's progress.

When the stabilizing device is completed, Marcia informs her colleague who sends Garrett to steal it. But Craig shows up, captures Garrett, and ties his hands behind his back. While Craig is taking him to the authorities, Garrett breaks his bonds and, after a brief scuffle, escapes. Craig examines the rope that had bound Garrett's hands and discovers that it had been partially cut. Only Dr. Benjamin's secretary could have cut them, Craig deduces. He quickly phones Sheila, who happens to be in Dr. Benjamin's laboratory, and warns her to keep her eye on the scientist's secretary. When she hangs up the receiver, Sheila notices a pair of scissors on the desk with several incriminating strands of rope lodged between the blades.

At that moment, the secretary enters and Sheila confronts her with the evidence. Marcia knocks Sheila cold and begins to change herself back into her normal body. But as this transformation is taking place, Sheila revives and is astounded. Marcia attempts to escape and Sheila pursues—right to the edge of a cliff. The girls grapple, and Marcia finally falls over the edge and hurtles to her death. When Sheila tells Craig of the phenomenon that she has observed, Craig realizes that the Purple Monster probably has this same awesome power and may be any one of the trusted scientists.

Following up a number of clues, Craig trails Garrett to a phone from which the mobster calls the Purple Monster. Craig is so astute that he can determine the number being called just by

Roy Barcroft making an auspicious entrance.

listening to the *sound* of the dialing. It is with some shock that he realizes the number is Dr. Layton's. After reporting this to Sheila, Craig prepares a trap. While Dr. Layton is away from his desk, Craig plants a movie camera in his office, hoping to record the transformation on film. Craig then calls Dr. Layton and tells him that he has learned that a rocket ship is being built somewhere in the observatory and is on his way over with the police.

The ruse works. The Purple Monster quickly transforms himself into a Martian and prepares to leave for Mars in the completed spaceship. The rocket blasts off just as Craig discovers the hidden rocket room. As the rocket ship hurtles through space, Craig grabs the electroannihilator (carelessly left behind), carefully aims it, and destroys the spacecraft with one well-directed ray.

The Royal Mounted Rides Again

13 Episodes
Universal, 1945

Directed by
Ray Taylor
and Lewis D. Collins

CAST

Frenchy	George Dolenz
Wayne Decker	Bill Kennedy
June Bailey	Daun Kennedy
Bucket	Paul E. Burns
Taggart	Milburn Stone
Price	Robert Armstrong
Dancer	Danny Morton
Jackson Decker	Addison Richards
Lode MacKenzie	Tom Fadden
Bunker	Joseph Haworth
Madame Mysterioso	Helen Bennett
Sergeant Nelson	Joseph Crehan
Superintendent MacDonald	Selmer Jackson
Ladue	Daral Hudson
Kent	George Lloyd
Grail	George Eldredge

Jackson Decker, mining operator of the northwest, orders his henchman Taggart to confiscate milling machinery owned by Tom Bailey. Soon after, Bailey, operating a rich vein, is mysteriously murdered.

Assigned to the case is the operator's son, Captain Wayne Decker of the Royal Mounted Police. He is joined in his search for the assassin by Corporal Frenchy and Bailey's daughter June. Their investigation clears Wayne's father, but points to an outlaw band attempting to gain possession of rich gold mines.

In a series of desperate encounters, Wayne narrowly escapes death and Taggart and a henchman, Bunker, are killed in a gun battle. Another henchman Grail, however, makes a last, futile effort to run the gold "blockade" imposed by Wayne.

The greedy outlaw murders two of his cohorts in an effort to corner the stolen Bailey gold and is murdered in cold blood by Price, operator of the Yukon Palace. The lawless action establishes Price as the leader of the outlaw gang, and he is placed under custody of the Royal Mounted Police by Captain Wayne.

Bill Kennedy, Tom Fadden, and George Dolenz listen to a miner's report on outlaw activities.

Keye Luke and Jan Wiley talk to Nazi-disguised Lloyd Bridges.

Victoria Horne makes a call, and Gene Stutenroth keeps his pistol trained on captured Lloyd Bridges, while Arno Frey looks bemused.

Secret Agent X-9

13 Episodes
Universal, 1945

Directed by
Ray Taylor
and Lewis Collins

CAST

Secret Agent X-9	Lloyd Bridges
Ah Fong	Keye Luke
Lynn Moore	Jan Wiley
Nabura	Victoria Horne
Solo	Samuel S. Hinds
Lucky Number	Cy Kendall
Marker	Jack Overman
Bach	George Lynn
Takahari	Clarence Lang
Hakahima	Benson Fong
Kapitan Graf	Arno Frey
Yogel	Gene Stutenroth
Mama Pierrie	Ann Codee
Drag Dorgan	Edward M. Howard
Bartender	Edmund Cobb

Facing a shortage of aviation fuel, Japanese warlords order the beautiful Nabura, head of the feared Black Dragon Intelligence Service operating on neutral Shadow Island off the China coast, to smuggle an agent into America and secure a secret formula for synthetic fuel.

Lynn Moore, an Australian agent posing as a quisling, learns of Nabura's plan and informs Secret Agent X-9 of the plot. Ah Fong, a Chinese agent posing as a fan-tan dealer, joins X-9 and Miss Moore in an attempt to thwart the evil scheme.

After several attempts to kill X-9 fail, Nabura orders Shadow Island bombed by the Japanese air force and plans to make her escape by submarine. But Ah Fong impersonates an aide of the Black Dragon leader and orders the Japanese flight commander to bomb the fleeing submarine on the ruse that it had been commandeered by allied secret agents. The sub is blasted to bits.

"Once we get the American formula for synthetic fuel, our armies will be victorious," Japanese scientist Benson Fong, seated, tells a pair of army cohorts.

Who's Guilty?

15 Episodes
Columbia, 1945

Directed by
Howard Bretherton
and Wallace Grissell

CAST

Bob Stewart	Robert Kent
Ruth Allen	Amelita Ward
Duke Ellis	Tim Ryan
Rita Royale	Jayne Hazard
Mrs. Dill	Minerva Urecal
Sara Caldwell	Belle Mitchell
Patton	
Walter Calvert	Charles Middleton
Henry Calvert	Davison Clark
Horace Black	Sam Flint
Curt Bennett	Bruce Donovan
Sergeant Smith	Jack Ingram
Morgan Calvert	Milton Kibbee
Pancho	Nacho Galindo
Jose	Roberto Tafur
Smiley	Wheeler Oakman
Burk	Charles King
Edwards	Anthony Warde

Walter Calvert calls upon his brother Henry at his eerie old house and demands a share of the family fortune. He says he will kill Henry if he doesn't get it. A few days later, Henry's car crashes and Henry is presumed dead. Bob Stewart, a detective whom he asked to investigate the matter if he should die, starts his investigation. Duke Ellis, a reporter, is with him. Bob meets the family at their mansion and questions Henry's sister, his half brother, his nephew, and his nephew's bride, and Ruth Allen, whose father was in business with Henry.

Henry's brother Patton and a shadowy figure known as the Voice plan to kill all the relatives and divide the fortune. As the murder attempts multiply, Bob and Ruth endeavor to track down the masterminds and bring them to justice.

Eventually, Bob proves that Henry is actually alive and is the mysterious Voice. When he attempts to murder Bob, Patton accidentally shoots Henry and is himself captured. With the mystery solved, the family plans to share the fortune.

1946

Douglas Fowley and Eddie Acuff at the posh Century Club.

Chick Carter, Detective

15 Episodes
Columbia, 1946

Directed by
Derwin Abrahams

CAST

Chick Carter	Lyle Talbot
Rusty Farrell	Douglas Fowley
Sherry Marvin	Julie Gibson
Ellen Dale	Pamela Blake
Spud	Eddie Acuff
Dan Rankin	Robert Elliott
Nick Pollo	George Meeker
Vasky	Leonard Penn
Joe Carney	Charles King
Mack	Jack Ingram
Jules Hoyt	Joel Friedkin
Frank Sharp	Eddie Parker

Detective Chick Carter finds himself on his most exciting case when Sherry Marvin, a singer at the Century Club, reports the robbery of the famous Blue Diamond, owned by Joe Carney, the proprietor of the club. Joe planned the theft in order to pay a debt to Nick Pollo, with the $100,000 in insurance money he would collect.

Sherry double-crosses Joe by wearing an imitation diamond. She had planned to throw the real one, hidden in a cotton snowball, to Nick during the floor show. However, Spud Warner, a newspaper photographer, there with reporter Rusty Farrell, playfully snatches a snowball from her basket. Nick receives an empty snowball and the Blue Diamond disappears!

The search is on, and Chick finds himself pitted against ruthless adversaries—Joe, Nick, and their henchmen Mack and Vasky. Aided by Ellen, a private investigator, Chick uncovers the various crimes committed by the evildoers and has them rounded up. Spud runs in from the alley clutching a snowball he's found, but it's empty. Almost moved to tears by Sherry's sincere repentance for her part in the affair, Spud takes a handkerchief from the pocket that held the snowball. Out drops the diamond, and the case is closed.

The Crimson Ghost

12 Episodes
Republic, 1946

Directed by
William Witney
and Fred Brannon

CAST

Duncan Richards	Charles Quigley
Diana Farnsworth	Linda Stirling
Ashe	Clayton Moore
Blackton	I. Stanford Jolley
Chambers	Kenne Duncan
Van Wyck	Forrest Taylor
Anderson	Emmett Vogan
Maxwell	Sam Flint
Parker	Joe Forte
Fator	Stanley Price
Wilson	Wheaton Chambers
Stricker	Tom Steele
Harte	Dale Van Sickel
Bain	Rex Lease
Zane	Fred Graham
Gross	Bud Wolfe

Professor Chambers, an internationally prominent physicist, has developed for the use of the government a counteratomic device called the Cyclotrode. This Cyclotrode has the power of short-circuiting all electric current within the radius of its powerful rays.

Alone, after demonstrating the power of the Cyclotrode to four of his associates—one of whom, unknown to the others, is the Crimson Ghost—he is confronted by two henchmen of the Crimson Ghost, Slim and Ashe, who demand the device. Rather than surrender it, Chambers smashes the Cyclotrode. Duncan Richards, a well-known criminologist and associate of Chambers, returns in time to prevent Chambers's abduction. A fight follows during which Slim is knocked out and Ashe escapes. Around Slim's neck is a metal band—when a professor pulls on it, an electrical flash occurs, killing Slim. Chambers explains what has happened, and also reveals that he has another Cyclotrode in safekeeping.

Later, at the order of the Crimson Ghost, Chambers is taken to an underground workshop

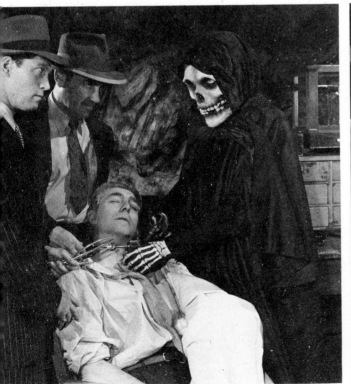

Clayton Moore (*left*) and the Crimson Ghost place the deadly collar on Kenne Duncan's neck.

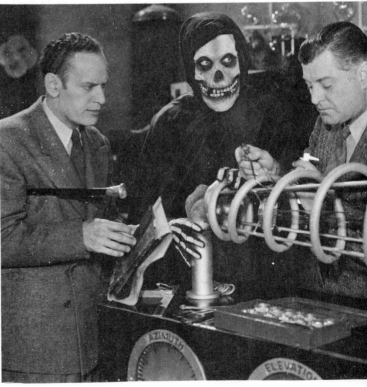

The Crimson Ghost and associates at work on the powerful Cyclotrode.

and is forced to wear one of the Crimson Ghost's collars, by which means his will can be controlled—anyone trying to remove it will meet instantaneous death. Diana Farnsworth, secretary to the group, advises Duncan of Chambers's disappearance.

Duncan, arriving at the vault where the Cyclotrode is stored, is spotted by Ashe and the Crimson Ghost. A battle ensues during which Ashe gets away with Chambers and the Cyclotrode, pursued by Duncan. The Crimson Ghost, focusing the device on Duncan's car, pulls the switch causing a powerful electrical flash, momentarily blinding Duncan. The car crashes through the railing of a bridge, leaving him unconscious in the river below. Duncan recovers and swims to safety.

Duncan persists in his struggle against the Crimson Ghost finally trapping him and revealing him to be Professor Parker, who seemingly had been helping Chambers combat the evil effects of the Cyclotrode.

Daughter of Don Q

12 Episodes	Directed by Spencer
Republic, 1946	Bennet and
	Fred Brannon

CAST

Dolores Quantaro	Adrian Booth
Cliff Roberts	Kirk Alyn
Carlos Manning	LeRoy Mason
Mel Donovan	Roy Barcroft
Maria Montenez	Claire Meade
Grogan	Kernan Cripps
Romero	Jimmy Ames
Tompkins	Eddie Parker
Norton	Tom Steele
Murphy	Dale Van Sickel
Rollins	Fred Graham
Riggs	Tom Quinn
Kelso	Johnny Daheim
Gray	Ted Mapes
Lippy	I. Stanford Jolley
Moody	Buddy Roosevelt

Kirk Alyn with pistol ready, as Adrian Booth employs a more ancient weapon.

Carlos Manning, antique-shop owner, discovers an ancient Spanish land grant that gives Don Quantero, an early California settler, a large tract of land that is now the business district of a city. Manning, one of the descendants of Don Q., avariciously plots to inherit the vast fortune himself by murdering his relatives.

In order to do this, he and gunman Mel Donovan seize the only copy of the Quantero family tree from Dolores Quantero. They plan a series of murders which Dolores and Cliff Roberts, a reporter, recognize as a plot to destroy the Quanteros.

Starting with a short list accidentally dropped by one of the villains, Dolores and Cliff proceed to warn the descendants of Don Q. of each attempt by Manning and his men to kill them off. Dolores and Cliff fight off murder attempts upon themselves until Manning is exposed, and it is discovered that Dolores is the real heir.

Hop Harrigan

15 Episodes   Directed by
Columbia, 1946   Derwin Abrahams

CAST

Hop Harrigan	William Blakewell
Gail Nolan	Jennifer Holt
Jackie Nolan	Robert "Buzz" Henry
Tank Tinker	Sumner Getchell
Arnold	Emmett Vogan
Gwen Arnold	Claire James
Dr. Tobor	John Merton
Ballard	Wheeler Oakman
Retner	Ernie Adams
Craven	Peter Michael
Barry	Terry Frost
Edwards	Anthony Warde
Fraser	Jackie Moran
Gray	Bobby Stone
Deputy Sheriff	Jack Buchanan
Carter	Jim Diehl

Jennifer Holt, William Blakewell, Robert "Buzz" Henry, and Sumner Getchell discuss the latest machinations of the Chief Pilot.

Hop Harrigan and his pal Tank Tinker operate a small airport. They are hired by J. Westly Arnold to fly an eccentric inventor, Dr. Tabor, to his secret laboratory where he has a revolutionary new power unit. But another faction, led by a mysterious character called the Chief Pilot, is also interested in the invention. Using a fiendish destroying ray, the Chief cripples Hop's plane and kidnaps Tabor!

But the determined Hop vows to bring the Chief Pilot to justice, and to rescue Tabor, despite murderous secret weapons and cunningly contrived death traps employed against him. Hop discovers that the Chief Pilot is assisted by two henchmen, Hunter and Arnold's secretary Craven, and pursues these men vigorously.

Hop succeeds in trapping the Chief Pilot and his henchmen. But Tabor escapes, goes mad, and plans to destroy the world with his invention! At the last moment, Hop finds the laboratory; Tabor and his power unit are blown to eternity.

Helen Talbot and Larry Thompson are about to be blown to bits, as Anthony Warde prepares the dynamite charge.

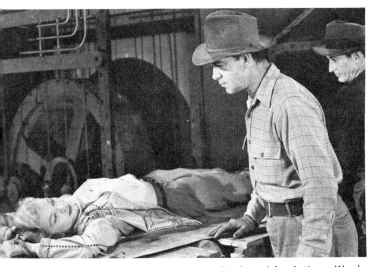

Helen Talbot has one last unkind word for Anthony Warde.

Larry Thompson and Helen Talbot face cremation.

King of the Forest Rangers

12 Episodes
Republic, 1946

Directed by
Spencer Bennet
and Fred Brannon

CAST

Steve King	Larry Thompson
Marian Brennan	Helen Talbot
Professor Carver	Stuart Hamblen
Burt Spear	Anthony Warde
Haliday	LeRoy Mason
Andrews	Scott Elliott
Judson	Tom London
Miner	Walter Soderling
Rance	Bud Geary
Harmon	Harry Strang
Bailey	Ernie Adams
Stover	Eddie Parker
Holmes	Jack Kirk
Martin	Tom Steele
Blaine	Dale Van Sickel
Lynch	Stanley Blystone

Strange prehistoric towers have been discovered in and near one of the great National Parks, and Professor Carver, an eminent archaeologist, heads an expedition to determine their origin and the purpose for which they were built. But his investigation, which is supposedly in the interests of science, is designed for his own selfish ends.

Tom Judson, amateur scientist, discovers the torn half of an ancient Indian rug into which is woven a weird pattern of animals and arrows. He shows it to Carver who recognizes it as the missing half of a rug, the remainder of which he already possesses. Together, the two halves form a cryptic code which leads to the vast wealth of the ancient builders of the towers. Carver orders Burt Spear, his chief henchman, to have Judson waylaid and robbed. Judson escapes the ambush with the rug but is fatally wounded.

Steve King of the Forest Rangers obtains the rug from Judson just before he dies. He brings it to the Trading Post run by Marian Brennan, where he shows it to a number of people, including Carver. Carver cunningly claims to see no significance in the pattern or anything which would suggest a motive for murder. King intends to send the rug to Washington for examination and asks Marian to place it in her safe for the night.

After closing hours, Spear and one of his men force Marian to surrender the relic. King arrives in time to engage the men in a fight in which one of them is killed. But Spear escapes with the rug and reaches the lake where another man is waiting for him in a motorboat. King pursues them in another boat. In a running gun battle, King's boat takes fire and he is forced to jump overboard. After several attempts to run King over in the water, Spear tosses a bomb in his direction. King eludes the bomb by diving underwater.

From this point on, Carver and his men carry on a series of murderous sieges in an effort to gain title to the plots of land upon which the towers stand. King learns that the towers mark the sites of the platinum mines of the ancient tribes and defeats Carver and his followers. The wealth of the land is made secure for its owners.

Lost City of the Jungle

13 Episodes
Universal, 1946

Directed by
Ray Taylor
and Lewis D. Collins

John Gallaudet, Jane Adams, and John Eldredge wend their way through the Lost City.

CAST

Rod Stanton	Russell Hayden
Marjorie Elmore	Jane Adams
Sir Eric Hazarias	Lionel Atwill
Tal Shan	— Keye Luke
Indra	Helen Bennett
Doc Harris	Ted Hecht
Dr. Elmore	John Eldredge
Caffron	John Miljan
Grebb	John Gallaudet
Kurtz	Ralph Lewis

Following the end of World War II, warmonger Sir Eric Hazarias sets the wheels in motion for World War III. His search for Meteorium 245, the only practical defense against the atomic bomb, leads him to the mythical city of Pendrang.

Obstructing Hazarias's sinister plan to rule the world are United Peace Foundation investigator Rod Stanton, Tal Shan, a Pendrang native,

259

and Marjorie Elmore, the daughter of scientist Dr. Elmore.

Rod and Tal Shan locate a secret entrance to the Lost City of the Jungle. Inside they find a tablet bearing mysterious hieroglyphics, which Dr. Elmore translates. The hieroglyphics describe the way to the tomb of the Glowing Goddess, where another tablet is found. Dr. Elmore's aide Grebb photographs the tablet and treacherously turns the photos over to Sir Eric.

Sir Eric has the new hieroglyphics translated and they direct him to the location of a chest deep within the Lost City containing the Meteorium 245. With Rod and Tal Shan close behind, Sir Eric and Grebb load the chest aboard a small plane and take off just in time to escape their pursuers.

But their victory is short lived. The two men begin to argue over possession of the priceless Meteorium. During their struggle the chest is opened, unleashing the awesome power of the element; the airplane is totally disintegrated in midair.

The Mysterious Mr. M

13 Episodes
Universal, 1946

Directed by
Lewis D. Collins
and Vernon Keays

CAST

Kirby Walsh	Richard Martin
Shirley Clinton	Pamela Blake
Grant Farrell	Dennis Moore
Marina Lamont	Jane Randolph
Derek Lamont	Danny Norton
Grandma Waldron	Virginia Brissac
Anthony Waldron	Edmund MacDonald
Wetherby	Byron Fougler
Captain Blair	Joseph Crehan
Shrak	Jack Ingram

Grant Farrell, federal investigator, is called upon by civic authorities to assist Kirby Walsh, a local detective, in solving the case of the disappearance of Dr. Kittridge, a noted submarine inventor.

Through an injection of the new drug Hypnotrene, the noted scientist is placed under a hypnotic spell by Anthony Waldron, a gang leader, who is taking instructions from a "Mysterious Mr. M." The injection proves fatal before Kittridge can divulge any information about his new underseas creation.

Through her attorney Mr. Wetherby, Mrs. Waldron, the grandmother of the notorious gang leader, offers a huge reward for the arrest of the traitorous and maniacal murderer the Mysterious Mr. M.

Unbeknownst to the investigators, Anthony Waldron has his secret laboratory located beneath Mrs. Waldron's mansion and, through secret panels and passageways, has access to most of what is going on within the building.

As Farrell and Shirley Clinton, a beautiful insurance investigator, follow up a clue leading to a nearby oil field, Waldron's henchmen learn of their plans and prepare a trap. As the investigators enter the refinery, the gangsters set off a dynamite explosion that destroys the huge oil storage tanks. Farrell and Shirley, however, flee to safety.

When Waldron learns that a valuable submarine generator is being sent to the investigators, he arranges for it to be hijacked en route. To prevent further thefts, Walsh and Shirley decide to fly a huge transport plane, filled with vital submarine gear, to its destination. As Walsh is piloting the plane, one of Waldron's henchmen, who has stowed away, knocks him unconscious and parachutes to safety as the plane goes out of control. Shirley establishes radio contact with Farrell at the airport and, with his guidance, manages to bring the plane in for a rough but safe landing.

Kirby is taken to a nearby hospital while Shirley, who had seen the face of the thug who clobbered the detective, goes to the Waldron mansion to see if Mrs. Waldron can help identify the assailant. While she is discussing the matter with Mrs. Waldron, Anthony appears and places them both under the influence of Hypnotrene. He sends Mrs. Waldron to her room and takes Shirley to his underground laboratory, to hold as hostage. As he is about to leave, Waldron notices that Farrell has entered the mansion, so the gangster prepares a trap. He tells the hypnotized Shirley to go upstairs and re-enter the house, lead Farrell down to the secret laboratory, and then pull a hidden wall lever, which will blow the house to smithereens, while he escapes in Mr. M's submarine, waiting offshore. Shirley proceeds to do as she's told, pretending accidentally to find the secret passageway leading to the laboratory. But Farrell is suspicious of her strange behavior and stops her just before she is about to pull the fatal lever. He administers a Hypnotrene antidote, and Shirley tells him of Waldron's plans to escape by submarine. The two quickly hop into a seaplane and begin to comb the shoreline.

Meanwhile, aboard the submarine, Waldron comes face-to-face with the Mysterious Mr. M,

Insurance investigator Pamela Blake listens as law officers Dennis Moore and Richard Martin (*third and fourth from left*) try to trace the whereabouts of Mr. M.

who is Mrs. Waldron's lawyer Wetherby. Both villains are arguing over their failure to obtain the valuable submarine plans, when the investigator's seaplane appears and Farrell drops a load of bombs, blasting the sub to the bottom of the sea and killing all aboard.

The Phantom Rider

12 Episodes	Directed by
Republic, 1946	Spencer Bennet
	and Fred Brannon

CAST

Dr. Jim Sterling)	
Phantom Rider)	Robert Kent
Doris Hammond	Peggy Stewart
Fred Carson	LeRoy Mason
Blue Feather	George J. Lewis
Ben Brady	Kenne Duncan
Nugget	Hal Taliaferro
Yellow Wolf	Chief Thundercloud
Cass	Monte Hale
Ceta	Tom London
Marshal	Roy Barcroft
Senator Williams	John Hamilton
Keeler	Hugh Prosser
Deputy Sheriff	Jack Kirk
Randall	Rex Lease
Tim	Tommy Coats
Logan	Joe Yrigoyen
Lyons	Bill Yrigoyen

Peggy Stewart, in the grip of an outlaw.

The Scarlet Horseman

13 Episodes
Universal, 1946

Directed by
Ray Taylor
and Lewis Collins

CAST

Jim Bannion	Paul Guilfoyle
Kirk Norris	Peter Cookson
Carla	Virginia Christine
Loma	Victoria Horne
Ballou	Danny Morton
Tioga	Fred Coby
Elise Halliday	Janet Shaw
Tragg	Jack Ingram
Zero Quick	Edward M. Howard
Idaho	Harold Goodman
Pecos	Ralph Lewis
Kyle	Edmund Cobb
Amigo	Cy Kendall

Comanches, led by the beautiful half-breed Loma, are receiving guns from smuggler Zero Quick, in preparation for a major Indian uprising. To avoid detection, Loma works as a maid for Carla Marquette, daughter of a discredited state senator.

As the uprising begins, Kirk Norris and Jim Bannion, Texas undercover agents, arrive to help quell the rampaging Indians. They decide to have Jim assume the identity of the Scarlet Horseman, the legendary champion of the Comanches whose leadership they have always followed. Although Loma manages to convince the tribesmen that this Scarlet Horseman is not their real champion, their awe of him does not vanish completely.

The agents discover that wives and daughters of influential Texas senators have been kidnapped by a mysterious traitor known only as Matosca. The captives are being held hostages as part of the traitor's scheme to pressure the senators into supporting the partitioning of Texas. When Elise Halliday, the daughter of a prominent senator, is taken prisoner, the Scarlet Horseman trails her captors and rescues her. Meanwhile, Kirk Norris has been intercepting Zero Quick's gun-smuggling henchmen, and has learned that Loma works under Matosca's orders. He reports this to Carla Marquette.

Realizing that the villains still intend to kidnap Elise, Jim and Kirk prepare a trap by announcing that Elise will be coming to live in town. When Matosca's henchmen kidnap the senator's daughter, the Scarlet Horseman takes Elise's place in a wagon, hoping that he will be led to the Legion of Lost Women. But Zero Quick recaptures Elise and signals a warning

to the wagon driver, who lights a dynamite fuse and leaps off the wagon. Fortunately, the Scarlet Horseman senses the danger and leaps from the wagon just as it explodes.

Kirk and a Wells Fargo agent named Idaho join forces and trace mud found in Quick's office to its source, only to ride into an Indian ambush prepared by Matosca and Quick, now working together. Kirk and Idaho are about to be burned at the stake when the Scarlet Horseman appears, routs the Comanches, and rescues the two captives. Matosca warns the senators that their wives and daughters will be put to death if a law is not passed permitting the Comanches to vote, thus assuring the traitor's possession of the valuable Plains territory.

In a final encounter with Quick, the Scarlet Horseman, Kirk, and Idaho learn of the location of the Legion of Lost Women. The Scarlet Horseman gallops to the rescue, then heads for the ranch of Carla Marquette, who reveals herself to be the diabolical Matosca. The Horseman arrives just in time to save Elise's life by shooting the gun from Matosca's hand and capturing the archtraitoress.

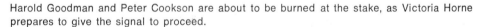

Harold Goodman and Peter Cookson are about to be burned at the stake, as Victoria Horne prepares to give the signal to proceed.

Son of the Guardsman

15 Episodes	Directed by
Columbia, 1946	Derwin Abrahams

CAST

David Trent	Robert Shaw
Louise Markham	Daun Kennedy
Roger Mowbry	Robert "Buzz" Henry
Allan Hawk	Jim Diehl
Red Robert	Hugh Prosser
Mark Crowell	Leonard Penn
Lord Markham	Wheeler Oakman
Sir Edgar Bullard	Charles King
Lord Hampton	John Merton
Duncan	Ray Bennett
Sir William Pryor	I. Stanford Jolley
Dame Duncan	Belle Mitchell
Morgan	Frank Ellis
Lynn	Al Ferguson

In medieval England, Dave Trent turns against his robber-baron uncle Edgar Bullard and joins a group of free men known as outlaws, who fight all evildoers. Young Roger Mowbry joins the fighters when his family is murdered by Bullard's men.

Bullard wants lovely Louise Markham and would give her in marriage to one of his allies. But, Trent in love with Louise, stops such action by defending her honor in a series of constant battles involving the outlaws and the tyrants. Roger Mowbry is found to be Prince Richard, heir to a throne being misused by a wicked regent. Bullard wages a last all-out battle to destroy the lad and the outlaws. However, Trent and his men prevail. Richard is crowned king, and David and Louise prepare to marry.

1947

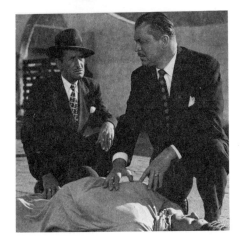

The Black Widow

13 Episodes (Republic, 1947	Directed by Spencer Bennet and Fred C. Brannon

CAST

Steve	Bruce Edwards
Joyce	Virginia Lindley
Sombra	Carol Forman
Ward	Anthony Warde
Ruth Dayton	Virginia Carroll
Jaffa	I. Stanford Jolley
Hitomu	Theodore Gottlieb
Dr. Curry	Ramsay Ames
Walker	Gene Stutenroth
Weston	Sam Flint
Bard	Tom Steele
Bill	Dale Van Sickel
Dr. Godfrey	LeRoy Mason
Bradley	Forrest Taylor
Blinkey	Ernie Adams
Burns	Keith Richards

To expedite his nefarious plan to dominate the world, Asian King Hitomu sends his daughter Sombra to America to steal the secret of a new atomic rocket engine. Armed with the latest electronic devices, Sombra hides behind the "front" of a fortune-telling establishment. She is aided by Ward, a gangster, and Jaffa, a corrupt, embittered scientist.

The Daily Clarion, hot on the scent of news about a series of spider-poison killings, hires the intrepid amateur criminologist Steve Colt to unravel the murders, and assigns Joyce Winters, a reporter, to assist him. When Steve stumbles on to the fact that the murder victims were all connected with Henry Weston, an atom bomb scientist now involved in the development of the atomic rocket engine, Steve rushes out to warn him, and arrives as Sombra, disguised as Weston's secretary, is escaping with the formula for the rocket's fuel sealed in a glass tube.

As Steve pursues her, Sombra eludes him by the use of a scientific device that enables her to change the color of her car while it is in motion. Meanwhile Hitomu arrives to join Sombra by means of a teleportation machine that allows him to materialize himself halfway around the world!

Realizing that Weston is the key to the Black Widow's apparent schemes, Steve has the scientist conduct his work in secret, in an abandoned mine. As work continues and Steve prepares to ship a planeload of advanced-design rocket motors to a scientific installation, Sombra plants a crate loaded with two of her henchmen on the plane. As the ship takes off, the two criminals emerge and try to seize control. But a fight ensues during which both spies are thrown to their doom.

Pretending to be injured, Steve sends out word that he has been hospitalized, hoping that Sombra will attempt to remove him in some way. The trap works. Sombra enters his room disguised as a nurse and tries to inject poison into his bloodstream, but Steve seizes her and has her jailed. Hours of intensive grilling prove useless; Sombra denies all guilt, insisting that she is a registered nurse. Steve leaves the police station for a while, and, when he returns, he finds Sombra gone. A guard explains that she died of a sudden heart attack and was driven to the morgue. When Steve gets to the morgue, he finds the driver regaining consciousness: he had been knocked out and his truck stolen.

Conferring with Weston, Steve learns that a serum which produced all the symptoms of heart failure without actually causing death had been developed by a scientist named Jaffa, who had subsequently been sent to prison for illegal activities. In jail he had died of—a bizarre coincidence—*heart failure.* Hearing this, Steve is certain that Jaffa is not really dead and is in league with Sombra. He and Joyce set off to find any acquaintances of Jaffa. Their investigation leads them to a local bookdealer named Hagen, who had been a former friend of Jaffa's. Hagen agrees to run an ad as bait, asking for information about the "late" scientist. But Hagen, too, is in league with the Black Widow and informs her of the trap.

A few days later Steve returns and learns from Hagen that there has been one response to the ad: a directive to go to a certain building on the outskirts of town for more information. As soon as Steve leaves, Hagen radios the news to Sombra. But a minute later Steve reenters Hagen's office to pick up a book he had left behind. In the "book" is a tape recorder, which has transcribed Hagen's message to Sombra. Hagen is arrested, and Steve and Joyce rush to the house mentioned in the advertisement. Meanwhile, Ward is wiring the house's phone to a load of dynamite. All Sombra has to do is dial the phone from her hideout, and the decoy building will be blown to smithereens. Ward then hides in the woods outside the house, waiting for Steve's arrival.

Steve and Joyce pull up, and while Steve goes into the house, Joyce waits outside in the car. As soon as he sees Steve enter, Ward notifies Sombra via his car radio, and Sombra begins to dial. But Joyce notices the reflection from Ward's car window and goes to investigate. Overhearing his message, she pushes Ward and manages to honk his car horn. Steve dashes from the house just as it blows up. Ward knocks Joyce unconscious and kidnaps her before Steve can arrive. Steve and the police conduct an intensive search of the entire area, but all they can come up with is Ward's car, with no sign of Joyce or any of the Black Widow's gang.

Steve gets a brilliant idea: he deduces that the two-way radio in Ward's car is tuned in to the frequency of the radio in Sombra's hideout, and that through radio triangulation he can pinpoint the exact location of the hideout. Staking out three short-wave radio receivers at key points, Steve relays a message to Sombra from Ward's car. In Sombra's headquarters, Joyce flings herself at the radio and issues a plea for help, but Ward hurls her away and turns off the short-wave set. However, Joyce's brief statement was enough to enable Steve's three radio operators to get a triangulation "fix" on the position of Sombra's hideout. Steve immediately orders a full contingent of police to converge upon the spot, which he recognizes as Sombra's fortune-telling establishment.

Fearing for Joyce's safety, Steve decides to enter alone, with the police to follow if they hear any shots. Meanwhile, Hitomu and the others prepare to escape and send Sombra to stall for time. As Steve bursts into her office, Sombra invites him to sit down, and proposes a

Sam Flint is forced to relinquish the rocket fuel formula to Sombra, disguised as Virginia Carroll, and her henchman Tom Steele.

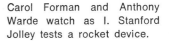

Carol Forman and Anthony Warde watch as I. Stanford Jolley tests a rocket device.

deal: her life for Joyce's. As she speaks, she presses a button which releases a poisonous black widow on the chair near Steve's neck. But Steve sees its reflection in a mirror on Sombra's desk and leaps forward, just as Ward enters. As Steve and Ward battle, Sombra, pistol in hand, is knocked into the deadly chair and is bitten by the spider. In the throes of death, Sombra fires, killing Ward.

Steve dashes into the back room and shoots Jaffa and Hitomu as they attempt to escape. Joyce is rescued, and her appreciation is matched only by her eagerness to phone in the story of the demise of the Black Widow threat.

Anthony Warde slugs it out with Bruce Edwards as another spy joins the fray.

Brick Bradford

15 Episodes
Columbia, 1947

Directed by
Spencer Bennet

CAST

Brick Bradford	Kane Richmond
Sandy Sanderson	Rick Vallin
June Saunders	Linda Johnson
Professor Salisbury	Pierre Watkin
Laydron	Charles Quigley
Albers	Jack Ingram
Black	Fred Graham
Dr. Tymak	John Merton
Byrus	Leonard Penn
Walthar	Wheeler Oakman
Queen Khana	Carol Forman
Creed	Charles King
Dent	John Hart
Carol Preston	Helene Stanley
Prescott	Nelson Leigh
Zuntar	Robert Barron
Meaker	George de Normand

Brick Bradford is asked by a United Nations official to protect the Interceptor Ray, an antiguided missile weapon which Dr. Tymak is perfecting. Brick and his friends Professor Salis-

Pierre Watkin and Linda Johnson face the deadly death ray. Charles Quigley points to the timing device as cohorts Fred Graham and Jack Ingram watch intently.

bury, the professor's daughter June, and Sandy Sanderson are spied upon by a gang led by Laydron, who want the invention for their own evil ends.

One of Dr. Tymak's more spectacular innovations is a "crystal door," entry into which enables one to be transported to the moon. Tymak uses this device to obtain the element Lunarium, necessary for his invention and available only on the moon. Tymak, however, runs into Lunarians who capture him and hold him prisoner. When Brick steps through the crystal door to rescue Tymak he meets members of an exile force who are trying to overthrow the evil rulers of the moon. Brick succeeds in helping them while rescuing Tymak.

Back on earth, Brick again rescues Tymak from Laydron's kidnap attempts. But having accomplished this, Tymak discovers that in order to continue his work, he needs a formula which was developed by an eighteenth-century Englishman and hidden in Central America. Brick and Sandy hop into the Time Top, a craft that can travel back into time. In order to obtain the formula Brick and Sandy are forced to combat natives and buccaneers before returning safely in time, where Laydron continues to harass Tymak.

Jack Armstrong

15 Episodes	Directed by
Columbia, 1947	Wallace Fox

CAST

Jack Armstrong	John Hart
Betty	Rosemary La Planche
Alura	Claire James
Billy	Joe Brown
Uncle Jim	Pierre Watkin
Grood	Charles Middleton
Professor Zorn	Wheeler Oakman
Blair	Jack Ingram
Slade	Eddie Parker
Vic Hardy	Hugh Prosser
Gregory Pierce	John Merton
Dr. Albour	Gene Stutenroth

Jim Fairfield, the head of an aviation company that develops atom-powered motors, learns from his chief scientist Vic Hardy that cosmic radioactivity is being employed in experiments outside the country. This information is revealed to Jim's nephew Billy, his niece Betty, and their best friend Jack Armstrong. The threesome decide to investigate the matter further before calling the police.

When Hardy is kidnapped by enemy agents, the trio's investigation takes them to an enchanted island where Grood, a villainous scientist, is masterminding a mad scheme to conquer the world. Jack, Billy, and Uncle Jim rescue Hardy, but Grood escapes to a secret airfield where a plane awaits him. Jack, however, follows his trail and, after a desperate struggle, kills the criminal with a hand grenade. Jack and his friends leave the island—the world is no longer threatened with destruction.

Jesse James Rides Again

13 Episodes	Directed by
Republic, 1947	Fred C. Brannon
	and Thomas Carr

CAST

Jesse James	Clayton Moore	Clark	Tristram Coffin
Ann	Linda Stirling	Bolton	Tom London
Lawton	Roy Barcroft	Tim	Holly Bane
Steve	John Compton	Wilkie	Edmund Cobb
		The Sheriff	Gene Stutenroth
		Hawks	LeRoy Mason
		Grant	Edward Cassidy
		Sam	Dave Anderson
		Captain Flint	Eddie Parker
		Goff	Tom Steele
		Brock	Dale Van Sickel

A reformed Jesse James tries to go straight on his Missouri farm, but he is warned by his friend Steve that he is about to be arrested for the Northfield Bank robbery in which he played no part. Knowing that he will not be able to prove his innocence because of his reputation, he and Steve flee into the South.

While riding through Tennessee, they stop to water their horses at the Bolton Farm in Peaceful Valley. There they learn that a band of hooded raiders has been attacking the farm in the valley. In the course of their conversation, the Bolton farm is attacked by the raiders and Jesse and Steve help drive them off.

The two fugitives discover that there is oil under Peaceful Valley and that sinister forces will stop at nothing to get at it. Jesse survives many attempts on his life, but he is able to expose the outlaws, led by Lawton, and exonerate himself completely.

Clayton Moore's disguise is discovered by the hooded raiders.

Clayton Moore, in a critical struggle with Roy Barcroft.

The Sea Hound

15 Episodes
Columbia, 1947

Directed by
Walter B. Eason
and Mack Wright

CAST

Captain Silver	Buster Crabbe
Tex	Jimmy Lloyd
Ann Whitney	Pamela Blake
Jerry	Ralph Hodges
Admiral	Robert Barron
Rand	Hugh Prosser
Manila	Rick Vallin
Murdock	Jack Ingram
Kukai	Spencer Chan
John Whitney	Milton Kibbee
Lon	Al Baffert
Black Mike	Stanley Blystone
Sloan	Robert Duncan
Vardman	Pierce Lyden
Singapore	Rusty Wescoatt

Captain Silver, cruising in tropical waters in his schooner *Sea Hound,* responds to an SOS from the yacht *Esmeralda* under attack by pirates in Typhoon Cove. His crew includes Jerry a young boy; Tex, a seagoing cowboy; Kukai, a Chinese scientist-inventor, and their dog Flecha. Stanley Rand, the yacht's owner; Ann Whitney, his guest; and Vardman, Rand's confidante, are cornered on the island by men in the employ of the Admiral, a ruthless sea robber posing as a trader and rubber planter.

Captain Silver and his friends drive the pirates off and learn that Rand and Ann had come to the island to meet Ann's father, who had supposedly discovered the location of legendary Spanish treasure. They had been searching for Whitney when they were attacked by the Admiral's men.

Silver and the group sail in search of a sunken galleon and Spanish gold, following directions on an old map in Rand's possession. Silver, using a diving outfit, finds part of the wreck, and the treasure chest, which proves to be empty. He learns that the galleon's treasure had been taken by natives, the Ryaks.

Back in port, Silver and his friends are beset by toughs in a cafe, but the Admiral and his henchmen, pretending friendship for Silver, help rout the bullies. The Admiral then invites Silver and his party to visit his rubber plantation in the interior. While they are his guests, the Admiral hears that Rand and Vardman had previously robbed a man, possibly John Whitney, of a secret map, and that Whitney was subsequently captured and taken into the interior by natives.

When Silver and his friends attempt to leave the plantation, they find their way blocked by the Admiral's gang, and a fight starts, with Silver and the others battling their way to freedom.

At night, the Admiral's henchmen steal aboard the *Sea Hound* and obtain a copy of the map which indicates the location of the Spanish treasure. Rand and Vardman promptly desert Silver for the Admiral, who wants them to decipher the stolen map.

But when they fail to produce conclusive facts the Admiral throws Rand and Vardman into the slave camp and orders them tortured, believing that they are concealing information about the Spanish treasure. The two are no sooner imprisoned than the Ryaks attack the slave camp and seize Rand and Vardman.

Silver learns that Whitney has been found by the Admiral and is being held prisoner aboard the *Albatross,* the Admiral's boat. He decides the rescue of Whitney is a one-man job, swims out to the ship, and succeeds in getting off the boat with Whitney, but with the Admiral's men after them.

Deep in the jungle, Silver and Whitney join forces with Tex, Jerry, and Ann and fight their enemies. Ann and her father are captured by Rand and Vardman, who turn their prisoners over to the Admiral. They have made a bargain with the Admiral to share in the treasure as reward for their evil act.

Whitney, the key to the treasure, escapes

from the Admiral. The Ryaks, meanwhile, capture Tex and Jerry and also the Admiral and two of his henchmen. When the Admiral bargains to save only himself, one of his men, angered, slays him. Silver saves the Ryak chief when this man tries to escape, using the chief as hostage. In the scrape the Admiral's henchman plunges over a cliff to his death. Grateful to Silver for saving their chief, the Ryaks release Tex and Jerry and reward the captain with the Spanish treasure. Silver and his crew and Ann, now permanently united with her father, sail away from the island.

Ralph Hodges and Buster Crabbe, on the lookout for the Admiral's men.

Son of Zorro

13 Episodes
Republic, 1947

Directed by
Spencer Bennet
and Fred C. Brannon

CAST

Jeff Stewart	George Turner
Kate Wells	Peggy Stewart
Boyd	Roy Barcroft
Sheriff Moody	Edward Cassidy
Judge Hyde	Ernie Adams
Pancho	Stanley Price
Stockton	Edmund Cobb
Thomas	Ken Terrell
Baldwin	Wheaton Chambers
Quirt	Fred Graham
Melton	Eddie Parker
Fred	Si Jenks
Hood	Jack O'Shea
Charlie	Jack Kirk
Leach	Tom Steele
Murray	Dale Van Sickel

Young cavalry officer Jeff Stewart returns to his home in the west after the Civil War to find that a ring of crooked politicians has taken over the country, bleeding the people with an exorbitant 50 percent toll tax on the main highway, and protecting the bandits that raid the ranches. With the permission of the state governor and the assistance of Kate Wells, the postmistress, Jeff plans to build another road to beat the toll. He also decides to resurrect an ancestor of his who, in a similar situation, took the law into his own hands—Zorro. With the aid of Pancho, Zorro manages to thwart the schemes of the conspirators and exposes the sheriff, Judge Hyde and, finally, Daniels (the mastermind) as participants in the crooked dealings in the country.

Roy Barcroft and his cohorts threaten the captured George Turner.

George Turner prevents Peggy Stewart from removing his mask.

Peggy Stewart and Edward Cassidy regretfully prepare to place George Turner under arrest.

The Vigilante

15 Episodes   Directed by
Columbia, 1947   Wallace Fox

CAST

Greg Sanders	Ralph Byrd
Betty Winslow	Ramsay Ames
George Pierce	Lyle Talbot
Stuff	George Offerman, Jr.
Prince Amil	Robert Barron
Captain Reilly	Hugh Prosser
Silver	Jack Ingram
Doc	Eddie Parker
Walt	George Chesebro
Miller	Eddie Cobb

The Vigilante, government undercover agent, is in reality Greg Sanders, western movie star. His dual identity is known only to his assistant Stuff. An assignment takes Greg and Stuff to the ranch of wealthy George Pierce. Other guests include Prince Amil, a mysterious potentate; his aide Hamid; Betty Winslow, a rodeo queen; Captain Reilly of the sheriff's squad; and Tex Collyer, a rancher.

Pierce, acting as a gang leader known as X-1, is after a string of pearls called "the 100 tears of blood," which have a mysterious origin. The "tears of blood" are actually blood-red pearls which have been concealed in the hooves of five stallions belonging to Pierce's guests.

Pierce and his men will stop at nothing in their efforts to obtain the pearls. There are numerous attempts upon the lives of those whom Pierce suspects of having the pearls. Prince Amil tells Greg that Hamid had stolen the pearls originally and that he is now trying to regain them in order to spare others the curse that went with their ownership.

The Vigilante, aided by Hamid, proceeds to accumulate evidence linking Pierce to these crimes. In a final showdown, Pierce is killed and Amil destroys the pearls with acid. The curse that haunted the owners of the "100 tears of blood" is removed forever.

George Chesebro and Lyle Talbot kneel over a fallen foe.

1948

Sam Flint, Noel Neill, Steve Darrell, and Clayton Moore discuss methods for raising money.

Adventures of Frank and Jesse James

13 Episodes
Republic, 1948

Directed by
Fred Brannon
and Yakima Canutt

CAST

Jesse James	Clayton Moore
Frank James	Steve Darrell
Judy Powell	Noel Neill
Rafe Henley	George J. Lewis
Powell	Stanley Andrews
Amos Ramsey	John Crawford
Thatcher	Sam Flint
Sheriff Towey	House Peters, Jr.
Dale	Dale Van Sickel
Steele	Tom Steele
Nichols	James Dale
Ward	I. Stanford Jolley
Marshal	Gene Stutenroth
Bill	Lane Bradford
Station Agent	George Chesebro
Stage Driver	Jack Kirk

Frank and Jesse James, fugitives from justice, together with miner Jim Powell and Judy his daughter devise a plan to repay the victims their gang has robbed. Jim is certain that, with a little more work, one of his mines will yield enough gold to pay off handsomely. Jesse borrows money from a friend, Paul Thatcher, to buy the necessary equipment, and work is begun.

When gold is located, mine foreman Amos Ramsey kills Powell and conceals the discovery. Ramsey then hires Rafe Henley's outlaw gang to prevent any attempts to work the mine. The James boys, posing as Judy's cousins, return to town in an effort to track down Powell's murderer and reopen the mine. When the Henley gang continues to block work in the mine by destroying equipment, Frank and Jesse do everything possible to raise money for new supplies, while, at the same time, fighting off gang attacks.

Through it all, Ramsey manages to hide his guilt, primarily because Henley's gang acts as a decoy for his machinations. But eventually, Frank and Jesse discover Ramsey's involvement and catch both him and Henley redhanded while they are extracting gold from the mine. In the battle that follows, both villains are killed.

Congo Bill

15 Episodes	Directed by
Columbia, 1948	Spencer Bennet
	and Thomas Carr

CAST

Congo Bill	Don McGuire
Lursen	Cleo Moore
Cameron	Jack Ingram
Bernie MacGraw	I. Stanford Jolley
Andre Bocar	Leonard Penn
Dr. Greenway	Nelson Leigh
Kleeg	Charles King
Zalea	Armida
Morelli	Hugh Prosser
Kahla	Neyle Morrow
Villabo	Fred Graham
Ivan	Rusty Wescoatt
Rogan	Anthony Warde
Tom MacGraw	Stephen Carr

Don McGuire tries to stop I. Stanford Jolley from reaching his pistol.

Congo Bill, wild animal trainer and jungle expert, undertakes to deliver a letter to Ruth Culver, the heiress to the $500,000 Culver Circus fortune, who has been missing in Africa. In Africa he learns of the rumored existence of a white queen in the jungle. His safari is beset by many evil forces, most formidable among them the henchmen of Andre Bocar, African trader, secretly in league with Bernie MacGraw, who hopes to inherit the fortune himself. Bill is aided by a mysterious stranger, Cameron.

Congo Bill meets Lureen, the white queen, and discovers she is the missing circus heiress. The queen's witch doctor, who is shipping illicit gold to Bocar, tries to do away with Bill. With the aid of Cameron, who turns out to be a member of the Colonial Intelligence seeking the gold, Bill recovers the precious metal and traps Bernie and Bocar and his gang. He and Lureen return to the States to sponsor a bigger and better circus than ever.

Virginia Belmont and Jim Bannon defend themselves from Mort's men.

Dangers of the Canadian Mounted

12 Episodes	Directed by
Republic, 1948	Fred Brannon
	and Yakima Canutt

CAST

Christopher Royal	Jim Bannon
Bobbie Page	Virginia Belmont
Mort	Anthony Warde
Skagway Kate	Dorothy Granger
Dan Page	Bill Van Sickel
Fagin	Tom Steele
Boyd	Dale Van Sickel
Belanco	I. Stanford Jolley
George	Phil Warren
Dale	Lee Morgan
Andy	James Dale
Oldtimer	Ted Adams
Danton	John Crawford
Marshal	Jack Clifford
Lowry	Eddie Parker
U.S. Commissioner	Frank O'Connor

In the town of Alcan on the international borderline that divides the United States from Canada, a prospector is brutally murdered by outlaw Mort Fowler, just after he'd stumbled upon an ancient Chinese junk. The junk is said to be one of the treasure-hunting ships sent out by Genghis Khan in the thirteenth century and is believed to hold the clue to a vast hidden fortune. A gang, headed by Mort, who takes orders from a mysterious "Chief," is searching for the secret riches.

Mort brings noted "Orientologist" Professor Belanco to the site of the junk, and forces the professor to study the artifacts and coins found on board.

When he learns that the territory is to be opened to homesteaders, Mort directs a series of attacks against the road builders which brings Captain Chris Royal of the Canadian Mounted Police to the scene to face a succession of terrifying adventures. The first occurs on a speeding train which Mort has wired with explosives. As the fuses sputter, Chris is knocked out and left by Mort to be blown up with the train. Chris narrowly escapes death by regaining consciousness and leaping from the train a few seconds before it explodes.

Chris identifies Mort through the serial number of his gun which he had dropped on the train. Knowing that Mort often visits Skagway Kate's boardinghouse, Royal lies in wait and trails Mort to his cabin where he attempts to place the outlaw under arrest. But a fight develops and Mort escapes in a car.

When Mort returns to his hideout, he finds that Professor Belanco has interpreted the ancient coins and uncovered a message that states: Secret of Treasure in altar in cave of a Thousand Tunnels. The men decide to move all of their gear to the cave of a Thousand Tunnels, located several miles away, to facilitate the interpretation of any hieroglyphics that might turn up in the cave. Belanco suggests that he needs more metal-cleaning compound and writes out a prescription in Latin for the formula. Porter, one of Mort's men, is sent into Alcan to have the prescription filled.

But the Latin prescription is in reality a plea for help, and the Alcan druggist immediately shows it to Royal. The message states that Belanco is being held prisoner and will be driving past a certain path that night. Royal tells the druggist to stall Porter, and promptly sets out to the spot mentioned in the message. Royal arrives in time to intercept Mort and Belanco but Mort's men, following him in another car, prevent Royal from rescuing the professor. Mort sends his men to the cave with Belanco, while he heads back to Alcan to warn Porter. Royal also has returned to Alcan, intending to give Porter a fake compound and follow him to the outlaw's hideout. But Mort arrives and yells a warning to Porter, who starts to run. When it becomes obvious that Porter is going to be captured, Mort shoots him to prevent him from talking.

In the "Cave of a Thousand Tunnels," Belanco and Mort uncover a hidden chamber containing a large stone idol. An inscription on the idol warns that anyone who proceeds further faces certain death. The professor feigns great fright and, despite Mort's many threats, refuses to unlock the idol's secret compartments. In order to keep abreast of Royal's activities, Mort has one of his men allow himself to be captured as a poacher and locked up in Alcan's jail. From this intimate vantage point, the outlaw is able to overhear all of Royal's plans, and relay this information by flashing a mirror from his cell window to an accomplice in the woods outside.

As part of a plan to get Belanco to proceed, Mort and his men attack a one-man Royal Mounted observation post and steal the officer's uniform. However, the Mountie's radio is on, and the command post overhears Mort's instructions to bring the uniform to the Cave of a Thousand Tunnels. Upon hearing this, Sergeant Royal sets out at once for the cave. Meanwhile, in the cave, Belanco is suddenly "rescued" by a Royal Mounted trooper who "shoots" the outlaw guarding the professor.

The grateful professor is explaining how to unlock the secret of the idol to his rescuer when the "Mountie" reveals his true identity as an outlaw. The "dead" guard stands up and Mort enters, laughing at his scheme's success. Just as Mort begins to manipulate the various levers and buttons on the idol as instructed by Belanco, the professor warns him that, if he does, the stone doors of the chamber will slide shut and a deadly gas will engulf them. Mort doesn't believe the professor, but blocks the doors with some timber as a precaution. Sure enough, as Mort uncovers the secret compartment within the idol and removes an ancient pouch, gas begins to pour in from the idol's interior.

At this point Sergeant Royal enters, but his pistol is struck from his hand by one of Mort's men. Royal and Belanco are knocked unconscious and left in the gas-filled chamber to die. The outlaws flee after removing the timber and allowing the stone doors to slide shut. Royal recovers and tries desperately to unlock the doors, but to no avail. Belanco recovers and tells Royal to pull the arm of the idol down. Royal does so and the doors swing open, allowing the two to escape.

Back in Alcan, Royal is troubled by the fact that Mort apparently is aware of all his plans. Suspecting a link between his prisoner and Mort, Royal loudly proclaims some "vital information" concerning his investigation, and catches the prisoner redhanded as he attempts to flash the news via a mirror. Royal heads for the woods behind the jail and has a Royal Mounted officer complete the false mirror-message: he knows of Mort's whereabouts and is on his way there. When the outlaw in the forest receives the message he takes off immediately to warn Mort. Royal follows him.

Meanwhile, the clues taken from the idol lead Mort back to the Chinese junk. Following directions, he discovers a hidden box containing the treasure. Just as he is about to leave, his cohort arrives with news of Royal's plans. Having followed close behind, Royal moves in, guns blazing. Mort flees on horseback, still clutching the treasure chest. Royal kills the remaining outlaw and takes off after Mort.

Mort heads straight for Skagway Kate's boardinghouse, and shows the chest to Kate, who promptly opens it and discovers that the "treasure" is a bottle of clear liquid. Royal arrives and places the two under arrest, correctly surmising that Kate is Mort's mysterious boss. In her anger Kate knocks the bottle to the floor, smashing it. But the liquid suddenly turns into diamonds. As they are being led to prison, Royal explains that the Mongols had discovered the secret of liquefying diamonds, and that the bottle's contents were indeed worth a vast fortune.

G-men Never Forget

12 Episodes
Republic, 1948

Directed by
Fred Brannon
and Yakima Canutt

CAST

Ted O'Hara	—Clayton Moore
Murkland	⎫
Cameron	⎬ ⌐ Roy Barcroft
	⎭
Frances Blake	Ramsay Ames
Parker	Tom Steele
Brent	Dale Van Sickel
Cook	Edmund Cobb
Benson	Stanley Price
Slater	Jack O'Shea
George	Barry Brooks
Hayden	Doug Aylesworth
District Attorney	Frank O'Connor
Miss Stewart	Dian Fauntelle
Fiddler	Eddie Acuff
Staley	George Magrill
Kelsey	Ken Terrell

Pistol in hand, Ramsay Ames helps a grateful Clayton Moore to his feet.

Vic Murkland, a notorious criminal, escapes from prison. His aide Dr. Benson, a plastic surgeon, changes his features so that the gangster looks like the local police commissioner. The real commissioner is kidnapped and held prisoner at Dr. Benson's sanitarium. Murkland then makes his headquarters in the commissioner's office where he can get the information he needs to operate his protective insurance racket.

Ted O'Hara and Sergeant Frances Blake are called in on the case of the prison break and the mysterious disappearance of Murkland. They discover that the Murkland gang plans to destroy the new Channel Island Tunnel in a conspiracy to "shake down" the builder. Their intercession leads them into a series of dangerous adventures. As they race to head off the plans of Murkland and his henchmen, the criminals execute a number of vicious schemes to create an impregnable protection racket in the city.

The escaped convict and his gang menace the G-men with poison gas, falling bombs, flaming gasoline, and a flooded tunnel before, in a decisive battle, Murkland's true identity is exposed and his mad ambitions are thwarted.

Roy Barcroft, Clayton Moore, and Ramsay Ames discussing plans to track down the elusive Murkland.

Clayton Moore looks anything but sick as he talks to a visiting Ramsay Ames.

Kirk Alyn as The Man of Steel.

Superman

15 Episodes	Directed by
Columbia, 1948	Spencer Bennet
	and Thomas Carr

CAST

Superman	Kirk Alyn
Lois Lane	Noel Neill
Jimmy Olsen	Tommy Bond
"Spider Lady"	Carol Forman
Driller	George Meeker
Anton	Jack Ingram
Perry White	Pierre Watkin
Brock	Terry Frost
Conrad	Charles King
Dr. Hackett	Charles Quigley
Dr. Graham	Herbert Rawlinson
Leeds	Forrest Taylor
Morgan	Stephen Carr
Elton	Rusty Wescoatt

A scientist on the planet Krypton rockets his infant son to Earth just before Krypton explodes. The boy is found on Earth by a farmer who names him Clark Kent. When Clark grows up, the farmer tells him of his origin and makes him promise to use his amazing powers only for good.

Disguised as a mild-mannered reporter, Clark gets a job on the *Daily Planet* and soon tangles with the Spider Lady, an underworld queen who is after the reducer ray. Meanwhile, a fragment from the ex-planet Krypton reaches Earth. It is the only substance that can render Superman helpless.

The Spider Lady forces Dr. Graham, a brilliant scientist, to develop a ray comparable to the deadly reducer and threatens to destroy the city if the government doesn't submit to her will.

But Superman stops the reducer-ray threat and, at the same time, neutralizes the dangerous Krypton fragment with the aid of a lead-lined uniform.

In the end, the reducing ray kills the Spider Lady and her henchmen, and Clark gets his first by-line.

Tex Granger

15 Episodes	Directed by
Columbia, 1948	Derwin Abrahams

CAST

Tex	Robert Kellard
Helen	Peggy Stewart
Tim	Buzz Henry
Blaze	Smith Ballew
Reno	Jack Ingram
Carson	I. Stanford Jolley
Adams	Terry Frost
Conroy	Jim Diehl
Sandy	Britt Wood

Robert Kellard blazes away with both six-shooters.

Heading toward the western town of Three Buttes, Tex Granger spies a young boy, Tim, guarding a gold shipment which he has just rescued from a stagecoach that had been held up by Blaze Talbot and Reno. Tex and Tim turn the gold over to its consignee Dance Carson, who uses his loan office to carry out unscrupulous land manipulations. Later, Tex and Tim meet Helen Kent who persuades Tex to purchase a newspaper, *The Frontier.*

Shortly thereafter, Blaze and Reno come to town. Blaze wins Carson's favor and is made marshal. Soon afterward, Reno attacks Carson's office, still seeking the gold. He is driven off, but Three Buttes is turned into a seething caldron of turmoil as the three villains and their henchmen alternately battle each other and combine against the masked Midnight Rider of the Plain—really Tex Granger—who appears mysteriously whenever he is needed. Both as the Rider and as the fighting newspaperman, Tex constantly skirmishes with the outlaws. When he finally subdues them, peace comes to Three Buttes once again.

283

1949

An armored George Reeves moves to the attack.

Adventures of Sir Galahad

15 Episodes
Columbia, 1949

Directed by
Spencer Bennet

CAST

Sir Galahad	George Reeves
Bors	Charles King
Merlin	William Fawcett
Morgan le Fay	Pat Barton
Sir Lancelot	Hugh Prosser
Lady of the Lake	Lois Hall
King Arthur	Nelson Leigh
Kay	Jim Diehl
Bartog	Don Harvey
Queen Guinevere	Marjorie Stapp
Ulric	John Merton
Cawker	Pierce Lyden

Sir Galahad, a young warrior, is refused admission to King Arthur's Round Table until he regains the missing magic sword Excalibur, which makes its possessor invincible. Meanwhile, Ulric the Saxon King invades England. Galahad, aided by Sir Bors, attempts to retrieve the sword from Bartog, Ulric's chief aide, who has secured it from a mysterious knight. Merlin the magician harasses Galahad at every turn. Morgan le Fay, Arthur's sister and a magician, helps him to fight both Merlin's magic and the Saxons. The Black Knight, a traitor within Camelot and in league with Saxons and outlaws, conspires to overthrow King Arthur.

When Queen Guinevere is seized by the plotters, Merlin finally sends Galahad to the Lady of the Lake, who gives him Excalibur, which he brings to Arthur. The Black Knight is unmasked as Modred of the Round Table, and Galahad takes his place as a full-fledged knight.

Batman and Robin

15 Episodes	Directed by
Columbia, 1949	Spencer Bennet

CAST

Batman	Robert Lowery
Robin	John Duncan
Vicki	Jane Adams
Gordon	Lyle Talbot
Harrison	Ralph Graves
Nolan	Don Harvey
Hammil	William Fawcett
Carter	Leonard Penn
Brown	Rick Vallin
Dunne	Michael Whalen
Evans	Greg McClure
Earl	House Peters, Jr.
Jason	Jim Diehl
Ives	Rusty Wescoatt

Batman and Robin, whose real identities are Bruce Wayne and Dick Grayson, are asked to help Police Commissioner Gordon of Gotham City in his search for a remote-control machine stolen by a cloaked, hooded figure known as "The Wizard." The machine was invented by eccentric Professor Hammil, aided by Carter. Bruce and Dick foil the Wizard and his gang. They raid a jewelry store for diamonds necessary for the successful operation of the remote-control machine. From that moment on, Batman and Robin engage in battle after battle against their insidious foe. After learning the true identity of the Wizard, they capture him and smash his gang.

John Duncan and Robert Lowery prepare to capture one of the Wizard's henchmen.

Bruce Gentry—Daredevil of the Skies

15 Episodes
Columbia, 1949

Directed by
Spencer Bennet
and Thomas Carr

CAST

Bruce Gentry	Tom Neal
Juanita Farrell	Judy Clark
Frank Farrell	Ralph Hodges
Dr. Benson	Forrest Taylor
Radcliffe	Hugh Prosser
Krendon	Tristram Coffin
Allen	Jack Ingram
Chandler	Terry Frost
Gregg	Eddie Parker
Ivor	Charles King
Hill	Stephen Carr
Gregory	Dale Van Sickel

Bruce Gentry, working with famed scientist Alexander Benson, sets out to uncover the origin of a deadly secret weapon: an electronically controlled flying disc which can be directed at moving or stationary targets. This disc was masterminded by an enemy agent known only as "The Recorder," because he speaks entirely via recordings. Aided by rancher Frank Farrell and his pretty sister Nita, Bruce tenaciously and consistently foils the Recorder's schemes, which are carried out by the villain's cohorts, Krendon, Allen, and Chandler.

After closing in on the villain's headquarters and confronting the enemy agents, Bruce learns that the Recorder is actually Benson, the scientist. While Bruce is apprehending the criminals, Krendon breaks his bonds long enough to release a deadly disc against the Panama Canal. Bruce quickly races to his plane, takes off in pursuit of the disc, and crashes into it, parachuting to safety just moments before a fiery death. Meanwhile, at the agent's headquarters, the disc's firing apparatus has exploded, killing all of the criminals.

Tom Neal throws a hard left at one of the Recorder's henchmen.

Federal Agents vs. Underworld, Inc.

12 Episodes	Directed by
Republic, 1949	Fred Brannon

CAST

Dave Worth	Kirk Alyn
Laura	Rosemary La Planche
Gordon	Roy Barcroft
Nila	Carol Forman
Steve Evans	James Dale
Professor Williams	Bruce Edwards
Professor Clayton	James Craven
Chambers	Tristram Coffin
Mort	Tom Steele
Professor Graves	Dale Van Sickel
Ali	Jack O'Shea
O'Hara	Marshall Reed
Zod	Bob Wilke
Native	Robert St. Angelo
Courier	George Douglas
Porter	Dave Anderson

Following the strange disappearance of Professor Clayton, famous explorer and archaeologist, Dave Worth, ace federal agent, is assigned to the case. It develops that Nila, an international thief and one of the main conspirators in an infamous organization known as "Underworld, Inc.," is behind the professor's disappearance.

During an expedition to Abistahn, Clayton has discovered the famous Golden Hands of Kurigal, the key to a fabulous fortune hidden in a foreign country. Nila has stolen one of the Hands, and, with her gang, is murdering people ruthlessly in a desperate attempt to track down the second Hand.

To find out more about Nila, Dave goes to the Immigration Bureau to examine files on the entrants from Abistahn. Nila, meanwhile, has sent her strong-arm man Gordon to destroy the records. The two men meet at the bureau. A fight follows in which Gordon manages to imprison Dave in a warehouse. Evans, a fellow federal agent, has picked up Dave's trail and goes to his rescue. At the warehouse, there is a gunfight and Dave is trapped behind a pile of huge packing cases, unaware that a heavy truck is bearing down upon him.

Evans manages to extricate Dave at the last moment. Meanwhile, Nila, who has disguised herself as a scrubwoman, gets past the museum guards to make a deal with Clayton's assistant Professor Williams, for the Hand. Dale and Evans, however, thwart that scheme, maintain the pressure on the underworld gang, and eventually succeed in foiling the crafty Nila. They round up her gang and locate the last of the Golden Hands.

Unaware that they're being attacked from behind, Kirk Alyn and James Dale keep pistols pointed at Roy Barcroft.

Ghost of Zorro

12 Episodes
Republic, 1949

Directed by
Fred C. Brannon

CAST

Zorro	Clayton Moore
Rita	Pamela Blake
Kilgore	Roy Barcroft
Moccasin	George J. Lewis
Crane	Eugene Roth
Mulvaney	John Crawford
Green	I. Stanford Jolley
White	Steve Clark
Marshal Simpson	Steve Darrell
Hodge	Dale Van Sickel
Brace	Tom Steele
Yellow Hawk	Alex Montoya
Fowler	Marshall Reed
Doctor	Frank O'Connor
Freight Agent	Jack O'Shea
Larkin	Holly Bane

George J. Lewis pulls a knife on Zorro as Pamela Blake tries to help.

Clayton Moore and Pamela Blake wait for Crane's next move.

Jonathan White and his daughter Rita, the owners of the Pioneer Telegraph Company, plan to extend their lines from St. Joseph to Twin Bluffs, a frontier outpost. They employ a work crew led by Ken Mason, an eastern surveying engineer. George Crane, the operator of a blacksmith shop, secretly plots to stop this expansion in order to prevent the exposure of his vast outlaw empire.

White is killed in an Indian attack arranged by Crane. Rita resolves to continue building the line and contacts Crane, who she believes is her friend. When Crane hears of Rita's resolution, he orders an Indian attack on the telegraph company's camp.

Meanwhile, Ken secretly meets Moccasin, an Indian with whom he was raised, and finds out that the original Zorro was his grandfather. With Moccasin's aid, Ken vows to ride as the Ghost of Zorro and stamp out the evil plaguing the territory.

Masked as the Ghost of Zorro, Ken frustrates Crane's malicious plans and is finally able to expose the master criminal.

King of the Rocket Men

12 Episodes
Republic, 1949

Directed by
Fred Brannon

CAST

Jeff King — Tristram Coffin
Glenda Thomas — Mae Clarke
Tony Dirken — Don Haggerty
Burt Winslow — House Peters, Jr.
Professor Millard — James Craven
Professor Bryant — I. Stanford Jolley
Chairman — Douglas Evans
Martin Conway — Ted Adams
Gunther Von Strum — Stanley Price
Martin — Dale Van Sickel
Knox — Tom Steele
Blears — David Sharpe
Rowan — Eddie Parker
Turk — Michael Ferro
Guard — Frank O'Connor
Phillips — Buddy Roosevelt

Diabolical Dr. Vulcan causes the death of Professor Drake and nearly kills Professor Millard of Science Associates, a privately operated desert research project. These events attract the interest of Glenda Thomas, photographer for *Miracle Science* magazine. She visits the project and meets Burt Winslow, the publicity director, and Jeff King, a young project member.

Later, Jeff is attacked by two of Dr. Vulcan's henchmen. Jeff routs the pair and secretly visits a remote cave where he has been hiding Professor Millard, in order to prevent another attempt on the scientist's life. The professor displays a rocket-propelled flying suit which he and Jeff have perfected.

Jeff dons the suit and, calling himself the Rocket Man, frustrates Dr. Vulcan's sinister plans to seize control of the Science Associates devices which, if controlled by the wrong party, could easily wreak world disaster.

After a number of his plans have been foiled, Dr. Vulcan surmises that Jeff and the

Don Haggerty, holding Tristram Coffin captive, faces the Rocket Man.

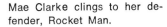

Mae Clarke clings to her defender, Rocket Man.

Rocket Man are the same man. While Jeff is preparing to transport a new device called the Sonutron, he is captured by Dirken, one of Vulcan's men. When Rocket Man suddenly appears, Dirken is astonished and flees, abandoning Jeff. Jeff returns to the cave with the pseudo Rocket Man, Professor Millard, who has donned the flying suit for the occasion.

Professor Millard has developed a powerful decimator capable of disintegrating rock strata. Dr. Vulcan steals the decimator and plans to use it to destroy the city of New York! He brings about an earthquake and tidal wave off New York harbor when the mayor refuses to meet his billion-dollar ransom demand.

Using scientific apparatus to locate the decimator, Rocket Man hurries to halt the weapon's penetration of a volcanic fault in the ocean floor, unaware that a squadron of bombers is also en route to blast its island location off the map. Rocket Man destroys the decimator, subdues Dr. Vulcan, and dives to safety just as the bombs fall. Vulcan and his men are killed in the blast, the city is saved from total destruction, and Dr. Vulcan's reign of terror is ended.

Rocket Man attacks one of Dr. Vulcan's henchmen.

Tristram Coffin, Mae Clarke (*seated*) and James Craven (*center*) are captured in their laboratory cave by Dr. Vulcan's gang.

1950

The oddly masked Atom Man warns Kirk Alyn against any attempts to rescue the wired Noel Neill.

Atom Man vs. Superman

15 Episodes
Columbia, 1950

Directed by
Spencer Bennet

CAST

Clark Kent ⎞	
Superman ⎠	Kirk Alyn
Lois	Noel Neill
Luthor	Lyle Talbot
Jimmy Olson	Tommy Bond
Perry White	Pierre Watkin
Foster	Jack Ingram
Albert	Don Harvey
Carl	Rusty Wescoatt
Beer	Terry Frost
Dorr	Wally West
Lawson	Paul Strader
Earl	George Robotham

Luthor, secretly the Atom Man, Superman's archenemy, blackmails the city of Metropolis by threatening to destroy the entire community. Perry White, editor of the *Daily Planet,* assigns Lois Lane, Jimmy Olson, and Clark Kent to cover the story.

The ingenious Luthor invents a startling number of deadly devices with which to plague the city, not the least of which is a disintegrating machine which can reduce people into their basic atoms and reassemble them in any given spot. But even this diabolical device is no match for Superman's cunning; he manages to thwart each of Luthor's mad schemes.

Since only Kryptonite can rob Superman of his power, it eventually occurs to Luthor to invent a synthetic Kryptonite, and, with this aim in mind, the evil scientist goes about obtaining the necessary ingredients: plutonium, radium, etc.

Luthor announces that he now has the necessary elements to make Kryptonite and stop the Man of Steel. Luthor plants the Kryptonite at the launching of a big ship, with Superman in attendance. Superman is exposed to the Kryptonite and passes out.

An ambulance pulls up and Superman is placed inside . . . right into Luthor's hands. Additional Kryptonite is held close to the helpless

Superman, and he grows even weaker. Inside Luthor's hideout, Superman is placed in a strange device, a lever is pulled, and the Man of Steel vanishes into "The Empty Doom," disappearing into thin air.

Crime in Metropolis increases markedly. Superman returns with his powers diminished and his efforts are futile. One day, Jimmy and Lois receive a mysterious message from Superman, telling them that he will return that night. The *Planet* prints Superman's message; Luthor reads it and is worried. He does not realize that the effect of the synthetic Kryptonite was temporary and has now worn off.

Luthor's final plan is to wreck Metropolis with his sonic vibrator and then to leave the Earth in his spaceship, taking Lois along as his prisoner. Havoc and destruction are inflicted upon the city; Superman is busy rescuing victims everywhere. Luthor and Lois are then launched in the spaceship and Superman flies off in search of them. Superman spots the ship, crashes through its hull, and flies back to Earth with Lois and Luthor. Luthor is imprisoned and Lois fails in an attempt to prove that Clark Kent is Superman. She laughs at the thought of suspecting the meek and mild Clark of being the Man of Steel!

Cody of the Pony Express

15 Episodes
Columbia, 1950

Directed by
Spencer Bennet

CAST

Archer	Jock O'Mahoney
Cody	Dickie Moore
Linda	Peggy Stewart
Ezra	William Fawcett
Doc	Tom London
Emma	Helena Dare
Mort Black	George J. Lewis
Slim	Pierce Lyden
Pecos	Jack Ingram
Denver	Rick Vallin
Durk	Frank Ellis
Irv	Ross Elliott
Eric	Ben Corbett
Chet	Rusty Wescoatt

Nugget City lawyer Mort Black is outwardly a respectable attorney but is secretly head of a band of outlaws, representing an eastern syndicate that plots to seize control of the surrounding frontier territory by acquiring all the transportation. To cope with the lawlessness in the territory, the army appoints Lieutenant Jim Archer as an undercover investigator assigned to discover who is responsible for the outlaw raids on the stagecoaches.

Archer and his aide, old Doc Laramie; Ezra, owner of the Graham's Corners Pony Express relay station; and young Pony Express rider Bill Cody arrive at Nugget City and learn of the outlaws' intentions to attack a gold shipment at Eagle Gap. Leaving Ezra, they arrive on the scene, mount the gold wagon during the attack and beat off the outlaws who are attempting to drive away. Back in Nugget City, Black is paid an unexpected visit from a representative of the eastern syndicate who informs him that more successful results are expected.

At Graham's Corners, word is received of a herd of ponies being driven in for use on the Pony Express, and all hands go to protect the animal shipment from possible attack. Linda Graham, Ezra's daughter, is left to guard Denver, a captured outlaw. When Denver escapes, Linda goes to warn her father and the others. She gets to the group just as the outlaws intercept and stampede the pony herd. While the others try to control the herd, the outlaws flee.

Cody, Archer, and Doc report to Fort Adams and learn that the outlaws are stealing army rifles and smuggling them to the Indians. Cody and Archer set out after the outlaws who have been spotted aboard a wagon known to be carrying contraband guns. They follow the wagon and see the outlaws as they rendezvous with Indian Chief Gray Cloud and present him with the rifles. When the villains leave, Cody and Archer inform the chief of the fact that the rifles were stolen from the army. When Pecos, one of the outlaws, who remains hidden, overhears the chief consent to a powwow at Graham's Corners, he follows the group and shoots down one of the accompanying Indians.

Through a distinctive tobacco pouch which Pecos has lost, Cody and Archer identify him as the Indian killer and demand that Black arrest him. Black does this, but secretly plans to rescue Pecos that night. Anticipating just such an attempt, Cody and Archer smuggle Pecos from the makeshift jail into a wagon. When the outlaws see the getaway wagon, they give chase. Pecos falls from the speeding wagon and is shot by one of his own comrades to prevent his recapture.

Returning to Nugget City, Cody and Archer report Pecos's death to Black. When Black suggests that the outlaw situation is under control, he is reminded by Cody and Archer that Pecos's killer is still at large.

Archer has very strong suspicions that Black is the man behind the outlaws, but absolute proof is needed. When Archer, accompanied by Cody, goes to Black's office to talk to him, he finds Black gone and an open safe containing a stolen government mail pouch that has been opened. As they are about to take the pouch as evidence to the fort, they are ambushed by Slim, Black's deputy, who, with his cohorts, ties Cody and Archer to a post and prepares to shoot them. Just then, lightning from a gathering storm strikes the post, apparently electrocuting Cody and Archer!

The lightning knocks Cody and Archer unconscious and causes the outlaws to flee. When they revive, Archer returns to find the incriminating pouch and take it to the fort while Cody goes to keep an eye on Black's doings in town. Meanwhile, Black, realizing that he has been discovered, plans one more villainous escapade —the robbery of a gold shipment lying over at Graham's Corners. Cody gets wind of the scheme, however, and warns the ranchers and Archer, who brings a squad of troopers. The raid is thwarted and Black and his outlaws are captured. With their job over, Archer draws Linda aside for a talk, while Cody and Doc plan to join the Army back east.

Dickie Moore (*left*) discusses a clue with Jock O'Mahoney.

Desperadoes of the West

12 Episodes
Republic, 1950

Directed by
Fred C. Brannon

CAST

Ward	Richard Powers
Sally	Judy Clark
Hacker	Roy Barcroft
Dawson	I. Stanford Jolley
Rusty	Lee Phelps
Larson	Lee Roberts
Colonel Arnold	Cliff Clark
Bowers	Edmund Cobb
Hard Rock	Hank Patterson
Reed	Dale Van Sickel
Gregg	Tom Steele
Kern	Sandy Sanders
Casey	John Cason
Jack	Guy Teague
Joe	Bud Osborne
Storekeeper	Stanley Blystone

A group of courageous ranchers under the leadership of Colonel Arnold and Ward Gordon, engaged in the cooperative project of drilling an oil well, is receiving fierce opposition from an unknown bandit gang.

"Dude" Dawson, a smooth eastern promoter, is the head of the outlaws. He is out to prevent the cooperative from striking oil before its lease expires so that he can secure the property for the eastern company he represents.

Dawson hires Larson and Hacker to commit a series of murders to prevent the completion of the well. When Ward, with the help of Colonel Arnold and his daughter Sally, arranges to bring in a new driller, the replacement is also killed and one of Dawsons' men takes his place.

The changed identity, however, is discovered by Ward and Sally. A terrific battle ensues and Dawson's men attempt to blow up the derrick. Ward manages to put out the fuse but bullets from the outlaws' guns detonate the dynamite and the derrick topples over, with Ward beneath it. But Ward escapes by an inch and drives off the attackers.

Finally, Dawson unwittingly brings about his own defeat. In a desperate last-minute move to wreck the drilling operation, he and his men attack Ward and the working crew and dynamite the well. The shock of the explosion brings in a gusher. The outlaws try to escape, but are brought to justice.

Judy Clark watches Richard Powers present some important evidence to Cliff Clark.

The Invisible Monster

12 Episodes	Directed by
Republic, 1950	Fred C. Brannon

CAST

Lane	Richard Webb
Carol	Aline Towne
Burton	Lane Bradford
Phantom Ruler	Stanley Price
Harris	John Crawford
Long	George Meeker
Doctor	Keith Richards
Martin	Dale Van Sickel
Haines	Tom Steele
Police Officer McDuff	Marshall Reed
Guard	Forrest Burns
Stoner	Ed Parker
Hogan	Frank O'Connor
Art	Charles Regan
Grogarty	Charles Sullivan
Night Watchman	Howard Mitchell
Harding	Bud Wolfe

The Phantom Ruler is a big-time criminal organizer who obtains assistants by smuggling in aliens not eligible for immigration. He brings in four intelligent, well-educated Europeans—a locksmith, an attorney, an aircraft engineer, and a chemist—and cows them into obedience by demonstrating his ability to make himself invisible by combining chemically treated clothing with a special type of light ray. After the locksmith obtains the combination to a bank vault, the Phantom Ruler, using his invisibility equipment, robs the vault.

Lane Carson, insurance company investigator, is assigned to the case. With the help of his assistant Carol Richards, he identifies the locksmith and trails him. After a fight with the Phantom Ruler's men, Lane captures the locksmith. But before Lane can question him, the invisible Phantom Ruler climbs in through the fire escape and kills the would-be informer. After the murder, Lane rushes to the window but sees only a truck parked below. When he follows it,

Lane gets on the trail of Burton and Harris, the Phantom Ruler's chief lieutenants. In a car chase and gunfight, Lane and Carol are closing in on the fugitives when Harris throws out a hand grenade. Miraculously, Lane and Carol are able to dodge the grenade which, a split second later, explodes and demolishes the car.

When the Phantom's men attempt to steal a truckload of the chemical that produces invisibility, the truck is intercepted by Lane. But the Phantom learns that the authorities have stored drums of the chemical in a warehouse. Donning his cloak of invisibility, the Phantom enters the warehouse and begins siphoning the drums into a truck parked outside. Lane arrives and notices the hose used by the Phantom to empty the cannisters. The Phantom, however, escapes.

Realizing how desperate the criminals are for the chemical, Lane and Carol consult the chemical's manufacturer, the Calhoun Company, and learn that someone has offered to pay a fabulous price for the chemical's formula.

When two of the Phantom's men come to the Calhoun Company skyscraper office to pay for the formula, Lane arrives and places the men under arrest. But as he does, one of the men tosses the plans out of the window, where they are snatched by the Phantom. Lane's pistol is knocked from his hand and a fight ensues, during which both Lane and one of the Phantom's men fall out the window. Lane grasps a nearby fire extinguisher hose and keeps from plummeting to the pavement below.

Lane and Carol have the chemical analyzed and discover that it has an illusory effect under certain types of light. They speculate that it could be used to produce invisibility. Tipped off that the gang may be using a telephone company repair truck in their work, Lane asks the police to keep him advised as to sightings of such trucks. He soon receives a report of a truck parked across from a bank and rushes to the scene. One of the Phantom's henchmen, pretending to be a repairman, is sitting high on a telephone pole directing the vital beam of light. When an armored car pulls up and the guards get out, the invisible Phantom enters the car and drives off.

Lane arrives, recognizes the Phantom's henchmen, and starts shooting. One of the men is wounded, but the other escapes in the telephone truck. Lane has the injured criminal brought to a suburban home for medical care, hoping to keep the location hidden from the Phantom. But the Phantom has two of his men keep Lane under constant surveillance, hoping that he will eventually visit the wounded man. The strategy works. Lane has no sooner begun to question the master villain's henchman, when the Phantom's two men enter and attempt a rescue. But the wounded man is too weak to leave, so his would-be rescuers fire several shots into his helpless body and flee. As Lane tries desperately to revive him, the dying man gasps the location of the Phantom's hideout. Lane loses no time in rushing to the site.

Meanwhile, the Phantom has decided that his four European informers have outlived their usefulness and plans to execute them. He plants two live wires on the floor of his headquarters chamber, intending to electrocute the unsuspecting Europeans. But before this plan can be affected, Lane and a police escort barge in. While attempting to escape, the Phantom steps on one of the live wires and is immediately electrocuted—a victim of his own diabolical scheme.

Lane faces certain death as the Phantom sets off a landslide that threatens to engulf Lane's car.

That flaming barrel under the wagon spells trouble for Keith Richards.

The James Brothers of Missouri

12 Episodes
Republic, 1950

Directed by
Fred C. Brannon

CAST

Jesse	Keith Richards
Frank	Robert Bice
Peggy	Noel Neill
Ace	Roy Barcroft
Belle	Patricia Knox
Monk	Lane Bradford
Marshal Rand	Eugene Roth
Lon	John Hamilton
Sheriff	Edmund Cobb
Duffy	Hank Patterson
Simpson	Dale Van Sickel
Slim	Tom Steele
Brandy	Lee Roberts
Citizen	Frank O'Connor
Dutch	Marshall Reed
Deputy Sheriff	Wade Ray
Pop Keever	Nolan Leary

Desiring to reestablish themselves as members of society, Jesse James and his brother Frank head for Rimrock, Missouri, where Lon Sawyer, a former member of their gang, has established a freight line. Under the aliases of John Howard and Bob Carroll, the James brothers arrive in Rimrock and find Sawyer Freight under attack by a raider group headed by Ace Marlin, the operator of a rival line. Ace and Belle Calhoun plot to wipe out the Sawyer line. Soon after the arrival of the James boys, Lon is robbed of a contract authorization and murdered.

Jesse and Frank determine to help Lon's sister Peggy to carry on the line. Despite a hijack attempt by Marlin's men, the brothers succeed in delivering a shipment of salt for Pop Keever, who, in appreciation, attends a mass meeting of shippers and urges them to desert Marlin's line and deal only with Sawyer.

Belle learns that Henry Simpson, the county land recorder, is a fugitive forger; Marlin forces him to change the county records so that it appears as though Marlin owns part of Rimrock Road, the most widely used town road. Marlin then proceeds to set up a prohibitive toll for use of his supposed section of the road.

Frank and Jesse discover that Marlin's men are on their way to Keyhole Pass with explosives to block the only other route left for freighting in and out of Rimrock. Frank and Jesse arrive as the outlaws are planting the explosives and a fight begins. The fight ends when a wagon full of explosives is detonated near Jesse, touching off a giant blast. Jesse leaps to safety just before the explosion, but the pass is blocked.

The brothers decide to check the official town atlas to determine whether or not Marlin actually owns part of Rimrock Road. They discover that the atlas has been tampered with and, despite several attacks by Marlin's men, succeed in delivering the atlas to the territory commissioner in Santa Fe, who declares Marlin's claim illegal.

Belle, who is really the brains behind Marlin, is furious. She orders a campaign of terror and looting against all shippers who use the Sawyer Line. In an effort to track down the outlaws, Jesse conceals himself in a false compartment on a freight wagon loaded with a dummy order. The wagon is held up by Marlin's men and brought to a cave where all of the loot is stored. Jesse slips away and returns later with Frank. Together they dynamite the entrance to the cave, sealing up the loot and preserving it as evidence.

One of Marlin's men is captured by the boys and confesses. He reveals that Marlin and Belle are behind the robberies. Jesse arrives in Rimrock to find Marlin demanding getaway money from Belle. As Jesse subdues Marlin, the outlaw's gun goes off, killing Belle.

The marshal, aware of the James boys' real identities, exonerates them and states for the record that the two fighting men Howard and Carroll are helping Peg Sawyer build her freight line into a monument of law and order in the West.

Pirates of the High Seas

15 Episodes	Directed by
Columbia, 1950	Spencer Bennet
	and Thomas Carr

CAST

Jeff	Buster Crabbe
Carol	Lois Hall
Kelly	Tommy Farrell
Whitlock	Gene Roth
Castell	Tristram Coffin
Kalana	Neyle Morrow
Lamar	Stanley Price
Roper	Hugh Prosser
Lotus Lady	Symona Bonifice
Wharton	William Fawcett
Carter	Terry Frost
Barker	Lee Roberts
Adams	Rusty Wescoatt
Durk	Pierce Lyden
Turner	I. Stanford Jolley
Shark	Marshall Reed

Jeff Drake sails his ship, the *Viking,* to the Pacific Island of Taluha in response to a call for help from his old navy buddy, Kelly Walsh, whose one-ship Pacific freight line is under constant attack by a mysterious pirate cruiser. Aboard the *Viking* is a group of adventurers which includes Frederick Whitlock, the owner of Taluha Island; Castell, a war crimes investigator; and Carol Walsh, Kelly's sister.

When they arrive on Taluha, strange events begin happening at a swift pace. Whitlock turns out to be a criminal genius who controls the movements of the phantom pirate ship, while Castell proves to be an escaped war criminal in search of his lost loot of precious diamonds. Jeff, Kelly, and Carol persevere and solve the riddle of the phantom ship. They identify Castell as a war criminal, and recover the precious diamond loot.

Buster Crabbe, ready for action.

Radar Patrol vs. Spy King

| 12 Episodes | Directed by |
| Republic, 1950 | Fred C. Brannon |

CAST

Chris	Kirk Alyn
Joan	Jean Dean
Ricco	Anthony Warde
Manuel	George J. Lewis
Nitra	Eve Whitney
Baroda	John Merton
Lord	Tristram Coffin
Sands	John Crawford
Miller	Harold Goodwin
Ames	Dale Van Sickel
Gorman	Tom Steele
Dutch	Eddie Parker
Chairman	Forbes Murray
Chairman	Frank O'Connor
Hugo	Stephen Gregory
Clark	Frank Dae
Trooper	Arvon Dale

Baroda, the sinister head of the most dangerous ring of saboteurs in the annals of military intelligence, has negotiated with the warlords of a potential enemy of the United States to sabotage plans for a vast defense system of radar stations along the American border. Chris Calvert, Radar Defense Bureau operator, prevents Baroda's agents from stealing secret orders from brilliant radar scientist Joan Hughes.

Nitra, Baroda's most trusted agent, kidnaps Joan from her experimental station through a clever ruse. But in order to escape a dragnet, she is forced to take refuge in an abandoned oil field, unaware that Calvert is on her trail.

In a gun battle between Chris and Baroda's agents, an oil well is accidentally ignited and its flames threaten to engulf the field where Joan is being held. As Nitra and her henchmen prepare to flee with the girl, Chris catches up with them and attempts a rescue. But he is knocked out and lies unconscious on the floor of a shed as the oil field blaze rages about him. A fiery derrick crashes down on the shed, apparently turning Chris into a human torch.

Somehow, Chris miraculously escapes a horrible death and, with his friend Manuel, a Mexican Police agent, continues his relentless fight against the enemy. Chris, Manuel, and plucky Joan Hughes encounter countless dangers before Baroda and his agents suffer a fitting demise and Nitra is taken prisoner.

Government officials leave the continued construction of a radar network around the nation in the capable hands of Chris, Joan, and their fellow workers.

Jean Dean, Kirk Alyn, and George J. Lewis intently study an electronic device.

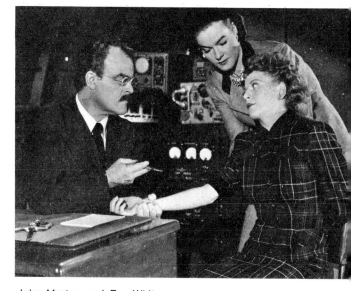

John Merton and Eve Whitney prepare to subdue an uncooperative Jean Dean.

1951

Don Daredevil Rides Again

12 Episodes   Directed by
Republic, 1951   Fred C. Brannon

CAST

Lee	Ken Curtis
Patricia	Aline Towne
Stratton	Roy Barcroft
Webber	Lane Bradford
Gary	Robert Einer
Hagen	John Cason
Sheriff	I. Stanford Jolley
Buck	Hank Patterson
Uncle Michael	Lee Phelps
Dirk	Sandy Sanders
Deputy Sheriff	Guy Teague
Black	Tom Steele
Miller	Michael Ragan
Turner	Cactus Mack

It's a long drop facing Ken Curtis as he tries to ward off one of Stratton's henchmen.

An old Spanish land grant made to Ricardo Moreno and later sold to Patrick Doyle is found by political boss Stratton to be a forgery. Stratton tries to cash in by having his men attempt to stake out mineral claims and homesteads on the ranches.

The plot is violently resisted by Patricia Doyle, granddaughter of the original owner, and her young neighbor Gary Taylor. Stratton, however, is able to back up his demands with the help of the crooked sheriff, and Gary and Patricia are faced with losing their property when Patricia's cousin Lee Hadley arrives from the East.

Having kept abreast of the situation from afar, Lee had anticipated Stratton's move and had already homesteaded the Doyle Ranch, forcing the racketeer to back down temporarily. The other ranchers follow suit, homesteading and mineral-claiming their own property, but Stratton organizes a gang of night riders to try to drive the ranchers off before they can prove their titles.

Since no help is forthcoming from the sheriff, Lee decides to take on the character of Don Daredevil, a character assumed by his grandfather during earlier troubled times. As the masked Don Daredevil, Lee is successful in driving off Stratton's terrorizing riders.

Stratton then lures Don Daredevil into an ambush but he escapes to an old ore shack overhanging a cliff. The shack is dynamited by Stratton's men but Don manages to escape by leaping from the shack just before the explosion occurs. Don tracks down the original land grant, and finds that it validates the legitimacy of the ranchers' claims, as well as Patricia's.

In a last desperate attempt to recover the grant deed, as well as the gold recently discovered on the property, Stratton attacks Lee and Patricia. In the fight, during which Stratton's aide is killed, a lamp is knocked over and the ranch building catches fire. Lee and Patricia escape but when Stratton rushes from the burning building, he is shot by his own men, whom he has posted to prevent Don Daredevil's escape.

Captain Video

15 Episodes
Columbia, 1951

Directed by
Spencer Bennet
and Wallace Grissell

CAST

Captain Video	Judd Holdren
Ranger	Larry Stewart
Tobor	George Eldredge
Vultura	Gene Roth
Gallagher	Don C. Harvey
Alpha	William Fawcett
Aker	Jack Ingram
Zarol	I. Stanford Jolley
Retner	Skelton Knaggs
Rogers	Jimmy Stark
Beal	Rusty Wescoatt
Elko	Zon Murray
Drock	George Robotham
Professor Markham	Oliver Cross
Professor Dean	Bill Bailey

Flying Disc Man from Mars

12 Episodes
Republic, 1951

Directed by
Fred C. Brannon

CAST

Kent	Walter Reed
Helen	Lois Collier
Mota	Gregory Gay
Bryant	James Craven
Drake	Harry Lauter
Ryan	Richard Irving
Steve	Sandy Sanders
Trent	Michael Carr
Watchman	Dale Van Sickel
Taylor	Tom Steele
Gateman	George Sherwood
Gradey	Jimmy O'Gatty
Curtis	John De Simone
Crane	Lester Dorr
Kirk	Dick Cogan

Dr. Bryant, a brilliant but eccentric scientist and builder of experimental planes, finding that a mysterious aircraft is hovering over his factory every night, hires Kent Fowler, a young aviator who operates a private plane patrol, to investigate.

Kent shoots down the mysterious craft and, when it lands, Dr. Bryant is on the spot to pick up Mota, a scientist from Mars. Mota explains that Martians are centuries ahead of this world in atomic development. He offers to work with Bryant in building atomic-powered planes and bombs if Bryant will help him organize a force to take over Earth and make it a satellite of the Martian dictator. Bryant agrees.

Bryant commissions his recently hired henchmen Drake and Ryan to steal some uranium from an adjoining plant, but Kent catches up with them. Kent, his windshield shattered by a bullet, swerves his car in front of their factory and ends up in a fiery crash, leaping from the car just in time to save his life. This marks the first of many dangerous adventures experienced by Kent and his pretty secretary Helen in their encounters with the enemy.

Mota's greatest asset is his atom-powered space vehicle, a craft capable of flying sideways and backward without turning around, ascending and descending like a helicopter, even hovering at a standstill in space. Mota's ship defies the law of gravity and can be operated by remote control.

For a time, Bryant successfully conceals from Kent his role in the evil plans but eventually Kent's suspicions are confirmed. When Bryant and Mota realize that Kent is becoming more convinced of their guilt, they immediately begin their campaign of terror. By dropping atomic bombs on bridges, factories, and towns, they intend to terrorize the government into submission. Helen is captured by Mota and is held captive in Mota's secret lair located in a volcano. Kent discovers the hideout and arrives to rescue her. As Kent battles Mota's men, an atomic bomb works loose and falls into the molten lava of the crater, starting an eruption. Kent and Helen escape in the bat plane while Mota and Bryant are engulfed by the molten lava.

Walter Reed discusses strange goings-on with James Craven.

James Craven and two of Mota's henchmen about to fire a devastating thermal disintegrator at an earth plane.

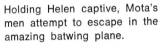

Holding Helen captive, Mota's men attempt to escape in the amazing batwing plane.

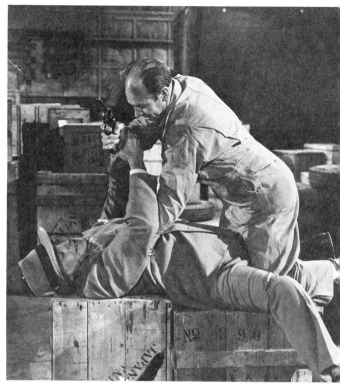

Pierce Lyden, Arthur Space, Mary Ellen Kay, Walter Reed, Mauritz Hugo, and George Meeker, at a meeting of the Truck Owners' Association. One of these men is the Villainous Voice.

Walter Reed desperately defends himself from Dick Curtis's deadly attack.

Government Agents vs. Phantom Legion

12 Episodes	Directed by
Republic, 1951	Fred C. Brannon

CAST

Hal	Walter Reed
Kay	Mary Ellen Kay
Regan	Dick Curtis
Sam	John Pickard
Cady	Fred Coby
Armstrong	Pierce Lyden
Willard	George Meeker
Patterson	John Phillips
Thompson	Mauritz Hugo
Turner	Edmund Cobb
Barnett	Eddie Dew
Coroner	George Lloyd
Brice	Dale Van Sickel
Brandt	Tom Steele
Crandall	Arthur Space
District Attorney	Norval Mitchell
Motorcycle Officer	Frank Meredith

To combat a wave of attacks on highway transportation, Government Agent Hal Duncan is assigned to work with the Truck Owners' Association. This group consists of four individual truck owners, Armstrong, Crandall, Thompson, and Willard, and their secretary Kay Roberts.

In his first attempt to track down the hijackers, Hal takes Armstrong's truck on one of its runs. Through a ruse, he stops the truck and is captured and tied up by Regan and Cady, two henchmen of "The Voice," the head of the gang which robs trucks and steals their cargoes for a foreign power.

Hal manages to break away and escape, but the truck is stolen. In an effort to trace it, Hal and his assistant Sam Bradley are led to a warehouse. A fight breaks out during which Regan and Cady escape through a trapdoor leading to an underground storage chamber.

Sam is knocked out but Hal follows the gangsters, who jump into a handcar loaded with grenades. Hal's shot punctures a gasoline drum, leaving a trail of gas between the rails. A blazing fire begins and Hal manages barely to escape with his life.

Hal believes the Voice to be one of the truck owners and he finally has a showdown with the master criminal, who turns out to be Armstrong. In a battle to the death, Armstrong is knocked down and impaled on a piece of broken glass.

Mysterious Island

15 Episodes	Directed by
Columbia, 1951	Spencer Bennet

CAST

Harding	Richard Crane
Pencroft	Marshall Reed
Rulu	Karen Randle
Bert	Ralph Hodges
Shard	Gene Roth
Gideon	Hugh Prosser
Nemo	Leonard Penn
Ayrton	Terry Frost
Moley	Rusty Wescoatt
Neb	Bernard Hamilton

Leonard Penn explains his latest invention to Gene Roth and Richard Crane.

In 1865 during the Civil War, Captain Harding, a prisoner of the Confederates, escapes in an enemy balloon together with Gideon, a war correspondent, Pencroft, a sailor, Bert, Pencroft's adopted son, and Neb, Harding's servant. For days the balloon drifts in space and finally lands on a desert island. Also landing on the island is Rulu, a beautiful visitor from the planet Mercury, who seeks a radioactive metal that will enable her to manufacture an explosive that could destroy the earth.

The castaways battle against the island's natives, pirates, and Rulu and her men. They are frequently aided by Captain Nemo, a scientific genius, who has been living on the island and who works to counteract Rulu's evil plans. Finally, Rulu sets off an explosion which totally destroys the island. The castaways are the sole survivors.

Roar of the Iron Horse

15 Episodes
Columbia, 1951

Directed by
Spencer G. Bennet
and Thomas Carr

CAST

Jim Grant	Jock O'Mahoney
Carol Lane	Virginia Herrick
Rocky	William Fawcett
Tom Lane	Hal Landon
Homer Lathrop	Jack Ingram
Cal	Mickey Simpson
Karl Ulrich	
(The Baron)	George Eldredge
Ace	Myron Healey
Scully	Rusty Wescoatt
Bat	Frank Ellis
Erv	Pierce Lyden
Campo	Dick Curtis
Lefty	Hugh Prosser

In the late 1890s, a railroad being built by a syndicate financed by government money seems to have more than its share of accidents. Tom Lane, chief engineer for the project, finally persuades Homer Lathrop, superintendent, to send to Washington for an investigator despite the objections of his foreman, Scully. Near Sombrero, the railhead, government investigator Jim Grant and a prospector, Rocky, are rescued from an outlaw attack by White Eagle, a young Indian chief hostile to Karl Ulrich because the latter forces his people to dig for a fabulous meteor supposedly filled with diamonds.

Jim later meets Tom Lane and Carol, Tom's sister. Finally forcing a showdown, Jim demonstrates that Lathrop and Scully are responsible for the trouble and are lead by Karl Ulrich, alias The Baron. In a desperate gun battle the Baron, Scully, and Lathrop are killed and the renegade gang wiped out. Rocky reveals that he has found the meteor. Jim and Carol ride together into the future.

Jock O'Mahoney takes aim while perched on the side of the "Iron Horse."

1952

Blackhawk

15 Episodes
Columbia, 1952

Directed by
Spencer Bennet

CAST

Blackhawk	Kirk Alyn
Laska	Carol Forman
Chuck	John Crawford
Mr. Case	Michael Fox
Olaf	Don Harvey
Stan } Boris }	Rick Vallin
Andre	Larry Stewart
Chop Chop	Weaver Levy
Bork	Zon Murray
Cress	Nick Stuart
Aller	Marshall Reed
Dyke	Pierce Lyden
Dr. Ralph	William Fawcett
Hodge	Rory Mallinson
Hendrickson	Frank Ellis

Led by Blackhawk, the International Brotherhood, an organization dedicated to the freedom of mankind throughout the world, uncovers a saboteur band led by the notorious female sabotage chief Laska, and sets about bringing the criminals to justice.

Their efforts lead them to the defense of the brilliant Dr. Rolph, a scientist who has perfected a deadly electronic ray. Rolph is abducted by Laska's men, along with the deadly ray. Close on the trail, Blackhawk bursts into the Laska stronghold, but, in the confusion, the saboteurs flee with Rolph. While state police dragnet the area for the missing scientist, Blackhawk and his comrade Chuck seek clues to the saboteurs by plane. Uncovering their whereabouts, Blackhawk rescues Rolph, but Laska and her gang escape.

Laska is ordered by her leader to fly to the town of Valdez, below the border. Blackhawk pursues him and engages the commandant of police to help in the hunt; they capture one of the saboteurs. However, Yaqui Indians ambush and overpower the Blackhawks. The owner of a nearby ranch, Señor Borego, comes to the aid of the Blackhawks and routs the Indians.

The Blackhawks capture another one of Laska's agents, Case. In a trap set for the Blackhawks by Laska, Case is killed but Blackhawk notices Case's wrist radio flashing a message from Laska. The Blackhawks arrange a meeting with her and a trap is set. However, Laska and her gang elude capture and race for the border. She is finally traced to the secret office of her leader. Enraged by what she believes are his attempts to betray her, she murders the leader as the Blackhawks enter and capture her. The last of the sabotage gang has been brought to justice by Blackhawk!

Kirk Alyn demonstrates a fancy wrist grip on one of Laska's cohorts.

King of the Congo

15 Episodes
Columbia, 1952

Directed by
Spencer Bennet
and Wallace Grissell

CAST

Thunda)	⬸ Buster Crabbe
Roger Drum)	
Pha	Gloria Dee
Boris	Leonard Penn
Clark	Jack Ingram
Kor	Rusty Wescoatt
Degar	Nick Stuart
Andreov	Rick Vallin
Nahee	Neyle Morrow
Alexis	Bart Davidson
Lipah	Alex Montoya
Zahlia	Bernie Goizer
High Priest	William Fawcett
Blake	Lee Roberts
Ivan	Frank Ellis

Captain Roger Drum of the United States Air Force shoots down an unidentified plane whose pilot was bound for Africa to deliver a microfilm message to a subversive group. Assuming the pilot's identity, Drum proceeds to Africa intent on unmasking the group. When his plane crashes in the jungle, Drum is rescued by the Rock People, led by the lovely Pha. Because of his strength, Drum is renamed Thunda, King of the Congo, by the Rock People.

The Rock People are attacked by enemies, the subversives, led by Boris, who are trying to contact Thunda, believing him to be their missing pilot. To fulfill his mission, Thunda pretends allegiance to the subversive group and hands them the microfilm message, thus earning the enmity of Pha and her people.

In his double-roled attempt to discover the plans of the subversive group, Thunda finds himself constantly rescuing Pha and her Rock Men from plots and traps devised by his "own" cohorts. To complicate matters still further, another tribe, the Cave Men, regularly attack both the Rock People and Boris's men.

Thunda eventually discovers that the subversives are attempting to locate a deposit containing a metal more radioactive than uranium. When another subversive spy, Alexis, arrives, he announces that Thunda is not the pilot who was sent on the mission. Boris orders Thunda to be executed, but the American escapes and teams up, once again, with Pha.

Together they encounter avalanches, gas bombs, exploding gunpowder, hungry leopards, and the ubiquitous Cave Men, in their attempts to prevent the enemy agents from accomplishing their aims. With the arrival of another American Air Force man, Lieutenant Blake, and the help of the Rock People, the subversives are overpowered, and as Boris and Alexis flee through the jungle they are killed by wild beasts.

With the enemy agents disposed of, Thunda and Pha look on happily as the Cave Men and Rock People vow to be friends.

Radar Men from the Moon

12 Episodes
Republic, 1952

Directed by
Fred Brannon

CAST

Commando Cody	George Wallace
Joan Gilbert	Aline Towne
Retik	⬸ Roy Barcroft
Ted Richards	William Blakewell
Graber	⬸ Clayton Moore
Krog	⬸ Peter Brocco
Daly	Bob Stevenson
Henderson	Don Walters
Zerg	Tom Steele
Alon	Dale Van Sickel
Hank	Wilson Wood
Robal	Noel Cravat
Nasor	Baynes Barron
Bream	Paul McGuire

Bartender	Ted Thorpe
Jones	Dick Cogan

America's defenses are being sabotaged by a series of mysterious explosions. The government contacts Commando Cody, a young scientist known as the Sky Marshal of the Universe, for aid. Cody is helped by his two assistants, Joan Gilbert and Ted Richards, who have worked with him to develop an amazing "flying suit" and a personal rocket ship for lunar flight.

Cody discovers two men about to destroy a troop train with an atomic gun. The villains manage to escape, but Cody finds that they are using an unknown element in the atomic weapon. By scientific deduction he determines that the element originated on the moon. To prove his theory, he prepares to fly to the moon, along with Joan and Ted.

On the moon, Cody discovers a huge, hidden city, ruled by Retik, the ruler of the moon, whose ambitious plans include conquering the earth. While on the moon, Cody uncovers the element used in the atomic weapon. But in detecting this substance (called "lunarium"), Cody is captured in Retik's vast laboratory and held prisoner.

After learning that a great portion of Retik's mad scheme depends on his ability to utilize his atomic weapon, Cody, Joan, and Ted escape. Despite Retik's attempts to stop them, the trio manages to return to earth. Retik sends two of his henchmen, Graber and Daly, to Earth with orders to kill Cody before he has a chance to warn Earth officials of the planned invasion.

In their determination to save the earth, Cody and his friends are subjected to ray-gun attacks, lava from an erupting volcano, and various rocket-ship chases and crashes. In a final, conclusive encounter, Cody succeeds in blasting Retik's rocket ship to bits. Retik and his henchmen are killed, and the madman's dream of world domination is ended.

George Wallace, garbed in his famous flying suit, and his lovely assistant Aline Towne.

George Wallace holds three of Retik's henchmen at bay: Clayton Moore, Peter Brocco, and Bob Stevenson.

The evil Retik, Roy Barcroft.

Aline Towne, George Wallace, and William Blakewell discuss suspicious happenings.

Son of Geronimo

15 Episodes
Columbia, 1952

Directed by
Spencer Bennet

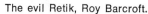

CAST

Jim Scott	– Clayton Moore
Tulsa	Bud Osborne
Frank Baker	Tommy Farrell
Porico	Rodd Redwing
Rance Rankin	Marshall Reed
Ann Baker	Eileen Rowe
Ace	John Crawford
Bat	Zon Murray
Eadie	Rick Vallin
Colonel Foster	Lyle Talbot
Geronimo	Chief Yowlachie

Jim Scott seeks to end the bloodshed between whites and Indians with the help of wagon-train boss Tulsa and frontier settlers Frank Baker and his sister Ann. Apaches headed by Porico, who claims to be the son of Geronimo, continually attack the settlers' wagon trains and new stage line. It isn't long before white outlaws, led by Ace Devlin and Rance Rankin, join the Indians.

After Jim succeeds in communicating with Porico, he convinces the young brave that the white settlers want peace, and that the outlaws are merely using the Apaches for their own selfish ends. Porico admits that he is not really Geronimo's son, and that he had used his false identity to rule the Indians. With his new Indian allies, Jim goes after the outlaws and rounds them all up, but not before Porico has shown his sincerity by personally stabbing Rankin.

Clayton Moore gives the sign of peace to Rodd Redwing.

315

Zombies of the Stratosphere

12 Chapters   Directed by
Republic, 1952   Fred Brannon

CAST

Larry Martin	Judd Holdren
Sue Davis	Aline Towne
Bob Wilson	Wilson Wood
Marex	Lane Bradford
Dr. Harding	Stanley Waxman
Roth	John Crawford
Mr. Steele	Craig Kelly
Shane	Ray Boyle
Narab	Leonard Nimoy
Truck Driver	Tom Steele
Telegraph Operator	Dale Van Sickel
Lawson	Roy Engel
Kerr	Jack Harden
Fisherman	Paul Stader
Dick	Gayle Kellogg
Policeman	Jack Shea
Elah	Robert Garabedian

Judd Holdren ponders his next move in his fight against invaders from space.

An invading rocket from another planet is detected by Larry Martin, an executive in the cosmic policing organization, the Inter-Planetary Patrol. He takes off in his flying suit to locate the strange craft. The invading rocket has brought two weird-looking, part-human Zombies, Marex and Narab, who are met by two earthmen assistants, Roth and Shane. As they transfer equipment from the rocket to a waiting truck, Larry lands on the truck and plants a direction finder with which he can later trace the truck.

Marex and his chief Zombie send the equipment to a cave that can only be entered through an underwater passage. Dr. Harding, a renegade scientist, is then persuaded to help in the fantastic scheme to construct a hydrogen bomb that will blow Earth out of its orbit and move the other planet in to capitalize on the earth's superior climate.

To ward off this disaster, Larry and his two assistants Bob and Sue follow a trail of clues as they try to prevent vital instruments and components from falling into the hands of the Zombies, their earth assistants, and a robot Marex has created—an iron monster operated by remote control.

Finally, while tracking down a stolen shipment of uranium ore, they are led to the hideaway cave where Larry and Bob nearly lose their lives in underwater fights with the Zombies, who can remain under water longer than earthmen. When they are trapped in the cave, Marex and Narab shoot Harding when he wishes to surrender. With their rocket poised in the mountain for a quick getaway, they set a detonator and manage to escape to their ship. But in a furious ray-gun battle, all the Zombies except Narab are killed. Larry finds Narab in the wrecked rocket and, discovering that the hydrogen bomb in the inner cave is about to explode and destroy the earth, Larry flies to the cave, goes through the water tunnel, and disconnects the bomb just before it can explode.

Wilson Wood, in the grip of a menacing robot.

Judd Holdren takes to the air in an attempt to capture fleeing spacemen.

Lane Bradford (*right*) gives instructions to a cohort.

1953

Canadian Mounties vs. Atomic Invaders

12 Episodes	Directed by
Republic, 1953	Franklin Adreon

CAST

Sergeant Don Roberts	Bill Henry
Kay Conway	Susan Morrow
Marlof (Smokey Joe)	Arthur Space
Beck	Dale Van Sickel
Commander Morrison	Pierre Watkin
Reed	Mike Ragan
Anderson	Stanley Andrews
Clark (Mountie)	Harry Lauter
Larson (Trapper)	Hank Patterson
Mr. Warner	Edmund Cobb
Corporal Guy Sanders	Gayle Kellogg
Mack	Tom Steele
Mrs. Warner	Jean Wright

A band of foreign agents who are engineering a mysterious operation in the frozen regions of Canada, are the subject of a widespread search by the Canadian Mounted Police. The search is spearheaded by Canadian Mountie Sergeant Don Roberts who is aided by Kay Conway, an undercover agent for the Canadian government. The theft of an ordinance map from Don's safe offers a clue to the operational locale of the agents—in the barren north country near Taniak.

To reach Taniak undiscovered, Don and Kay join a party of settlers who are moving into the district. In the meantime, the foreign agents, headed by Marlof who masquerades as an old trapper called Smokey Joe, plan to build rocket-launching platforms from which their country intends to bombard American and Canadian cities with guided atomic missiles preparatory to invasion. Marlof dispatches his two assistants Reed and Beck to the Taniak region to construct the launching platforms.

When the assistants learn that Don is masquerading as a civilian with the band of settlers, they infiltrate the group and try to prevent them from making the trip. With Don's "cover" broken, the trek across the frozen wasteland becomes a running battle both with the treacherous trappers and with avalanches, wolves, fearful gorges, bottomless icy lakes, and reindeer stampedes. Marlof's identity is finally discovered and his gang of agents is rounded up.

The Great Adventures of Captain Kidd

15 Episodes	Directed by
Columbia, 1953	Derwin Abbe
	and Charles Gould

CAST

Richard Dale	Richard Crane
Alan Duncan	David Bruce
Captain Kidd	John Crawford
Buller	George Wallace
Devry	Lee Roberts
Long Ben Avery	Paul Newlan
Dr. Brandt	Nick Stuart
Moore	Terry Frost
Jenkins	John Hart
Captain Culliford	Marshall Reed
Native	Eduardo Cansino, Jr.
Princess	Willetta Smith

Richard Dale and Alan Duncan, British Naval officers assigned by the Admiralty to track down the infamous Captain Kidd, join Kidd's crew and slowly come to realize that Kidd is not really a pirate, but a man fighting for his country.

One of Kidd's shipmates, Buller, mutinies and lures half of Kidd's crew away to a life of piracy. Buller teams up with another notorious pirate, Captain Culliford, and they deliberately lead naval authorities to believe that Kidd is responsible for their acts of piracy.

When the British fleet arrives, Kidd helps the fleet destroy the pirate headquarters. For his troubles, he is placed under arrest. Richard and Alan plead Kidd's case and try to rally support for him to no avail. Kidd goes to the gallows, and Richard and Alan leave England for America, firmly convinced that Kidd was the greatest man who ever sailed the seas.

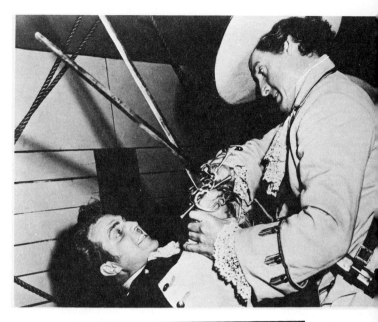

John Crawford faces an uphill battle against Marshall Reed.

Jungle Drums of Africa

12 Episodes	Directed by
Republic, 1953	Fred C. Brannon

CAST

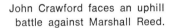

Alan King	Clayton Moore
Carol Bryant	Phyllis Coates
Bert	Johnny Spencer
Naganto	Roy Glenn
Regas	John Cason
Kurgan	Henry Rowland
Gauss	Steve Mitchell
Chief Douanga	Bill Walker
Ebola	Don Blackman
Nodala	Felix Nelson
Matambo	Joel Fluellen
Tembo	Bill Washington
Second Constable	Tom Steele
First Native	Robert Davis
First Constable	Roy Engel
Second Native	Bob Johnson

Sent to Africa to discover and develop uranium mining properties on the tribal lands of Chief Douanga, mining engineer Alan King and his assistant Bert Hadley run into trouble when the chief's messenger, whom they are to meet, is mysteriously killed. In an endeavor to track down the killer, they meet Regas, an itinerant hunter and trader, who feigns friendliness and offers to take them to the chief. Instead, he sabotages their jeep and leaves the pair to the perils of the jungle, where they are not only menaced by wild animals but attacked by natives led by the Witch Doctor Naganto, who is acting under Regas' direction.

Alan and Bert are rescued by Carol Bryant, whose father, until his recent death, was a medical missionary with Douanga's tribe. She is carrying on his work and is considered a sort of white witch doctor by the natives. Carol uses her reputation as a witch doctor to aid the two Americans. It isn't until later that they find the man behind their dangerous adventures is Kurgan, a foreign agent, who wants the uranium for his own country.

Despite attacks by natives and animals, dynamite plots, tiger traps, and fire and water hazards, Alan, Bert, and Carol persist in their struggle to overcome Kurgan. In the end, they defeat him and save the uranium for peaceful use.

Phyllis Coates, grabbed by John Cason.

Clayton Moore, Phyllis Coates, and Johnny Spencer talk to native chief Bill Walker.

Clayton Moore keeps his eye on the knife as he battles an unfriendly native.

The Lost Planet

15 Episodes	Directed by
Columbia, 1953	Spencer Bennet

CAST

Rex Barrow	Judd Holdren
Ella Dorn	Vivian Mason
Tim Johnson	Ted Thorpe
Professor Dorn	Forrest Taylor
Dr. Grood	Michael Fox
Reckov	Gene Roth
Karlo	Karl Davis
Ken Wolper	Leonard Penn
Hopper	John Cason
Darl	Nick Stuart
Lah	Joseph Mell
Jarva	Jack George
Alden	Frederick Berest
Robot No. 9	I. Stanford Jolley
Ned Hilton	Pierre Watkin

A cosmojet from the planet Ergro crashes into the side of Mount Vulcan, and reporters Rex Barrow and Ella Dorn (whose scientist-father has mysteriously disappeared), accompanied by photographer Tim Johnson, are assigned to investigate the scene. When Rex and his companions arrive, they are captured by Dr. Grood, an electronics genius from Ergro, who intends to conquer the universe. As phase one of his ambitious scheme, Grood has kidnapped Professor Dorn and has had him imprisoned on Ergro, where his incredibly keen scientific talents are being utilized.

Rex and his friends are brought to Ergro and forced to mine Ergro's mystery metal, cosmonium. Secretly aided by Professor Dorn, the trio manage to escape from the mine and hide in a nearby cave. However, Grood has been watching their flight on his television screen and, in an attempt to annihilate them, turns his death ray at the cave.

But, before he is subdued by Grood's men, Professor Dorn succeeds in blasting the death ray with a cosmic-ray gun. Grood then sends his robotmen after the earth people, but only Tim is captured. The two reporters try to rescue Tim but are blocked by the robotmen who capture Ella. Rex sneaks into Professor Dorn's laboratory where, with the professor, he makes a startling discovery: there is another mystery metal on Ergro, dornite. When combined with cosmonium, the two metals produce an invisibility ray.

Rex and Professor Dorn formulate a plan to render Rex invisible and send him back to earth aboard a cosmojet. Grood, discovering that his supply of dornite is missing, dispatches his robot to find it. Not yet invisible, Rex is discovered hiding in the cosmojet by the robot. In order to kill Rex, Grood gives the order to destroy the spaceship with a thermic disintegrator, a weapon that produces intense heat. But before the disintegrator is fired, Rex renders himself invisible and escapes.

Michael Fox, Judd Holdren, and Forrest Taylor in the underground laboratory on the planet Ergro.

The effects of the invisibility ray soon wear off, however, and Rex is captured again. He is sent to assist Professor Dorn who whispers to Rex that there is a hidden spaceship that can take him back to earth.

By means of his television screen, Grood watches as Rex and Dorn prepare to blast off in the hidden ship. As the ship takes off, Grood fires a salvo of nuclear rays at it. But luckily a piece of cosmic waste matter falls between the cosmojet and the ray, and Rex is saved from destruction.

Back on earth, Rex is contacted, by means of interplanetary transmission, by Professor Dorn, who warns him that Grood is also back on earth in his mountain laboratory. Intending to capture Grood, Rex returns to the secret laboratory but discovers that Grood has rocketed back to Ergro.

Rex returns to Ergro and is captured by the robots. As Rex is about to be destroyed in a hypnotic ray machine, Dorn renders him invisible, thus saving his life.

Meanwhile, Ella and Tim are prisoners in a cell located deep inside a dead volcano. Rex frees them, and they attempt to escape along the side of the volcano. But Grood, this time by means of the solar-thermo furnace, melts the rocks and causes a lavalike flow heading down toward the earthpeople.

Professor Dorn, however, has created a de-thermo flame by reversing the charge at the solar-thermo generating plant. He uses the device, and Rex, Ellen, and Tim find themselves enveloped by harmless *cold* flame!

The friends manage to make their way to a rocket ship and blast off for earth, landing near Grood's mountain laboratory which they proceed to destroy. On their way back to Ergro they are detected by Grood, who fires a guided missile at their rocket ship. But Rex puts the ship into a steep dive and the missile whizzes past.

To escape, Grood jumps aboard a cosmojet and orders a robot to set the ship's course for space. But the robot sets the control panel for *infinity,* and Grood is launched on a trip through space that will never end.

1954

Gunfighters of the Northwest

15 Episodes	Directed by
Columbia, 1954	Spencer Bennet

CAST

Joe Ward	Jack Mahoney
Bram Nevin	Clayton Moore
Rita	Phyllis Coates
Otis Green	Don C. Harvey
Lynch	Marshall Reed
Bear Tooth	Rodd Redwing
Inspector Wheeler	Lyle Talbot
Arch Perry	Tom Farrell
Wildfoot	Terry Frost
Arnold Reed	Lee Roberts
Fletcher Stone	Joe Allen, Jr.
Hank Bridger	Gregg Barton
Running Elk	Chief Yowlanchie
Dakota	Pierce Lyden

Man with the Steel Whip

12 Episodes	Directed by
Republic, 1954	Franklin Adreon

CAST

Jerry Randall	Richard Simmons
Nancy Cooper	Barbara Bestar
Crane	Dale Van Sickel
Barnet	Mauritz Hugo
Tosco	Lane Bradford
Chief	Pat Hogan
Sheriff	Roy Barcroft
Harris	Stuart Randall
Lee	Edmund Cobb
Sloane	I. Stanford Jolley
Price	Guy Teague
Quivar	Alan Wells
Gage	Tom Steele

Saloon owner Barnet is fomenting trouble between ranchers and the Indians on a nearby reservation. Barnet wants to obtain a section

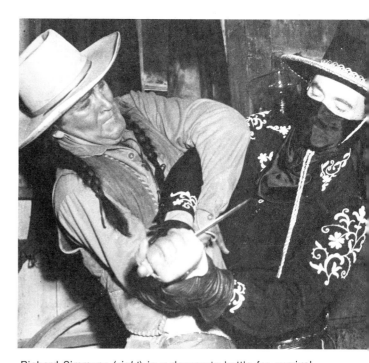

Richard Simmons (*right*) in a desperate battle for survival.

of the reservation on which a rich vein of gold has been discovered. His henchmen Crane and Tosco hire renegade Indians who raid settlers, stagecoaches, and stock. The ranchers, convinced that the reservation Indians are to blame, organize to attack.

Jerry Randall, a young rancher, persuades the ranchers to let him investigate before they take action. He and Nancy Cooper, former schoolteacher on the reservation, create a supposedly legendary figure, El Latigo, to gain the Indians' confidence. When Jerry appears as a masked rider in an elegant Spanish costume, they believe he is the spirit of a former benefactor. One of them who has been helping with Barnet's plot even tips off El Latigo about a coming raid on a road camp. While Nancy sends for the cavalry, El Latigo races to warn the

camp. The troops arrive during the attack and drive off the renegades as El Latigo engages in desperate hand-to-hand combat with one of the Indians who puts a torch to a powder wagon.

After avoiding the explosion, El Latigo and Nancy narrowly avert death at the hands of Barnet's gang as they take a load of much-needed food to the reservation Indians. Frustrated and furious, Barnet redoubles his deadly efforts. Desperate at news that the Indians are selling part of their reservation to incoming settlers, Barnet plots an elaborate plan, first to murder El Latigo, and second, to rob the stagecoach bearing an official order from Washington for the settlers to occupy the property. But El Latigo, warned again by his Indian friends, catches up with Barnet, defeats him, and brings justice to the community.

Riding with Buffalo Bill

15 Episodes
Columbia, 1954

Directed by
Spencer Bennet

CAST

Bill Cody	Marshall Reed
Reb Morgan	Rick Vallin
Maria Perez	Joanne Rio
Ruth Morgan	Shirley Whitney
Ace	Jack Ingram
Rocky Ford	William Fawcett
Bart	Greg Barton
Jose Perez	Ed Coch
Elko	Steve Ritch
Darr	Pierce Lyden
King Carney	Michael Fox
Zeke	Lee Roberts

Famous hunter and Indian scout Bill Cody comes to the aid of miner Rocky Ford when outlaws attack his ranch. Ford tells Cody that the man behind the local terrorism is King Carney who is trying to keep the new railroad out of the territory in order to carry on his illegal operations. Ford asks Cody to don the disguise of a legendary masked rider who once before smashed outlaw rule in the vicinity. Cody enlists the help of settlers Reb Morgan and his sister Ruth and pits his wiles and physical endurance against the outlaws—ultimately crushing them and restoring law and order to the territory.

Marshall Reed rides like the wind with Joanne Rio hanging on.

Trader Tom of the China Seas

12 Episodes   Directed by
Republic, 1954   Franklin Adreon

CAST

Tom Rogers	Harry Lauter
Vivian Wells	Aline Towne
Barent	Lyle Talbot
Major Conroy	Robert Shayne
Kurt Daley	Fred Graham
Rebel Chief	Richard Reeves
Gursan	Tom Steele
Bill Gaines	John Crawford
Native	Dale Van Sickel
Wang	Victor Sen Yung
Khan	Jan Arvan
British Colonel	Ramsey Hill
Ole	George Selk

Deep in the South China Seas territory lies the strategic little country of Bumatra, a United Nations protectorate, where a revolution is being hatched that will spread to every country along the trade routes!

Young Tom Rogers, an inter-island trader plying the China Seas, accidentally uncovers the plot and secretly volunteers his services to the United Nations undercover agents.

Tom is joined by Vivian, the daughter of a United Nations agent, in tracking down the foreign spies, led by Barent and his colleague Kurt, who are smuggling arms and ammunition to foment the revolution. News reaches Tom and Vivian that a cargo of poison gas is being smuggled in on a steamer. A terrific battle rages after they get aboard, during which the ship is scuttled on a reef. When the enemy agents attempt to salvage the cases of poison gas, Tom blows it up with an expert rifle shot.

Tom and Vivian trace the spies to activities in a neighboring country where a revolt is about to break out. When they arrive, the United Nations' Troop Commander tells them that he cannot interfere in the rebellion without a request from the ruling khan. Tom and Vivian sneak through the rebel lines and make their way to the khan who gives Tom a document requesting troop assistance. After fighting their way back

to the commanding officer, Tom and Vivian give him the document, which is all he needs to send his troops into action and quell the rebellion.

Returning to Bumatra just in time to thwart further subversive action, Vivian is taken prisoner and used as a hostage. She is forced to phone Tom for help. Then she is tied up, the house soaked with gasoline, and an ambush set for Tom. Warned by a secret signal during his telephone talk with Vivian, Tom approaches the house without being seen and drops a package of firecrackers down the chimney. The explosion diverts Barent and Kurt and Tom breaks in. During the fight that follows, the exploding firecrackers touch off the gasoline, and the house is soon a sea of flames. Tom knocks out the foreign agents, picks up the helpless Vivian, and barely has time to get out of the blazing building. Barent and Kurt meet their just doom in the holocaust, thus ending forever their attempts to disrupt the peace.

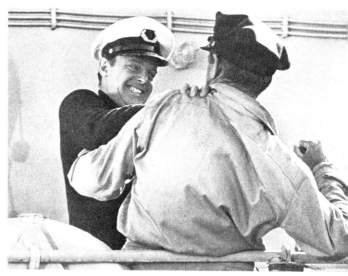

Harry Lauter slugs it out with Fred Graham.

While cohort Fred Graham looks on, head villain Lyle Talbot radios orders to his henchmen.

1955

Adventures of Captain Africa

15 Episodes   Directed by
Columbia, 1955   Spencer Bennet

CAST

Captain Africa	John Hart
Ted	Rick Vallin
Omar	Ben Welden
Princess Rhoda	June Howard
Nat Coleman	Bud Osborne
Hamid	Paul Marion
Borid	Lee Roberts
Greg	Terry Frost
Balu	Ed Coch
Prime Minister	Michael Fox

Nat Coleman, a wild animal trapper in the Near East, and adventurer Ted Arnold become interested in the mysterious Omar, Nat's Arabian assistant who once was rescued from an attacking leopard by the legendary Captain Africa. They follow Omar to a jungle meeting attended by the pretty Arabian girl Rhoda, at which Hamid, a deposed caliph, is trying to gather allies to help him regain his throne. When he is attacked by a guard, Ted seeks refuge in a cave but he is trapped by burning oil!

Ted saves himself by crawling through a small hole in the cave wall. Omar is attacked by Boris and Greg, the leaders of a group trying to liquidate Hamid and his followers, but Captain Africa routs the attackers.

Ted and Nat win Omar's confidence, and Omar consents to take Ted and Captain Africa to Hamid, his caliph.

At a meeting in Hamid's tent, Ted and Captain Africa learn that Hamid's prime minister has been taken to a nearby castle to be held for ransom. Ted and Captain Africa sneak into the castle to rescue the prime minister but Captain Africa is trapped and knocked unconscious when the huge spikes of the castle gate come down on him.

Captain Africa revives and rolls out from under the gate just as the spikes come down. He and Ted discover where the prime minister has been taken. Ted remains behind as Captain Africa hurries to inform Hamid. The prime minister is rescued by Ted but is wounded in the ensuing chase.

Ted, Omar, and Hamid lead the fight to take the palace. Captain Africa surprises two of Boris's men who are prepared to demolish the palace and all it contains if Hamid's forces win. Captain Africa prevents the explosion just in time. Inside the palace, as a great battle rages, Hamid duels with the tyrant caliph, vanquishes him, and becomes the new caliph. Ted and Rhoda plan their future together, and Captain Africa returns to the jungle he loves.

You know there's a train due momentarily as Harry Lauter lies unconscious.

King of the Carnival

12 Episodes
Republic, 1955

Directed by
Franklin Adreon

CAST

Bert King	Harry Lauter
June Edwards	Fran Bennett
Daley	Keith Richards
Carter	Robert Shayne
Zorn	Gregory Gay
Art	Rick Vallin
Jim	Robert Clarke
Travis	Terry Frost
Sam	Mauritz Hugo
Hank	Lee Roberts
Bill	Chris Mitchell
Mac	Stuart Whitman
Matt	Tom Steele
Garth	George de Normand

Bert King and June Edwards, high-wire acrobats in a circus run by Jess Carter, are told by Bert's friend, Treasury Department operative Art Kerr, that counterfeit money is being passed by an employee of the circus. Kerr asks Bert to be on the lookout for counterfeit bills. Daley and Travis, two riggers with the circus, arouse Bert's suspicions when he discovers them searching his quarters.

Daley and Travis are indeed members of the counterfeiting ring; their press is concealed in the watertight cabin of a submerged wreck just beyond the surf. The cabin is entered through an air lock with the use of diving helmets. Another crook, Zorn, operates the press. The mysterious boss of the gang gives his orders via a concealed radio.

Bert's obvious interest in the counterfeiting case results in a series of attempts on his life, which begin when his high trapeze rope breaks while he is performing directly above a cage of lions. Bert escapes death by grabbing a nearby guy wire as he falls.

Bert and June then plant a radio direction-indicator in the suspected outlaws' car. The indicator leads them to the beach. Before Bert can obtain a diving helmet and explore the wreck, he and June are involved in several furious chases and battles with Daley, Travis, and Zorn as well as two other members of the gang who are killed in the desperate encounters.

When Bert finally explores the submerged wreck, Zorn is waiting for him, armed with a knife. The counterfeiter is killed in a hand-to-hand struggle, following which Bert joins his T-man friend in a battle with Daley and Travis in a nearby cave. When the shooting is over, both Daley and Travis are dead.

Meanwhile, back at the circus, June has become suspicious of Jess Carter. But the circus master, the head of the counterfeiting ring, flees by climbing the acrobatic bars to the top of the tent. Bert pursues him and the two men desperately struggle. Carter finally loses his grip and crashes to his death far below.

Panther Girl of the Congo

12 Episodes
Republic, 1955

Directed by
Franklin Adreon

CAST

Jean Evans	Phyllis Coates
Larry Sanders	Myron Healey
Dr. Morgan	Arthur Space
Cass	John Day
Rand	Mike Ragan
Tembo	Morris Buchanan
Chief Danka	Roy Glenn, Sr.
Ituri	Archie Savage
Commissioner Stanton	Ramsay Hill
Orto	Naaman Brown

Dr. Morgan, a famous chemist, has developed a hormone compound which causes ordinary crawfish to grow into monsters. He and his henchmen Cass and Rand use these creatures to frighten African natives out of the district where Morgan has discovered a jungle diamond mine.

Morgan's activities are threatened when Jean Evans, the Panther girl, and guide and big-game hunter Larry Sanders arrive. While taking moving pictures of jungle animals, Jean accidentally photographs the claw monster. Morgan realizes that if Jean's films reach the authorities, there will be an instant investigation. First he tries to frighten Jean and Larry out of that section of the jungle. Then when that attempt fails, his henchmen, with the aid of a renegade Returi tribe, attack Larry, steal the films from him, and destroy them.

Jean and Larry immediately set out to take more films of the monster. They track a monster and get the movie footage they need. But this time, taking no chances, they decide to develop the film themselves. Larry goes off to a nearby town to buy the necessary developing chemicals. While he's gone, Cass and Rand sneak up on Jean and capture her. Jean refuses to give them the film, and both men suspect that Larry has it. When they spot Larry returning by canoe, they tie Jean to the village's dock and use her as bait. As Larry begins to untie Jean, Cass and Rand appear from behind a pile of crates and a fistfight ensues. As Larry is about to win the fight, Jean falls off the dock. Larry dives into the water to rescue her, and the outlaws escape.

That night, Jean, Larry, and District Commissioner Stanton watch the movie of the claw monster, and the commissioner is totally convinced of its existence. While the threesome discusses the problem, Cass and Rand toss a bomb through the window. Quick-thinking Larry flips a heavy table on its side and all three hide behind it, thereby escaping injury when the bomb explodes. Stanton determines to return to his headquarters and send two deputies to round up the monsters, Cass, and Rand.

When Stanton's men arrive, the entire group heads for the abandoned gold mine, where Larry suspects that Cass and Rand may be hiding. On the way, they run into a party of Returis who are guarding the mine. The Returi natives are quickly subdued, and the two deputies escort them back to town; alone, Jean and Larry go on to the mine. When Jean and Larry enter the mine, Cass and Rand are surprised and quickly jump behind some crates and start shooting. In the midst of the gun battle, Cass lights a stick of dynamite. But just as he is about

Myron Healy, rescued from drowning by Phyllis Coates, points out the enemy's location.

to hurl it, he is hit by a bullet. The dynamite explodes, killing both outlaws.

Jean and Larry examine the mine and discover evidence of diamond mining. They also notice a bottle of a special acid, available only to licensed chemists. Since Dr. Morgan is the only chemist in the area, it becomes obvious that he is responsible for the claw monsters. Jean and Larry then decide to go to Morgan's bungalow. Just outside the bungalow they discover a crate containing a claw monster. This seems to be conclusive evidence.

When confronted in his laboratory, Morgan produces a bottle of deadly gas and threatens to hurl it at the couple unless they hand over their weapons.

As he gathers up the pistols, Morgan places the bottle on a table. Jean seizes the moment to toss a plate at him, while Larry leaps to attack. In their struggle the bottle crashes to the floor and Jean and Larry barely manage to escape, leaving Dr. Morgan to perish from his own evil gas formula.

Arthur Space, John Day, and Mike Ragan plan new ways to throw the Panther Girl off their trail.

1956

Blazing the Overland Trail

15 Episodes	Directed by
Columbia, 1956	Spencer Bennet

CAST

Tom Bridger	Lee Roberts
Ed Marr	Dennis Moore
Lola Martin	Norma Brooks
Captain Carter	Gregg Barton
Rance Devlin	Don C. Harvey
Alby	Lee Morgan
Bragg	Pierce Lyden
Carl	Ed Coch

Rance Devlin, an unscrupulous rancher, schemes to get wealth and power by raiding the Overland Trail. Devlin bribes a band of Indians to attack a wagon train, then has two of his men disguise themselves as redskins and make off with a wagon full of gold.

Army Scout Tom Bridger and his friend Ed Marr, an agent of the Pony Express, help drive off the Indians and save the wagon train, then set out after the robbers. But Devlin and his men avoid capture, and, using his stolen wealth to hire more men, the outlaw increases the number of raids on settlers pouring into the western frontier via the Overland Trail. Ultimately, Tom and Ed locate the outlaw hideout, disguise themselves as two of Devlin's men to gain entry, and capture the villain, turning his whole gang over to the army.

Lee Roberts gets the upper hand as he takes on an outlaw.

Perils of the Wilderness

15 Episodes	Directed by
Columbia, 1956	Spencer Bennet

CAST

Laramie	Dennis Moore
Sergeant Gray	Richard Emory
Donna	Eve Anderson
Randall	Kenneth R. MacDonald
Little Bear	Rick Vallin
Homer Lynch	John Elliot
Kruger	Don C. Harvey
Baptiste	Terry Frost
Mike	Al Ferguson
Jake	Bud Osborne
Sergeant Rodney	Rex Lease
Amby	Pierce Lyden
Brent	John Mitchum

Bart Randall, ruthless overlord of crime in the wilds of the Canadian Northwest, is sought for murder and bank robbery by Laramie, a deputy marshal from Montana posing as an escaped outlaw.

Laramie is aided in his hunt by Sergeant Gray of the Royal Northwest Mounted Police, and by lovely Donna Blane, who is at first suspected of giving information to Randall, but who actually is a Canadian secret agent investigating Randall's trading of guns to the Indians. After a number of battles between Laramie and the Mounties and the outlaws, the Randall gang is smashed.

It's the outlaw on top in a battle with Richard Emory.

Index

Whiteford, Blackie, 80
Whitehead, Joe, 247
Whitley, Crane, 206, 225, 232
Whitlock, Lloyd, 31, 34, 43, 46, 48, 93, 97
Whitman, Gayne, 18, 154
Whitman, Stuart, 331
Whitney, Eve, 302
Whitney, Shirley, 327
Who's Guilty?, 251
Wilcox, Robert, 171
Wild West Days, 119
Wilde, Lois, 97, 99
Wiley, Jan, 182, 245, 246, 250
Wilke, Bob, 289
Wilkerson, Guy, 196
Wilson, Charles C., 212
Williams, Clark, 74
Williams, Guinn "Big Boy," 41, 103, 104, 189, 190

Williams, Maston, 48, 111, 133
Williams, Robert, 224
Williams, Roger, 80, 110, 120
Willis, Norman, 118, 168, 184
Wills, Walter, 129
Wilson, Al, 26
Wilson, Charles, 136
Wilson, Lewis, 212, 213
Winkler, Robert, 141
Winners of the West, 177
Withers, Grant, 52, 55, 63, 108, 109, 113, 135
Witney, William, 111, 115, 120, 124, 125, 130, 133, 141, 142, 144, 150, 154, 158, 168, 171, 181, 182, 186, 188, 200, 203, 206, 216, 255
Wolf Dog, The, 44
Wolfe, Bud, 255, 298
Wong, Beal, 205
Wood, Britt, 283

Wood, Ward, 210
Wood, Wilson, 313, 316, 317
Woodbury, Joan, 238
Woods, Donald, 191
Woods, Edward, 42
Woods, Harry L., 60, 61, 73, 92, 177
Worlock, Frederick, 220
Worth, Constance, 216, 217
Worth, Harry, 154, 181
Worth, Lillian, 3, 4
Worthington, William, 18, 50
Wright, Humberstone, 27
Wright, Jean, 320
Wrixon, Maria, 245

Y

Yaconelli, Frank, 119
Yetter, William, 220
York, Duke, Jr., 86

Young, Carleton, 107, 115, 125, 138, 144, 150, 154, 181
Young, Clara Kimball, 53, 80, 110
Young Eagles, 57
Yowlatchie, Chief, 177, 193, 315, 326
Yrigoyen, Bill, 261
Yrigoyen, Joe, 261
Yung, Victor Sen, 328

Z

Zimmerman, Victor, 161, 198
Zombies of the Stratosphere, 316
Zorro Rides Again, 120
Zorro's Black Whip, 233
Zorro's Fighting Legion, 150
Zynda, Henry, 206

341